(P9 24)

Have you seen the one I love?

CONTEMPLATIONS ON THE SONG OF SONGS

His Holiness Pope Shenouda III

Transcription and translation by St. Mark's Coptic Orthodox Church, Boston, MA

Library of Congress Cataloging-in-Publication Data

Shenouda III, His Holiness Pope, 2005-
  Have You Seen the One I Love / His Holiness Pope Shenouda III
      p.   cm.
    Includes bibliographical references and index.
    ISBN: 1-4196-9705-6 (pbk.)   9781419697050
    1. Bible.

Library of Congress Control Number: 2008904065
Publisher: BookSurge Publishing
North Charleston, South Carolina

HaveYouSeentheOneILove.com
Printed in the United States of America.
First Edition/First Printing

Contents

1   My Beloved is Mine, and I am His   9

2   I Am My Beloved's, And His Desire Is Toward Me   27

3   Your Name Is Ointment Poured Forth   47

4   Draw Me Away! We Will Run After You   65

5   Tell Me, O Whom I Love, Where You Feed Your Flock   83

6   I Sought Him, But I Did Not Find Him   101

7   By Night On My Bed I Sought The One I Love, Part 1   117

8   By Night On My Bed I Sought The One I Love, Part 2   135

9   By Night On My Bed I Sought The One I Love, Part 3   155

10   I Sleep, But My Heart Is Awake   171

11   I Am Black And Beautiful, O Daughters Of Jerusalem, Part 1   189

12   I Am Black And Beautiful, O Daughters Of Jerusalem, Part 2   205

13   I Am Black And Beautiful, O Daughters Of Jerusalem, Part 3   223

14   Who Is This Coming Out Of The Wilderness   241

15   I Have Compared You, My Love, To My Filly Among Pharaoh's Chariots   259

16   Behold, You Are Fair! You Have Dove's Eyes   281

17   The Voice Of My Beloved! Behold, He Comes   297

18   Behold He Comes Leaping Upon the Mountains   313

My Beloved is Mine, and I am His

Song of Solomon 2:16

In the Name of the Father, the Son, and the Holy Spirit, One God. Amen.

At the beginning of a new Year, I would like to talk to you about an important subject in our relationship with God so that everyone of us may have an appropriate start. For this reason, I have chosen a verse from Song of Songs in which the human soul addresses the Lord:

> *My beloved is mine, and I am his.*
> *He feeds his flock among the lilies.*
>
> Song 2:16

My beloved is mine, and I am his indicates that the relationship between the human soul and God is one of love.

Many people's relationship with the Lord stops at obedience. While it is commendable that man abides by the Lord's statutes and keeps His commandments, obedience without love is not acceptable in the sight of the Lord. It is possible for you to keep the commandments and avoid sin, and yet you do not love goodness, virtue or even God Himself. Outward obedience is not true obedience. The Lord wants obedience that springs forth as a fruit of love. For this reason Jesus says, *If you love Me, keep My commandments*, (John 14:15). That is to say, keeping the Lord's commandments should result from true love for the Lord and for goodness, not as a reflection of mere obedience.

There are others whose relationship with the Lord is based on fear and trepidation. They fear that the Lord may throw them in hell and eternal fire. They fear God's punishment and wrath. Fear is not an appropriate spiritual level that is fitting for the children of God, His righteous and holy ones. While fear may be the basis upon which man's relationship with God may start, man should not continue this relationship on just that level.

Fear may characterize this relationship at its onset, but as man keeps a commandment, he will find pleasure in fulfilling it. Once man finds this certain pleasure in abiding by the Lord's statutes and keeping the commandments, he will transcend this initial stage and do the right thing out of love of righteousness and out of love for the Lord, not out of fear of punishment. You are supposed to love the Lord.

There are other people whose relationship with the Lord is based on ordinances, practices and rituals. In other words, while they pray, fast, prostrate, attend church and take communion, there is a dearth of love. Be certain that prayer without love is void and meaningless. True prayer is a reflection of love for the Lord, yearning for Him and longing to talk with Him.

There are many people who pray, yet their hearts

are devoid of the love of the Lord. There are also many people who fast and yet their love for the Lord is poor and deficient. There are even those who attend church, practice confession, take communion, prostrate and engage in various spiritual activities, yet their love for the Lord is scarce and inadequate.

True prayer is a reflection of love for the Lord, yearning for Him

True relationship with the Lord is, in short, whether you love the Lord or not. If you love the Lord, then prayers are a natural expression of that love. Fasting will also be an expression of that love. Your love for the Lord will transform all worldly desires such as the hunger and yearning for food to become inconsequential and trivial. That is to say, you fast out of love for the Lord. There are people who fast, but they do not love the Lord.

For example, I have read much of the practices such as Yoga that Indian ascetics engage in simply for self control, discipline and health, yet these practices are not related to the love of the Lord. They have absolutely nothing to do with the love of God. There is a vast difference between those who fast out of love for the Lord and those who fast in pursuit of self control or to attain a certain virtue, regardless of God's place in this equation.

My beloved is mine, and I am his. Your relationship with the Lord should be based on love. *My beloved is mine, and I am his* indicates that this love is mutual and shared: God loves you and you love Him at the same time. As it is written, *We love Him because He first loved us,* (1 John 4:19). God so loved you that He created you. God loved you; that is why He created you in the best possible image. He created you in His image and His likeness. He gave you understanding, wisdom, spirit, eternity, and beauty in

11

everything.

Love should be reciprocal. It is supposed to be firm and solid. There are those whose relationships with the Lord are always oscillating, wavering and fluctuating. Sometimes this relationship is strong and firm, but at other times it is lukewarm and apathetic. Sometimes there is penitence and contrition, but at other times there is the return to sin and old ways. There is no steadfastness, persistence nor resoluteness in this relationship. The love of a spiritual person for God grows day by day. There is no turning back to former ways. He would not hear such words as *I have this against you, that you have left your first love,* (Rev 2:4).

True love is firm and unwavering. It is resolute and unshaken regardless of the crisis which may befall a person. Sometimes, we see a student who fails an exam. Then he becomes upset and argues with the Lord, "How could You allow that to happen to me?" In truth, there is no reason whatsoever to be angry or upset with God. However, this is an example to show how the relationship with the Lord may undergo certain fluctuations and vacillation.

Love for God should be firm and steadfast regardless of circumstances

Or, you have been praying for a certain sick person. If that sick person does not get better, you murmur in your heart, "Why is it the Lord does not heed or answer my prayers?" You become upset with God. Love for God should be firm and steadfast regardless of circumstances, crisis or tribulations. You love the Lord, not simply because you expect something good from Him. Rather, you love Him for who He is. Outside factors will have no impact on your relationship with Him.

My beloved is mine, and I am his. This means that God is for you and you are for Him. This characterizes that special, unique relationship between man and God. Man will not feel lost or confused in the midst of this vast universe. Man will not feel that God belongs to the multitudes, the crowd, or the affluent and rich. Hardly! God is yours and yours only! It is true that God is the Lord of everyone, yet He is specifically yours. The Lord's relationship with you is personal.

This relationship of love is characterized by its special yearnings, feelings and emotions. In other words, a person prays because he yearns and longs for the Lord. He is not doing this because of a certain commandment that impels him to pray, or to escape from the pricks of conscience. Neither does he pray merely because praying is a must as one of the traits of saints and holy men. Rather, he prays out of pure yearning for the Lord. This is reminiscent of David's:

As the deer pants for the water brooks,

so pants my soul for you, O God.

My soul thirsts for God, for the living God,

Ps 42:1

Is your love for the Lord likewise characterized with such emotions and feelings? Or, is it some kind of lukewarm feeling devoid of passion and fervor? Do you experience feelings of joy and delight when you go into the house of the Lord, *I was glad when they said to me 'Let us go into the house of the Lord,'* (Ps 122:1). Do you say to the Lord, *My soul follows close behind You,* (Ps 63:8)?

Or *My voice You shall hear in the morning, O Lord; in the morning I will direct it to You, and I will look up,* (Ps 5:2), as David the prophet used to say? Do your feelings for the Lord have this ardor and fervor, this zeal and passion? Or is God a distant Being, very far away in the heaven of heavens, and with Whom you do not have a personal relationship? It is this personal relation, this intimate bond between you and God that we should seek and pursue.

You need to know how to love the Lord, how to pray with zeal and enthusiasm. You will find that your heart is ablaze and your emotions burning and aflame, feeling the presence of the Lord in front of you and knowing that you are in His presence. You will experience these special feelings that exist and bind you, emotions of yearning and longing for Him. This is real love.

Does our love for the Lord entail formalities? No! There are no formalities in our relationship with the Lord. The Lord Himself does not like formalities. He likes expressions of love, *My son, give me your heart, and let your eyes watch my ways,* (Pro 23:26). Such are the feelings that God desires in His relationship with you.

You will thereby feel that the Lord dwells in your heart, and you dwell in His. You will feel that the Lord abides in you, and you in Him. You feel this mutual firmness and steadfastness in this relationship. You feel that the Lord longs for you just as you long for Him. You feel that the Lord is with you, and you are with Him. You experience Him walking on the way alongside with you. You feel secure in His bosom while asleep. You feel that the Lord protects and keeps you from every obstacle along the way. His eyes are watching you all day long.

This is how you feel the presence of the Lord. In this context, I would like to mention that I enjoy Elijah's words: *As the Lord God of Israel lives, before whom I stand,* (1 Kin 17:1). He continuously feels as if he is standing in the presence of the Lord. The Lord is ubiquitous; he is standing before Him on the way, in his thoughts, in his deeds and conduct. He is simply standing before Him in everything. This also recalls to mind what David the Prophet says, *I have set the Lord always before me; because He is at my right hand I shall not be moved*, (Ps 16:8). It is a relationship of love.

I wish we could rid ourselves of the formalities that may exist in our relationship with the Lord. We should rid ourselves of the "dos" and "don'ts," that fail to please the Lord. All God desires is your love. Do not worry too much about doing this or not doing that. Liberate yourself from the tyranny of the law and the commandment. Transcend these and replace them with love. With love, you will naturally and spontaneously abide by, and execute, all that the Bible contains. Love will purify your very nature.

You need to know how to love the Lord, how to pray with zeal

My beloved is mine, and I am his. If you are truly dedicated to the Lord and He is for and with you, there will be nothing in your heart that will be at variance with God's presence. Neither will you love anything or anyone more than the Lord. What is Adam's sin? Is it merely what we oftentimes take to be the mere eating from the tree of the knowledge of good and evil? No! Eating from that tree was simply a reflection and an expression of something more serious. Adam's problem was that, in addition to his love for God, he loved something else that conflicts and clashes with his love for the Lord.

Rather than consecrating his whole heart to the love of the Lord, something strange entered Adam's heart: a love that was foreign to Adam had managed to creep into his heart. Was it love of knowledge? Was it pride? Was it a desire to be equal with the Lord? Whatever it was, it was definitely some kind of love that was alien and foreign. In his heart, there was something else wrestling with God for supremacy. God no longer fully reigned supreme there. In addition to God, there was something else sharing Adam's heart.

Therefore, you should ask yourself, "Has any kind of foreign love managed to creep into your heart?" We all know how the love of Sodom, its fertility and the prospect of profit and gain entered Lot's heart. Samson's love for Delilah was also foreign and strange and at variance with Samson's love for the Lord. The love of money and glamorous appearances found their way to Ananias and Sapphira. Saul, the King, was also tempted by the love of power and dominion and had, therefore, persecuted David. Joseph's brothers and Jesus' disciples were enticed by the love of leadership, prominence and being first. The love of one's ego may infiltrate the heart. The love of the world and the desires of the flesh can also gain access to the heart.

Your love for God should be sincere and genuine

What has crept into your heart? What muddles your love for the Lord? What spoils it? Is there something alien that has managed to find its way into your heart and soul and has now confused and clouded up that pure wholesome relationship with the Lord? Ask yourself!

Love of God is not a commandment unique to the New Testament. It has been there in the Old Testament as well. In Deuteronomy, we read, *You shall love the Lord your God with all your heart, with all your soul, and with all your strength,* (Deut 6:5). It is not merely a commandment to simply love the Lord with your heart. That would be too easy. It is a commandment to love Him with ALL your heart. In other words, all the heart is consecrated and dedicated to the Lord.

It is therefore noteworthy to mention here that the

common saying, "An hour for your heart and an hour for God" is erroneous and misleading. In fact, it contains a number of errors. First, it shows that man's love for God is wavering and inconsistent: you can spend a day to satisfy the needs of your heart and another day to worship God.

Second, there is a division between the heart and the Lord: saying, "An hour for your heart and an hour for God," indicates that the heart is not with the Lord. During this time when you are fulfilling the desires of the heart, the Lord is not there. Rather, He is set aside. That means your heart is wayward and disobedient. Thus, you are on the wrong track. By the same token, when you dedicate time to the Lord, it means you are not attending to the desires of the heart.

Finally, the saying indicates this oscillation and vacillation, this unsteadiness and wavering in man's life. There is this lack of a definite fixed aim, a clear vision and a lucidly defined objective. Man is fluctuating between the world and the Lord. The Lord says, *My son, give me your heart,* in love that is firm, steadfast and unwavering.

It is not possible that you love the Lord unless you have come to know Him and found Him pleasing. Someone may like sin and find pleasure in committing it. He may even feel that God is somehow forced on him; he has to like Him in spite of himself. Yet, this is not the way. Your love for God should be sincere and genuine. You cannot love sin and decide to forsake it merely as a gesture to please God, or as a sign of generosity on your part towards Him. You cannot be condescending with God.

Neither can you do that merely because you are afraid of Him and fear His wrath and punishment. This is all futile and useless. You have to love the Lord genuinely and sincerely. This will not take place unless you love goodness and righteousness.

Many contemporary atheists resist the Lord because they are after the lusts of the world and they feel that God is an obstacle and a hurdle to their fulfilling their worldly desires. That is why they hate Him. They want nothing to do with Him. Thus, man cannot love the Lord unless he loves goodness and righteousness.

Carefully examine yourself and scrutinize your thoughts. Consider your values and ponder your principles. Let the love of goodness and righteousness into your heart. If you loved goodness, you are bound to love God, and if you loved God, you are bound to love goodness. If you wonder which one comes first, do not be troubled by that. You may start with either: the one would lead you to the other. It is very easy for those who have sound moral values and rigorous wholesome principles to proceed along the paths of the Lord. The pervert and deviant, however, will find God and His commandments burdensome and heavy.

When you truly and sincerely love the Lord, you will allow nothing strange to seep and infiltrate into your life. Everything that distances you from the Lord is foreign and alien to your holy nature. I sometimes find it strange when someone erroneously states, "This is my nature. This is me!" When he is angry and out of control, he says, "This is my nature." He swears and uses abusive language and says, "This is me!" In fact, man's nature is holy. God did not create anything bad or evil. Evil is alien to you; it is foreign. It is not innate. Rather, it is a parasite that has invaded your holy nature.

You should rid and liberate yourself from these strange and foreign things, such unorthodox and unusual behaviors, that may find their way to your soul. Rest assured that your soul yearns for righteousness and goodness. Be certain of that. No matter how viciously evil wrestles with you, your nature is essentially one that is righteous and good.

At the creation of the world, God only created righteous and good things. There was no evil, whatsoever. Had man's will not deviated from the goodness created by the Lord, evil would not have existed. Evil is the result of the freedom of choice that the Lord has given His creation.

The saint Abba Hor used to say to his disciple, "Look son! Do not allow a strange word to enter into this cell." He wanted to spend time with the Lord alone, nothing in his thoughts or in his heart except his love for the Lord. He wanted nothing strange to gain access to his heart. He wanted his mind to be the sphere of nothing other than his spiritual ruminations and ponderings. He would not allow any strange thought to enter his head. He called such thoughts strange or foreign: "Do not allow a strange word to enter into this cell."

Rest assured that your soul yearns for righteousness and goodness

If a strange topic, an unrighteous thought or anything inappropriate found its way into a conversation you are having with a friend about the Word of God, you should be aware that, *Strangers have risen up against me, and oppressors have sought after my life,* (Ps 54:3). That is to say, the mighty devils are seeking my soul to destroy it.

Try to consecrate your soul to the Lord; let nothing strange or foreign enter in your relationship with Him. Be determined to dedicate all your heart to the Lord. I do not want foreign thoughts, weird feelings or a strange sin to enter and spoil my relationship with the Lord. *My beloved is mine and I am his*. I am entirely for the Lord and He is for me. He is my lot and my inheritance. I have none but Him. The world will pass away and all the lust therein. The

Bible warns us not to *love the world or the things in the world,* (1 John 2:15). Only God is eternal and everlasting. So, how have you been conducting yourself since the beginning of this year? How have you been thinking? How have you been feeling? On what is your heart set?

Take time to contemplate, ponder, and examine yourself. Rid yourself of appearances that you impose on yourself to ease your conscience. Such practices, as praying without real passion or zeal; reading the Bible without understanding, contemplation, feeling or living it; following some rituals, or vainly committing yourself to some spiritual activities; all these are futile and meaningless.

Checking your daily calendar for performing these spiritual activities and practices reduces you to the rank of a mere employee for God. However, you are not an employee working for the Lord. Nor will God supervise you as supervisors do in a place of employment. Our Lord is a loving God and His vast loving heart seeks and craves the outpouring of your loving heart. Formalities and appearances have no place here.

Make sure that you are firmly and always abiding in the Lord

Ask yourself, What is the extent of your love for God? How deep is it? Are all the spiritual practices that you observe saturated with love for the Lord? Are your prayers filled with love? Do you fast out of love for the Lord? Does your reading of the Bible abound with love? Are your various spiritual practices permeating with love for the Lord? Are your prostrations and kneeling done with true love and submission for Him? Have you truly come to know God? Have you become His friend and spent time with Him? Have you lived with Him and experienced His existence in your life? Or, is God a stranger to you, abiding in the sky, in the heaven of heavens, and you have no relationship with Him? No, my beloved!

You ought to go up to Him in His heavens, or He may come down to you on earth. The important thing is that you abide firmly in Him, and He abides firmly in you. That is what we should strive for at the beginning of this year. We need to plant the love of God in our hearts, feel that God is everything for us, the One that fills the heart, pervades the thought and ignites our feelings and passion. He is our every craving and yearning; He is our very passion and desire. He is the One that truly satisfies your every need, and with Him you lack absolutely nothing.

That being said, I would like to warn you that having firmly secured your love for the Lord will not prevent the devils from fighting you. You will find them planting things even while you are praying. Resist and fight back. Make sure that you are firmly and always abiding in the Lord.

The love of some to God has induced them to devote themselves wholeheartedly and completely to Him. They dedicate all their lives to the Lord. Others may be busy with a number of things in the world. We cannot expect every human being to consecrate their lives completely to God. There are those who have families to provide for, those who have jobs to perform, those who have schools and school work to do, and others with various responsibilities. If you cannot dedicate your time to God, you can consecrate your heart to His love. If you cannot devote your time, you can live with love, devote your heart and do whatever you do in the name of the Lord.

Do not separate your work from the Lord. Rather, make sure that He is in everything you do. Your work ought to be done in the Name of the Lord. It is for His sake that you ought to be honest and trustworthy in all what you do, just like Joseph the righteous who was honest and industrious in distributing the wheat in Egypt during the famine. He looked upon his responsibilities as holy and godly, and considered himself entrusted by God to feed the people and sustain them.

Make God part of everything you do. Consult with Him on every word you utter to see whether or not it becomes His will. Before you give utterance to a word, pray as is written in the Psalms, *O Lord, open my lips, and my mouth shall show forth Your praise,* (Ps 51:15). Ask God to open and control your mouth when you speak; do not speak on your own.

Some show their love for God by serving others: through serving others, one is serving the Kingdom of heaven. It is a service done for the sake of the Lord. There is, of course, a big difference between someone who serves others out of love for the Lord, and someone who serves others as a social activity or obligation. These are worlds apart. That special holy feeling that the work is done through God imbues it with holiness and sanctity. The service is done with passion and zeal, conscientiously, wholeheartedly, and unreservedly. There is no room for formalities.

In every word you say, place the Lord always in front of you and it is bound to be a word of truth and righteousness. He who strays away from righteousness is bound to alienate himself from God. Truth and Righteousness are among God's attributes, *I am the way, the truth, and the life,* (John 14:6). There is a difference between a person who walks in truth as merely a reflection of a social virtue, and another who walks in truth as a reflection of a divine virtue and as an indication of one's steadfastness in the Lord.

There is a great discrepancy between your desire to do the right thing to avoid making mistakes in the society in which you live, and that desire to do the right thing to avoid being separated from the Lord. When a holy man makes a mistake, he feels separated from the Lord, *For what fellowship has righteousness with lawlessness? And what communion has light with darkness?* (2Cor 6:14).

Keep the Lord in your life

Keep the Lord in your life. When you serve someone, be confident that you are serving one of God's children, His people, His sheep, and His creation. Make sure that you are serving for His sake and out of love, not because of formalities and appearances. Allow God to lead you in every step of the way. Do everything for the sake of the Lord, and do not drive a wedge between anything you do and God. Do not separate your work from God.

You eat in the name of the Lord. You also hunger for the name of the Lord. You experience happiness in the name of the Lord, but for His name you also suffer and endure. You wake up for the name of the Lord, and you sleep for His name, so that one may receive the rest it needs to be able to continue to serve Him. Every work that you engage in should be for the sake of the Lord and in His name. How apt are the apostle's words:

> *For if we live, we live to the Lord;*
> *and if we die, we die to the Lord.*
> *Therefore, whether we live or die,*
> *we are the Lord's.*
>
> *Rom 14:8*

All your life is the Lord's.

There is something I would like to tell you. Your life at present is not one of continuity and stability. Rather, it is more of an experiment. Your life on earth is one of an experiment; the Lord is testing your freedom of choice so as to determine your eternity. Life on earth is not everlasting, continuous or steadfast. Where will you go later in the after life, in eternity? This is where I would like to ask you the question that I wish you will ask yourself. In eternity, will you live with God?

One single sin can disrupt all your life

Therefore, if you cannot stand to live with God here on earth, how will you be able to live with Him in heaven? If you cannot talk to the Lord for just half an hour a day here on earth, how will you be able to talk to Him when you go to eternity? Where will you go? If you had no relationship with the angels and the saints here on earth, how will you live with them when you meet them in heaven?

If you love material possessions, crave the fulfillment of physical desires, and lust after worldly desires, what will you do when you go to heaven and the material and physical desires are nonexistent? What will you say then? Will you apologize and say, "I am sorry. The heavens will not do for me. Send me back to earth!" That would be futile and useless, my beloved.

You should start establishing a relationship with eternity right away. You ought to familiarize yourself with the surroundings of eternity in this world. You should lead that spiritual life that you will eternally experience in the world to come. You should live with the Lord, His angels and His saints while you are here on earth for you will live with them there forever. What will that man who lives for the satisfaction of worldly desires do when the world and all its desires pass away? What can he possibly do?

Form a relationship with the Lord because a relationship with Him starts here, but it will never end. Your relationship with the world will come to an end one day. It will end no matter how long you live. However, your relationship with the Lord, the angels, the saints will not end. Neither will your relationship with righteousness, virtue and goodness. Never think that your life on this planet will last. Never! Life on earth will come to an end. Only the good and righteous deeds that were done in this life remain. God will scrutinize all your life and consider what goodness and love was manifested. These are the things that will last.

It is very possible that one single sin can disrupt all your life. He who loves the Lord should love Him not only steadfastly and firmly, but completely and wholeheartedly as well. Just as a single drop of ink in a cup of water like this one would muddle the whole cup, so will a single or tiny sin. A small, tiny sin in your perspective can likewise spoil your whole life. The question is one of love. Do you love the Lord or not? If you love Him, then there should be no place for sin. No sin whatsoever!

If you love the Lord, the world will shrink in your sight. It will readily be reduced into something inconsequential and trivial. It will all become, *vanity and grasping for the wind*, (Eccl 1:14). As St. Paul the Apostle says, *Yet indeed I also count all things loss for the excellence of the knowledge of Christ Jesus my Lord, for whom I have suffered the loss of all things, and count them as rubbish, that I may gain Christ*, (Phi 3:8). The whole world will be reduced to *rubbish* in your eyes. The whole world became nothing to those saints who have loved and pleased the Lord. St. Augustine said that he was on top of the world when he desired and feared nothing.

When you love the world, it shrinks and loses its glamour in your view. You feel like you are on the top of the world. You will feel lighter, more elevated and detached from worldly matter. You will also be able to tower and soar up into the skies and experience the heavens. The world will be at your feet. Then, you have been able to rid and liberate yourself from the world and its lusts. The love of the Lord will drive away every evil from your heart.

May the name of the Lord be blessed now and forever.

Let us pray.

May God have mercy upon us and bless us, and make His face shine with His Countenance upon us and have compassion upon us. With the prayers and intercessions that are raised on our behalf by the Mother of God, the Pure Saint Mary, and all the angels and apostles, and the prophets, and the martyrs, and the confessors, and the anchorites, and the saints who we ask to pray for us for peace at all times, and the blessings of the saint of this blessed day, and the blessing of Saint Mary first and last, may their holy blessings and the prayers and intercessions be with us all. Amen.

Peace be with you all.

May God make us worthy to say, Our Father...

I am My Beloved's and His Desire is Towards Me

Song of Solomon 7:10-12

In the Name of the Father, the Son, and the Holy Spirit, One God. Amen.

Tonight, I would like to talk to you about some of the verses in Song of Songs. In Chapter 7, we read,

> *I am my beloved's,*
> *And his desire is towards me.*
> *Come my beloved,*
> *Let us go forth to the field;*
> *Let us lodge in the villages.*
> *Let us get up early to the vineyards;*
> *Let us see if the vine has budded,*
> *Whether the grape blossoms are open,*
> *And the pomegranates are in bloom,*
> *There I will give you my love.*
>
> *Song 7:10-12*

These verses refer to service. They reflect the love that binds man to God: *I am my beloved's, and his desire is towards me.* Yet, despite this yearning to this beloved, man is seeking the company of the beloved *to go forth to the field.* The *field*, the *villages* and the *vineyards* are a reference to service. In other words, man's love for the Lord is by no means solely restricted or limited to prayers. It is also manifested in service in the fields, in the vineyards, and in the villages where, as indicated, *I will give you my love.*

We will be misled if we think that the love of the Lord is merely restricted to prayers, seclusion, meditation and contemplation. Service also reflects a great love and exhibits an overwhelming zeal for the Lord.

However, there are some who oftentimes opt to avoid service and prefer to live a life of seclusion and meditation as if service will alienate them from the love of God. On the contrary. Service can strengthen man's love for the Lord beyond limit. The Lord will gently urge them: *Come my beloved, let us go forth to the field; let us lodge in the villages. Let us get up early to the vineyards. There I will give you my love.*

Those people who lead a life of prayer and contemplation, such as monks, are usually referred to as the *earthly angels* or the *heavenly people.* Servants can also be angels. The term is not used exclusively to refer to monks. Has not the Lord called the shepherds of the seven churches *angels?* He said, *To the angel of the church of Ephesus write,* (Rev 2:1) and *To the angel of the church of Smyrna write,* (Rev 2:8) to Sardis, to Philadelphia etc. Those are also considered angels.

Angels were also highly praised in their service. St. Paul's words in Hebrews 1:14 are extremely apt and relevant here: *Are they not ministering spirits sent forth to minister for those who will inherit salvation?* This indicates that angels also do serve, and that they are sent forth to minister and serve those who will inherit salvation.

The Bible abounds with instances of the services that the angels render. This is obvious with children whom the angels encircle to protect and keep safe. It is also evident with adults: *The angel of the Lord encamps all around those who fear Him, and delivers them,* (Ps 34:7). It is also manifest in certain occurrences in which the Lord sends an angel to render a certain service. Well! If the angels in the heavens descend to serve the people on the earth, how more pertinent and necessary it is for the people on earth to serve one another! When people serve others, they are considered angels as well.

Saint John the Baptist served and prepared the people by preaching and urging them to repent. It was written about him, *Behold, I send My messenger before Your face, who will prepare Your way before You,* (Mark 1:2). That is why St. John the Baptist was considered an angel in his service.

The angels perform any type of service with which the Lord entrusts them, be it a material or a spiritual service. An example of a material service is found in God's sending an angel to provide Elijah the prophet with food. Another example is found when the Lord sent His angel to free Saints Paul and Peter from jail. God may also send an angel to punish someone. **Service can strengthen man's love for the Lord beyond limit** An example of this is the angel who struck all the firstborn in the land of Egypt. Further, God may send an angel with glad tidings such as the angel whom He sent to the Virgin to announce the birth of Christ, or He may send an angel to warn or alert people, etc.

The angel would be swift in carrying out an order. He will readily respond to the Lord regardless of the type of service to be rendered.

Angels are essentially loving and caring

Some say that there are angels for serving and others for praising. Angels of praise, like the seraphim, are like those whom Isaiah the prophet saw and talks about in Chapter 6 in the Book of Isaiah. He heard them crying to one another, saying, *Holy, Holy, Holy is the Lord of hosts; the whole earth is full of His glory,* (Is 6:3)

In fact, I marvel at this chapter that deals with the seraphim, those angels who are particularly known for their continuous praising of the Lord. I am truly amazed. Why is that? When Isaiah saw the Seraphim praising and glorifying the Lord with their pure and sanctified lips saying, *Holy, holy, holy,* he witnessed *the posts of the door were shaken, and the house was filled with smoke.* Alarmed, he said,

Woe to me, for I am undone!
Because I am a man of unclean lips,
and I dwell in the midst of people of unclean lips;
for my eyes have seen the King,
the Lord of hosts.

Is 6:4-5

The minute the seraphim heard Isaiah utter these words, they could not bear to it. Preoccupied as the seraphim were in glorifying the Lord and standing in His presence as angels of praise saying, holy, they had to do something. This is what the Bible says:

Then one of the seraphim flew to me,
having in his hand a live coal which he had taken
with the tongs from the altar.

And he touched my mouth with it, and said,

'Behold, this has touched your lips;

your inequity is taken away,

and your sin purged.

Is 6:6-7

The word seraphim is a Hebrew word. The singular is Seraph. As soon as this seraph heard Isaiah utter the words *Woe to me, for I am undone! Because I am a man of unclean lips*, he swiftly flew to the altar, took a live coal from it, touched Isaiah's lips, and said to him, *your inequity is taken away, and your sin purged.* Isaiah's lips were no longer impure. They have been purged and purified.

It is important to mention that the Bible does not state that the Lord sent one of the seraphim. Nor is it stated the God entrusted one of the seraph to do that job. However, that intense, keen and ardent love—that love that exists amongst the seraphim, angels who are essentially committed and dedicated to praising the Lord—that love could not stand motionless upon hearing that a human being is perishing because he is of impure, unclean lips. He therefore hurried to purge him.

What an exquisite example for angels! An angel is never nonchalant or indifferent. It does not become an angel to be passive at seeing others perish. No! Angels are essentially loving and caring. Even while standing in front of the throne of the Lord like the seraphim, the minute an angel hears that someone will perish, he will run quickly, leave the throne and bring a live coal with which to touch the unclean lips.

This is the true love, one that man can demonstrate towards others through service. That is why we read, *Come my beloved, let us go forth to the field; let us lodge in the villages. Let us get up early to the vineyards.* We should check on them and look after them: *Let us see if the vine has budded, whether the grape blossoms are open, and the pomegranates are in bloom.* That is to say, we need to check the outcome of our previous service: have the grapes that we planted blossomed or not? Are the pomegranates in bloom or not?

A question now arises. When I leave you, O Lord, and head to the fields and the villages to serve, will I not miss my prayers, contemplation, and the beautiful time I spend with You? Hardly! *There I will give you My love.* There in the field I will give you My love. There, while you are looking after people in the villages I will give you My love. It is not that I give you My love solely in your prayers, your fasting or in your meditations. No! I will give you My love while you are spending time, exhausted and weary, in the villages.

This is God. God desires the salvation of everyone. He loves everyone, and He wants you to also love everyone. He wants you to offer and sacrifice yourself for others just as He did for us. As you do so, *There (He) will give you (His) love.*

Well! You may be tempted to ask: Is a person who has spent the whole day long in praying the same as one who will come to pray at night after he has spent the whole day serving others? Trust me, dear brethren, that as long as this person truly loves the Lord, on his way back from service the Lord will assuredly bestow upon him His Divine inspiration and pour into his heart His love. In a short time, he will most likely acquire more spiritual blessings than others.

I would like to provide you with some examples for those people who have combined between the two elements: ardent, enthusiastic and fervent service on the one hand, and keen, devoted and dedicated solitude and seclusion, on the other. There are examples that cannot be questioned.

I would like to bring to your attention examples of those who have combined service with solitude. Elijah the prophet offers us one such example. He lived an austere and ascetic life on mount Carmel. His was a life of complete solitude to which everyone had attested. Then, he started serving others. It was Elijah who purged the earth from idol worshipping. It was Elijah who reproached Ahab the king for permitting the worshipping of idols. It was Elijah who became mightier than Obadiah, the prophet who was actually engaged in service. It was Elijah who was able to open and close the heavens at will. He was as successful in his service, as he was successful in his solitude. Nobody has ever claimed that his spirituality has deteriorated or suffered in the least. As evidence for this, the Lord had chosen to take him in a fiery chariot unto the heavens. This is the first example.

He loves everyone, and He wants you to also love everyone

Another example is offered to us in St. John the Baptist. He spent 30 years in solitude. Nobody ever saw him. Later, he appeared to the people to serve them. In an overwhelmingly successful service that had lasted no more than six months, St. John the Baptist prepared the whole people for repentance. Thousands upon thousands went out to him, were baptized in the Jordan, confessing their sins. St. John combined successful service with a successful life of seclusion and solitude.

Undoubtedly, God would acknowledge his work as he served, received and urged people to repent to *make ready a prepared people for the Lord*, (Luke 1:17).

Meanwhile, the Lord would comfort and encourage St. John saying, *Do not ever think that you have lost your relationship with me, for on the River Jordan I will give you My love.* That actually took place on the River Jordan when Jesus appeared and gave him His love for his services.

Before starting to serve others, He spent thirty years in solitude

St. Paul offers us a third and rather strange example. His was a service that was eccentric and astounding to the extent that he had to put up with more than any of the other disciples, as he said. However, he attributed this ability to the Grace of God that worked within him:

> *I am more: in labors more abundant... in journeys often. in perils.... in weariness and toil...*
>
> *besides the other things, what comes upon me daily: my deep concern for all the churches. Who is weak, and I am not weak? Who is made to stumble, and I do not burn with indignation?*
>
> *2 Cor11:23-29*

His service was zealous and full of fervor: *I have become all things to all men, that I might by all means save some,* (1 Cor 9:22). Does his ardent service mean that he had completely lost himself to it? Hardly! The Bible shows that St. Paul was:

> *Caught up to the third heaven... whether in the body or out of the body I do not know,*
>
> *God knows— caught up into Paradise and heard inexpressible words,*
>
> *which it is not lawful for a man to utter.*
>
> *2 Cor 12:3-4*

Now, who amongst the monks who live in isolation was caught up to the third heaven? St. Paul who frequently toiled and exceedingly labored did that. This is striking! This is the point. He combined the two things: meditation and contemplation on the one hand, and isolation and solitude on the other. He spent three years in solitude in the wilderness, and he was able to ascend to the third heaven even though he served day and night.

Throughout his service and journeys, whether at sea when he was shipwrecked or even as he was stoned half to death, the Lord comforted him saying, *Paul, do not think that your relationship with Me is any less now that you do not pray and fast, contemplate and meditate as much. In the midst of all your labor and toil, I will give you My love.*

So far, we have talked about Elijah, St. John the Baptist, and St. Paul. A greater example is offered by Christ Himself. While Jesus used to spend the whole day long serving people, He spent His nights in prayers on Mount Olive. Before starting to serve others, He spent thirty years in solitude. We hardly know anything about this stage which He spent in solitude and seclusion. Christ Himself combined service on the one hand with meditation and solitude, on the other.

St. Virgin Mary also led a life of meditation, solitude and seclusion worshipping in the temple. She emerges from this solitude and seclusion only to go to Elizabeth to spend three months with her to serve her during her pregnancy. When St. Elizabeth had finally given birth to her son and started to get back on her feet, St. Mary returns to her former solitary life. Again, St. Mary had combined service and solitude.

In the Song of Songs, the Lord portrays His Divine love, *My beloved is mine, and I am his. He feeds his flock among the lilies,* (Song 2:16) and *His left hand is under my head, and his right hand embraces me,* (Song 2:6).

Just as He says these words about His Divine love, the Lord also says the following concerning serving others: *Come my beloved, let us go forth to the field; let us lodge in the villages. Let us get up early to the vineyards.*

The expression *let us lodge in the villages* has a different meaning: service should not be restricted to cities where churches may abound, where plenty and well-known preachers serve, and where numerous spiritual meetings are found. We ought to go and serve in the villages, these places where spiritual possibilities and potential may be lacking and deficient. Service in the village is essentially more difficult than service in the city, and its reward is therefore greater. How so?

Those who serve in the city usually have no trouble finding a church populated with its parishioners. They simply deliver their sermons in peace and leave without dealing with a lot of problems. Also, let us consider the role of Sunday school teachers. They come to church by car or public transportation, find their students waiting for them in their classes, give their lessons and then leave. They do not have to deal with problems either.

Nor do they even visit their Sunday school children anymore. They demand a bus or a van to transport them to the homes of their Sunday school children. Yet, incidentally, walking has its special reward and blessing! This kind of service is easy.

Service in the village, conversely, requires arduous effort and hard work. A servant may go to a certain place where he can not even find a place for the children to gather together. Sometimes, he will have to stop at the doors of farmers, go from one house to the other to gather the children from their houses, the fields or other places of employment. Some of the children are busy, others unavailable. Yet, he continues to work laboriously and go from one place to the other. This is similar to what was said about Jesus: He also used to roam the cities as well as the villages. He went about the villages *preaching the gospel of the kingdom and healing all kinds of sickness and all kinds of disease among the people,* (Matt 4:23).

Come my beloved, let us go forth to the field; let us lodge in the villages. Lodging in the villages is even more demanding and challenging than merely going to them. Not only will I go to the village, but I will also lodge there. To lodge in the village means I will not sleep in my home; rather, I will sleep in the village, in a far off place. When I wonder how I could leave my home, His comforting voice comes to me: *There I will give you my love.* As you spend nights in the village, working arduously and laboriously, leaving the comfort of your home behind, and leaving your immediate surroundings and your family *there I will give you my love.*

Service should not be restricted to cities where churches may abound

When did the Lord give His love to Abram? When he left; when he got out. The Lord said to Abram, *Get out of your country, from your family, and from your father's house, to a land that I will show you,* (Gen 12:1). When Abram left to that place it was, *There I will give you my love.*

You may be tempted to argue that you want to stay and enjoy your family. There is a time for your family, and there is also a time in which you ought to leave your family and your children and go out into the fields and lodge in the villages. There, the Lord confirms, *I will give you My love. Come, my beloved!*

When you serve people, you are thereby offering

Me true love because those whom you serve are My children. In fact, you are reconciling those people whom you serve with Me; through your service you are essentially making ready a prepared people for Me.

I wish that we all take this matter very seriously. Let us consider how to go forth to the fields, how to go to the villages, and how to look after our brethren and attend to their needs.

Service is not merely restricted to servants of the church. Service comprises everyone. Everyone who has come to know and experience God's love should make this love known to others, however the means, forms or ways may be. It is not necessary that everyone be a teacher. Even the Bible instructs us: *My brethren, Let not many of you become teachers*, (Jam 3:1). Some people simply do not have the gift to be teachers. There are others who have not been entrusted by the church to teach. However, the least thing you can do is to bring someone to church and introduce him to the house of the Lord.

God desires to see your heart filled with love for others

There are those who can preach, and there are those who can lend their car temporarily to perform matters related to service. They can use it to transport people and things on the day of service. Others may donate money or take part in serving others in villages. There are many ways, and each one of them will be the cause of blessings.

You are here in one of the biggest neighborhoods of Cairo, yet not very far away from you there are a great number of villages and poor neighborhoods here and there. Go there, save no effort in searching for people, check on and look after them. Go check to *see if the vine has budded, whether the grape blossoms are open, and the pomegranates are in bloom*. Do note try to find excuses. Do not say, *Lord, isn't it enough that I have planted a pomegranate tree last summer?* No. This is not enough. It is not adequate.

You need to nurture the tree. You need to supply it with what it needs of fertilizers, chemicals and water. You have to protect and shield it from the winds, insects and all kinds of harm. Go forth and look if the pomegranates are in bloom. If they are, you ought to thank the Lord for His love and Grace that have made your service successful and fruitful. As you contemplate the blooming pomegranates, the Lord's voice is heard, *Right there next to these blooming pomegranates, I will give you My love. Here am I with the children whom God has given me.* (Is 8:18)

God will ask you in the Day of Judgment, *How many have you brought to Me?* How many persons have you introduced to the Lord? How many have you brought to church? How many have you led to repentance? In the midst of your toil and hard work, as you go here and there to talk to and convince people and lead them to the Lord, the Lord will strengthen you and encourage you not to lose heart or become weary for, *there I will give you My love.*

I am my beloved's, and his desire is towards me. This desire does not mean utter seclusion and solitude with the Lord only. God desires to see your heart filled with love for others. While some love to satisfy their egos, others love for the Lord. Those who love for themselves and want to satisfy their egos only use others to get what they want. As for those who love for the Lord essentially love everyone to lead them to Him. They introduce and reconcile them with the Lord. The Lord will reward the latter group of people, *As you have loved and checked on them, I will also give you My love.*

You will be amply rewarded for all your labor and

toil. Nothing will go to waste. That is impossible. The Lord will never forget even a cup of cold water you give to a thirsty person.

Some Christians live in different environments. However, they have no fruits in the environments in which they live. There are no fruits coming forth: their vines have *not* budded, their grape blossoms are *not* open, and their pomegranates are *not* in bloom. Nothing happened! On the other hand, there are others who are impassioned and imbued with the spirit of service. They are willing to labor and toil for their service and they show a serious attitude towards it: *Let us get up early to the vineyards.*

One may ask: what can possibly be meant by *getting up early to the vineyards?* There are vineyards that need judicious and timely attention. If you are tardy to such vineyards, the little foxes may spoil them. When you go to check them out, you will hardly find any grapes left. In other words, there are some cases that need prudent and immediate attention; otherwise, they will grow out of proportion and will be completely lost.

There are cases that will not be served by patience and tolerance. Rather, they require zeal, enthusiasm, passion, eagerness, quick rescue attempts and a swift response. This is implied in, *Let us get up early to the vineyards,* before it is too late. For just as you go early to the vineyard to serve, the little foxes also go there to consume what's in it. That is why we are being cautioned to, *Catch us the foxes, the little foxes that spoil the vine,* (Song 2:15).

Let us get up early to the vineyards. We have to be judicious and alert before it is too late. Let us examine the problem before it becomes more complicated and insolvable. Let us search for and identify sin in its first stages before it becomes gravely deadly and fatally incurable. Let us gather God's children into His Divine bosom.

Are there villages that no one goes to? You may have been a little tardy going to serve in a certain village and now this village has been ransacked by others who have spoiled the minds of its people, their beliefs and their virtues and morality. It is very possible! That accounts for the urgency entailed in *Come, my beloved, let us go forth to the field. Let us get up early to the vineyards.* Let us go there quickly before it is too late, before they are spoiled.

Now, what is the meaning of *Let us go forth to the field?* There are those who are self centered and egotistical: they are absorbed by the self, the ego. All that they care about is their own interests, their comfort and their future. Their main interest is to build and establish themselves.

Service, however, starts when a person manages to get out of and liberate himself from the self. Then a person can make the right contact with the society in which he lives. He can make contact with others. No longer will this person live for himself. That is why the message to us is to *Come, my beloved, let us go forth.* It is a call to stop being egotistical and self centered and adopt an attitude of philanthropy and selflessness.

You will be amply rewarded for all your labor and toil

There are, unfortunately, many servants who shun service for egotistical and personal reasons, *I cannot do that today. I am exhausted today. I have other commitments today. Today. I have to attend to this and that today. My friends are visiting me today,* etc. So, how about the service to which you have been called? Are you that self centered?

Free yourself of this self centeredness. Liberate

yourself from the ego and go to the field. *Come, my beloved, let us go forth to the field*. Rid yourself from the narrow circle of the self so as to go out into the big circle of the society that surrounds you. This is the case of a person who has come to love the Lord. Such a person wants all people to love Him as well.

That is exactly what had happened to the Samaritan woman. Once egotistical and self centered, interested only in those whom she loved, and absorbed as she was with her own desires, the Samaritan woman rushed into the city, and said to the whole city, *Come, see a Man who told me all things that I ever did*, (John 4:29).

What was the power behind liberating this woman from her self centeredness? What made that possible? Divine love: *Let us go forth to the field; let us lodge in the villages*. Let us leave our families, our responsibilities and even our children for *He who loves father or mother more than Me is not worthy of Me. And he who loves son or daughter more than Me is not worthy of Me*, (Mat 10:37). So, get out. Get out of this small, narrow circle, and get out into the big, wide field out there.

Liberate yourself from the ego and go to the field

But what will happen when I get out into the wide, open field? Will I have to forget and neglect myself? Hardly! You will not be neglected. *There I will give you my love*. Trust me, many a time when someone sits in seclusion in his room, he only finds that he has become weighed down and inundated by a shower of problems and depressing thoughts. When he goes out into service, however, he experiences relief and his problems and troubles tend to lessen and disappear. By going out into service, he has been able to enter the vast heart of the Lord: *There I will give you my love*.

Come my beloved, let us go forth to the field. The expression *Let us go* is particularly apt and fitting here. It is as beautiful as the expressions *Let us lodge, Let us get up early, Let us see,* etc. It is as if the Lord is saying, *Come my beloved, you will not go forth to the field alone! Let US go! You will go, and I will go with you. We will go TOGETHER. You will be accompanied by the Holy Spirit; you will go with Me, with Grace. You will not be working alone.*

Let us lodge in the villages. When you lodge there, I will be there with you. We will be lodging together in the villages. *Let us get up early to the vines; let us see if the vine has budded.* All of these expressions are in the plural form. It is as though the Lord is confirming: *I will never ever leave you alone in your service. I will serve with you. I will go forth to the field with you. I will lodge with you in the village. I will get up early with you to go to the vines. I will accompany you always. You are not working alone.*

During our prayers we beseech the Lord and say, *Take part in the work of your servants.* About himself and coworker Apollos, St. Paul says, *For we are God's fellow workers,* (1 Cor 3:9). So, you will not be working alone. This is the meaning of the fellowship with the Holy Spirit. The Lord's hand is working with you as you serve and labor. God works with you, in you and through you. You will be a tool in His Divine Scheme, in His Godly hand. And He will invite you to go, *Come my beloved, let us go forth to the field.*

Just as My angels have the opportunity to be praising Me, and other times when I send them forth as serving angels *for those who will inherit salvation,* (Heb 1:14), so also will you be. You also will be just like an angel: there will be time for praising and other times in which you will pick up a live coal from the altar with which to touch, purge and purify defiled and unclean lips. *Come my beloved, let us go forth to the field; let us lodge in the villages. Let us get up early to the vineyards.*

The Lord has used the expression *My beloved* in reference to those who go forth into the fields and villages because he who loves Him loves His children, His church, and His Kingdom. He who loves the Lord will labor to *make ready a prepared people for the Lord*, (John 1:17), gather His scattered, dispersed sheep unto Him, build the Lord's temple and populate it with ardent, living pillars and rocks.

Do you think that the disciples enjoyed Jesus' love and company during the 40 holy days only? While it is true that He did spend 40 days with them during which they enjoyed His love, He then told them, *I will go to Him who sent Me.* His disciples' question, *So, what shall we do? Shall we come after You?* must elicited the Lord's definitive *No! No! No! Wait!* And He instructed them to *Go into all the world and preach the Gospel to every creature*, (Mark 16:15). And to their thought, *But Lord, how about the beautiful time we spent together in praying, in Gethsemane, and on the mount?* the Lord instructed them to *Go into all the world and preach the Gospel to every creature.* (Mark 16:15), *and make disciples of all the nations baptizing them in the name of the Father, and of the Son and of the Holy Spirit, teaching them to observe all the things that I have commanded you,* (Mat 28:19-20), and *He who believes and is baptized will be saved*, (Mark 16:16). Their final comment, *What will happen when we do that?* must have been met by the Lord's assurance that *There I will give you My love.*

Do you think that the Lord would have been pleased with Joseph the righteous had he neglected the financing of Egypt and left it a prey to the consuming famine, choosing instead to go into an inner room and lock himself in to pray? That would have been quite impossible!

Rather, Joseph abandoned his solitude, went forth into the fields, built storehouse, planned judiciously, and relieved all of the hungry people of their hunger and suffering. As Joseph was doing that, the Lord's encouraging voice must have come to him saying, *I am pleased with you, Joseph. I am happy to see you in the storehouses. There I will give you My love.*

The Lord will give you His love wherever you carry out His Divine will. He will give you His love in bed as well as in the field. He will give you His love in the two places as long as you fulfill His will in both places.

You will be a tool in His Divine Scheme, in His Godly hand.

Extremism is always inappropriate. Thinking that love can only be found in the seclusion of the bedroom is an example of extremism. You may say to yourself, *I am exhausted and/or bored because of service. I will spend some time with the Lord.* What a tired excuse! Have you not been with the Lord while you were serving? If not, then it was not true service. It might have been some sort of a social activity or you may call it whatever you want.

True service is one in which you truly feel that you are with the Lord. *Believe me, O Lord, while I am standing in the midst of the people talking to them about You, You are in my heart and in my mind. You are the One talking through me and I feel Your love just as much as I feel it when I kneel down to pray.* There is hardly any difference. I cannot think of leaving service under the pretext that I will spend some time with the Lord. I am already with Him while I am serving. He who does not feel the presence of the Lord as he serves is merely exerting some human effort and performing some social activity. His service is hardly godly nor Divine.

Have You Seen the One I Love

Come my beloved, let us go forth to the field and villages. When you become tired, I will give you comfort. I will spend time with you; you will sit in My shade; you will eat from My fruits and I will give you My love.

May the Lord be with us in prayers, in service and always. To Him be the glory for ever, Amen.

Let us pray.

May God have mercy upon us and bless us, and make His face shine with His Countenance upon us and have compassion upon us. With the prayers and intercessions that are raised on our behalf by the Mother of God, the Pure Saint Mary, and all the angels and apostles, and the prophets, and the martyrs, and the confessors, and the anchorites, and the saints who we ask to pray for us for peace at all times, and the blessings of the saint of this blessed day, and the blessing of Saint Mary first and last, may their holy blessings and the prayers and intercessions be with us all. Amen.

Peace be with you all.

May God make us worthy to say, Our Father...

Your Name Is Ointment Poured Forth

Song of Solomon 1:2-4

In the Name of the Father, the Son, and the Holy Spirit, One God. Amen.

Let us read some verses from Chapter One in the Song of Songs:

> *Your name is ointment poured forth;*
> *Therefore the virgins love you.*
> *Draw me away!*
> *We will run after you.*
> *The King has brought me into his chambers.*
> *We will be glad and rejoice in you.*
> *We will remember your love more than wine.*
> *Rightly do they love you.*
> *Song1: 2-4*

The verse, *Your name is ointment poured forth*, is magnificently sublime and exquisitely superb. The same graceful words are used by the priest during the Mystery of the Evening Incense. Addressing the Lord, the priest says: *Your Holy Name is a sweet-scented ointment poured out for us. Incense is offered to Your Holy name in every place as a pure offering.* Just like aromatic fragrant ointment, the Name of the Lord has a sweet-smelling fragrance that delights and invigorates the soul and revives and rejuvenates the heart. It is ubiquitous; it spreads everywhere. It is also refreshing and sweet-scented. *Your name is ointment poured forth; Therefore the virgins love.*

The Name of the Lord is sweet and attractive; it pleases the children of the Lord. Therefore, in the Holy Psalmody we say, *Your Name is sweet and blessed in the mouths of Your saints.* It delights and rejoices the mouths that utter that blessed Name. David the prophet reiterates the same words when he says, *I will extol You, my God and King, and bless Your name forever and ever. Every day I will bless You, and I will praise Your name forever and ever*, (Ps 145:1-2). He acknowledges that he loves the Lord's Name so much that he never ceases to praise and extol It. He delights in It. He experiences joy and happiness by sounding it.

This is similar to a situation in which a person likes someone so much that they never tire of talking about them. Such a person will seize any opportunity to talk about the other person, to the extent that other people may come to believe that they are obsessed with them. It is as though they have nothing else to think or talk about. That beloved person is constantly the topic of almost every conversation. Conversely, those names that are hardly ever mentioned may be taken as a reflection of the insignificant position and low esteem that one attaches to them.

Your name is ointment poured forth is reminiscent of the alabaster flask of the costly oil of spikenard that the woman has poured on the feet of Jesus. The whole place is instantaneously filled and enriched by the sweet aroma of the ointment. The Lord's Name is also like ointment rich in its fragrance and full of sweetness and splendor. It spreads everywhere. It tickles the senses and enriches the spirit. It delights and gladdens the heart.

The Name of the Lord has always had a great impact on man: *The name of the Lord is a strong tower; the righteous runs to it and are safe*, (Prov 118:10). Therefore, we perceive the Name of the Lord as a fortified castle and a strong fortress that we seek for protection and shelter.

The Lord's intervention in a problem is the surest solution.

Therefore, we ought to call upon the Name of the Lord should we ever face any tribulations or encounter any hardships. If we call the Lord's Name, we will find Him there for us. The Name of the Lord instills fear in the devils and wrong-doers and fills the righteous with peace and tranquility. It encourages, sustains and fortifies them. In his confrontation with Goliath the mighty Philistine, David declares, *You come to me with a sword, with a spear, and with a javelin. But I come to you in the name of the Lord of hosts*, (1 Sam 17:45). By merely calling upon the Name of the Lord, the devil trembles in fear.

The Lord's intervention in a problem is the surest solution. The Name of the Lord causes the devil to shake in trepidation. It performs wonders. When the lame man laying at the gate of the temple asks St. Peter the Apostle for charity, St. Peter responds saying, *Silver and gold I do not have, but what I do have I give you: in the name of Jesus Christ of Nazareth, rise up and walk*, (Acts 3:6). The name of the Lord avails us not only in times of war but also in times of need and want.

The Name of the Lord is always used in prayers during our Holy Sacraments, *baptize them in the name of the Father, the Son and the Holy Spirit*, (Matt 28:19). Because of our profound love of the name of the Lord, we never start anything except in His name. The first thing we do is cross ourselves, *in the name of the Father, the Son, and the Holy Spirit*. We do this before we start studying, eating, sleeping, going out or coming in, and in everything we do in our life. We do this incessantly because *the name of the Lord is a strong tower*.

When we keep the name of the Lord in front of us, we will always remember Him

The Name of the Lord is beseeched in every endeavor upon which we embark so that we may secure His blessing and ascertain its success. When we entreat and beseech the name of the Lord, He will always be there leading and directing us. When we keep the name of the Lord in front of us, we will always remember Him. The God in front of whom we are standing is a living God, *As the Lord God of Israel lives, before whom I stand,* (1 Kin 17:1).

Sinners and wrong-doers are panic-stricken and intimidated by the name of the Lord. Fearsome and terrifying is the lot of those who invite the wrath of the Living God. The righteous, on the other hand, find joy and pleasure in the name of the Lord. They delight in hearing and saying the name of the Lord again and again. His blessed name is music to their ear.

We therefore never tire of saying and mentioning His blessed name which is constantly mentioned in our prayers, sacraments, readings, and in every aspect of our daily lives. It is a cause for joy, a source of happiness. We delight and rejoice in His name. In the story of St. Cyprian, we know that the evil spirit was cast away at the mere utterance of St. Justina's name. How much more powerful and effective would the name of the Lord be? *Your name is ointment poured forth; Therefore the virgins love you.*

This is the true meaning of happiness and joy that are rooted in the name of the Lord and the delight that engulfs the soul when He dwells within us and when we maintain a relationship with Him. Consequently, *the virgins love you.* This is an indication that the Song of Solomon is a revelation about Divine Love. It is not about worldly, sensuous or physical love. The latter kind of love is dominated by overwhelming egotism, an irresistible desire to possess and an overpowering need to control.

A woman in love with a certain man will be extremely jealous if she knows that another woman loves that same man. She would be devastated and distraught. In the verses we are now contemplating, however, we read *the virgins love you.* They all do. Moreover, she is thrilled and happy for this. This is how she expresses her love: *We will be glad and rejoice in you,* using, as she does, the plural form *we.* She even goes on to say: *We will remember your love more than wine. Rightly do they love you.* By saying this, she declares that all the people love him and she acknowledges her happiness, nonetheless.

This is a perfect example of the human soul that delights and rejoices for everyone to love the Lord, *Rightly do they love you.* We all love you. This is completely opposed to worldly love that is dominated by selfishness and egotism. Self-centeredness reigns full supreme in this kind of love, *only me* is the guiding principle. It should not come as a great surprise, then, that a mere glance could lead to confusion, jealousy and hatred. This is typical of worldly love as it is characterized by both the desire to possess and control, and the inherent feelings that others' love is unwelcome and unwarranted.

A spiritual person, on the other hand, is

predominantly motivated by the desire that all the others would join the flock and come to know and love the Lord. Such a person saves no effort in inviting others to the love of the Lord. No spiritual person tries to dominate or monopolize the love of the Lord. Rather, they would try their hardest to bring others to the Lord. They will go to the end of the world preaching in the name of the Lord.

The Samaritan woman provides us with a striking example here. The minute she came to know and accept Jesus, she went her way to the city to tell everyone about Him, *Come, see a man who…* (John 4:29). Another example that shows the same attitude is provided by the disciples. Now that the disciples had come to know Jesus and experience His love, they filled the whole world with their good news about Him. Even when the head priests commanded them to stop talking about Jesus, they declared that they could not do so, *…and the Lord added to the church daily those who were being saved,* (Act 2:47).

St. Paul the Apostle reverberates the same idea in, *I would to God that not only you, but also all who hear me today, might become both almost and altogether such as I am,* (Acts 26:29). Also, *I have become all things to all men, that I might by all means save some,* (1 Cor 9:22). When man really comes to know and experience the Lord, he desires that all peoples may come to know and experience Him as well. *Therefore the virgins love you.* Every virgin runs to gather other virgins so that all may be in the presence of the Lord.

Before we proceed any further, we would like to dwell upon the meaning of the word *virgins*. What does this word mean? Are the virgins the only group that can have a share and an inheritance with the Lord? Is the Lord for everyone or not?

The word *virgin* is a reference to a woman who has

never given herself to a man, or vice versa. This typifies the human soul that has opted to lead a life of celibacy and consecrate itself only to the Lord. To such people who adopt this kind of life, God is everything. It is for this reason that we find that the Bible likens the saved ones, those who are going to inherit the Kingdom of Heaven, to five wise virgins. The specific reference to the number five is meant as an analogy to the five senses that characterize human beings and which are employed to perceive God. The number refers to the whole of humanity. So why were they called virgins? Simply because there is no one else in their hearts.

The word *virgin* refers to those who are married as well as those who live in celibacy. It includes everyone. Among those to whom the label *virgin* applies are Abraham, Isaac, and Jacob. It is true that they were married, but their souls enjoyed a state similar to that which virgins experience. Their minds were occupied with no one other than the Lord. Also, the Church itself was likened to a virgin. St. Paul the Apostle declares that, *I have betrothed you to one husband that I may present you as a chaste virgin to Christ*, (2 Cor 11:2).

There is no one else other than the Lord in her midst.

The word *virgin* in this verse is a direct reference to the Church. Likening the Church to a virgin is apt and fitting since the Church has not busied itself with anyone else's love. There is no one other than the Lord in her midst. A man would refrain from betrothing a woman who is preoccupied with another man. Similarly, if the Lord is to betroth the Church, it must be His alone, unoccupied by anything or anyone else. This is the meaning of the celibacy of the human soul. This is by no means a reference to the body. Rather, it is a reference to the soul that relinquishes everything else in its serious pursuit of the Lord. It is the human soul as it strives to *love the Lord from all (the) heart, the mind...* Aside from the Lord, nothing else exists.

In order for you to really love the Lord, you have to completely empty your heart from any other love that wrestles and competes with His love and thereby constitutes an obstacle and an impediment. Let us now try to understand the kind of love that is considered an impediment or an obstacle in the way of loving the Lord.

In order for you to really love the Lord, you have to completely empty your heart from any love that wrestles and competes with His love

One's love for one's family does not contradict one's love for the Lord. It is, in fact, part of the love of the Lord. Therefore, the human soul is still chaste and pure and, to stretch the metaphor, a virgin.

In addition to this kind of love, we also wish that all people may be saved and delivered; we want our biological parents and children as well as our spiritual parents and children to be saved. This, too, is part of the love of God. The heart is still pure, chaste and undefiled. However, one ought to rid oneself from the other kinds of love that contradict the love of God and impede it. By so doing, the soul becomes chaste and pure. So, the verse *therefore the virgins love you* indicates that these chaste and pure hearts and souls may have indeed experienced other kinds of love, but kinds that neither defile nor contradict His. *Your name is ointment poured forth; Therefore the virgins love you.*

These chaste and pure hearts found the fragrance of Your Holy Name and Your sweet-smelling ointment irresistibly appealing. They could not but follow You. This should not come as a surprise to us. Sweet scents are often a symbol of good things. This is particularly true in the realm of the spiritual world.

We oftentimes hear that a certain person had a saintly spirit and when that person's hour to depart had come, people were able to recognize the aroma of sweet-smelling incense in the room. It is also commonly believed that saints are themselves regarded as sweet-scented incense in the presence of the Lord. Their prayers are likened to incense, and when they depart they leave behind them sweet-scented fragrance. This beautiful fragrance is a symbol of their pure and chaste spirits. We even hear of stories about experiencing the smell of sweet-scented fragrance when a spiritual gathering is visited by the anchorites. They feel that the place is filled with the Holy Spirit. Incidentally, this is in sharp contrast to what one may experience in the presence of evil and defiled spirits. They are foul, repulsive and distasteful.

We regard the prayers of the saints as incense in the presence of the Lord. The sweet-scented incense that we raise and which fills the Church with its sweet aroma and fragrance brings the remembrance of the saints and their life histories. These saints are like the sweet smell of incense before the Lord. The Lord delights in them. The Offerings and the various presents offered to the Lord are also like sweet incense, a *delight and a joy to the Lord*, as we read in the Book of Leviticus. Sacrifices, offerings, the life histories of saints, holy and chaste spirits are all examples of sweet smelling fragrance. Beautiful and fragrant though these are, they fall exceedingly short when contrasted with the Lord's Holy Name. We can, therefore, only imagine how powerful, pungent and forceful these words are, *Your name is ointment poured forth; Therefore the virgins love you.*

When virgins are in Your presence they are intoxicated by the fragrance and beauty of Your Holy Spirit with which You fill the air. Your Holy Spirit permeates the place and saturates it with sweet-smelling aroma. In You they have found the *ointment* that they earnestly seek and desire.

In preparation for a wedding ceremony, the bride is prepared to be presented to her husband at her best. Fragrance and perfume are gracefully applied and all manners of beautification are lavishly and tastefully used, *prepared as a bride adorned for her husband*, (Rev 21:2). In Esther, we read that a queen had to spend a whole year in preparation for the day in which she was to be presented as a bride to the king. Their parents would spend six months applying perfumes and scents and another six months applying other kinds of ointments. As we can imagine, she was finally presented to the king as though drenched in perfumes and fragrant scents.

A godly and righteous human soul is similarly soaked with virtues; it is one that is drenched in sweet smelling spiritual aroma. Whereas sweet perfumes and fragrant scents are used to anoint the body, the soul can only be made beautifully chaste and sweet-smelling by righteous and virtuous deeds. To extend the metaphor, the soul's sweet smell, that special spiritual aroma, can only be realized through virtue, godliness, and sanctification.

It is important to understand that *Your name is ointment poured forth* indicates that the Lord's name is the *ointment* itself, not merely that sweet-scented ointment is poured upon it. Rather, His name is itself *ointment*. Therefore, everyone upon whom Your Holy Name is called will be filled with ointment and will have that special aroma.

One cannot but wonder about the beautiful aroma

of the Kingdom of Heaven. The mere remembrance of the name of the Lord is similar to experiencing sweet-scented poured ointment. Saints and angels also have this special beautiful aroma. We can, therefore, only imagine the beautiful aroma of the Kingdom of Heaven. What an exquisitely unparalleled special aroma and unprecedented spiritual scent would our heavenly Jerusalem offer? One will surely be blissfully intoxicated and ecstatically overjoyed there. One would never want to leave such a serene and delightful place.

Spiritual life depends solely on love

God created paradise and filled it with beautiful aromatic scents. The Song of Solomon abounds with images that reflect this beauty. We read that the human soul is like a *lily among thorns* (Song 2:2) and *an apple tree among the trees of the woods*, (Song 2:3). There are many other images that we will consider later.

Therefore the virgins love you. Spiritual life depends solely on love. Many people claim that faith, righteousness, or godliness are the basis of a sound spiritual life. That is untrue. A sound spiritual life is based wholly on love. There is no other way, *God is love, and he who abides in love abides in God, and God in him*, (1 John 4:16). Spiritual life revolves around this verse, *Therefore the virgins love you*. No matter how hard one tries to expound or illustrate the many different aspects of righteousness and sanctity as they occur in the Bible, the few words, *the virgins love you*, are more powerful and poignant.

They explain these aspects better because the verse here depicts the human soul as a *virgin* soul, hardly concerned with the material world, neglectful of the love of matter, oblivious of the self and completely unattached to and unmindful of the desires of the flesh. The soul's main objective and ultimate desire is the love of God. So if you love the Lord, then you are a believer and you are on the right track. If you do not, then you still do not know Him, nor have you started your journey with Him. Love is the key. Even if you try your hardest to keep the commandments, obey the Lord, and *give (your) body to be burned*, (1 Cor 13:3) without love, it profits you nothing. If you pray day and night without love, it leads you nowhere.

God seeks love; He yearns for that love that springs from the hearts of virgins

If you fast all the fasts of the year and you do not have love, it avails you nothing. If you read the Holy Gospel and even memorize it without love, it is of no use. If you preach day and night and you do not have love, you have, *become sounding brass or a clanging cymbal,* (1 Cor 13:1). The pivotal point of a sound spiritual life lies in the love of the *virgins*. Your love for the Lord indicates that you are well on your way to the Lord's path. If, however, you do not love the Lord, then you are still outside and away, in *a far country,* (Luke 15:13).

God seeks love; He yearns for that love that springs from the hearts of *virgins*. It is inconceivable to try to win the Lord's love when you are not completely devoted to His love. It is unthinkable to mix His love with the love of the world. This simply indicates that your soul is not a *virgin*. You are not consecrated and dedicated to Him. Rather, you are like the Samaritan woman who was married to five husbands: the world, the devil, carnal lusts, the desires of the flesh, the ego...etc. What makes the soul a *virgin* is the capacity to love the Lord from all the heart.

Two questions come to mind in this respect. The first question is, Do you have that 'virgin' soul? And the second is, Do you love the Lord? The two questions are closely related; they are two faces for the same coin: if you love the Lord, you will have a virgin, pure and chaste soul. Conversely, if you have a pure, chaste, and virgin soul, you will naturally love the Lord.

The verse *therefore the virgins love you* is used in every church liturgy: *Do not love the world nor the things which are in the world, for the world shall pass away and all its desires...* The Bible instructs us that the love of the world is enmity with the Lord. This enmity springs from the fact that the love of the world deprives the soul from its virtuous and pure state; the soul thereby loses its virginity and becomes wed to the world and, consequently, begets numerous and countless desires and lusts. In the First Epistle of John, we read, *If anyone loves the world, the love of the Father is not in him,* (1 John 2:15). It is for this reason that the *virgins* love You. They can love Him because they have not concerned themselves with the love of the world or its desires or the ego and its egotistic, selfish needs. They remained *virgins*, wholeheartedly consecrated to the Lord. *Therefore the virgins love you.*

Since *the virgins love You*, the question that now arises is, How can one's soul become like a virgin that loves You? The answer to the question is rendered in, *Draw me away! We will run after you.* If one truly wants to become like one of the *virgins*, the only choice is to ask the Lord to *draw (one) away.* One may be tempted to follow other gods due to one's inherent weakness. We are dust and unto dust we oftentimes return. We seek transient, ephemeral glory and desire fleeting, short lived splendor. The only solution, then, is to *draw me away* to run after You and rid ourselves of this dust and this corruption.

This is attainable. The Lord confirms, *And I, if I am lifted up from the earth, will draw all peoples to Myself,* (John

12:32). This is by no means a mere reference to the Lord's Resurrection. It is very relevant to our everyday life on earth. Jesus has ascended and He has since been drawing us to Him, *Follow Me, and I will make you a fisherman of men*. To Matthew, the tax collector, He beckoned: *Follow Me*. Instantaneously, St. Matthew followed the Lord.

The phrase *Follow Me* was neither a command nor an invitation. Rather, it was an irresistible, enthralling and miraculous power that has passionately and forcefully transformed Matthew. The Lord's words are powerful, effective, and living. They are like a double edged sword. They were like an immense, powerful magnet that rendered Matthew helpless in the presence of the Lord.

They had therefore accomplished their purpose in completely severing all of St. Matthew's ties with the world. They were an enormous energy that allured and enticed him to the extent that he became disenchanted with the world, hardly mindful of his worldly responsibilities or interests, and unconcerned with material possessions and fleeting riches. He started to follow in the footsteps of the Lord. Therefore, the only logical way to follow the Lord is to implore, *Draw me away, We will run after you*.

Here is a story that I may have mentioned before. One of the guards who was entrusted with watching Jesus' clothes recounted that after the soldiers cast their lots, *on my clothes they cast lots*, he ended up with the Lord's sandals. When he put on the Lord's sandals, he found himself drawn into paths that he never trod before and places to which he had never previously been. Those sandals, he maintained, finally led him to Mount Olive where he found himself kneeling beside a tree and praying for the first time. The Lord's sandals had drawn him.

You may go through a similar experience with the

Lord. Only implore Him to *draw* you with His Holy Spirit, His Grace, His blessings, His angels, or any other means available. *Draw me away, We will run after you.*

Once one is drawn away to the Lord, one will undoubtedly start running after Him. Examples abound. St. Augustine experienced this. He saved neither time nor effort in running after the Lord as soon as he was drawn to Him. He soon ascended to great pinnacles to become a leader and an authority in Divine matters.

One cannot cease to wonder about those sinners who were drawn by the Lord, some of them were not merely transformed into penitents but far transcended this stage and became saints. Examples of such sinners who became saints are St. Mary the Egyptian, who even transformed and became an anchorite. St. Augustine, St. Moses the Black, St. Pelagia, and many others who were drastically and thoroughly transformed.

Draw me away, We will run after you also indicates the work of the Lord in one's life. It is as though one feels as if one cannot help but run after the Lord. *Run in such a way that you may obtain it...therefore I run thus,* (1 Cor 9:24), as was said by St. Paul the Apostle. Now, one is earnestly running in the path of the Lord steadfastly, unwaveringly and showing no signs of hesitation or slothfulness.

Once one is drawn away to the Lord, one will undoubtedly start running after Him

Nor should we lose sight of the plural pronoun *we* in the verse, *Draw me away, We will run after you.* It indicates that one will not run alone. Rather one will attract every one to run along after the Lord. When the prisoner of Philippi was saved, he was baptized along with all the members of his family. Also, when Cornelius came to know the Lord, he followed with all the members of his family in the footsteps of the Lord. Just draw me, O Lord, and I will run after you with all the people that I know. I will not come alone. I will come with thirty, sixty and one hundred.

When the Lord drew the Samaritan woman, all the men in her town were lured into coming to meet Him. Also, when the Lord drew the twelve Apostles, they all followed Him accompanied by three thousand souls the first day, then five thousand and, later, whole towns and cities followed Him. *Draw me away, We will run after you.* This is what happens to anyone whose heart is touched by the Lord and whose life is visited by the Holt Spirit. Such a person will not run after the Lord alone. He will be accompanied by those souls whom God gave him.

It is not important for me to know where You will be leading me

Draw me away. Let me follow You wherever You go, even to Golgotha. It is not important for me to know where You will be leading me. The important thing is to follow You anywhere, even if You are taking me to the Golgotha, or to Gethsemane. I will follow You even if there are persecutions and tribulations. If You lead me to the banks of the river, I will be there with You. If You take me to the Mount of Transfiguration I will be there. Where You are taking me is inconsequential. I set neither limits nor conditions. It just suffices to be with You.

Just, *draw me away, we will run after You.* When we run after You, we will experience joy and happiness in fellowship. *The King has brought me into his chambers. We will be glad and rejoice in you.* This is the lot of all those who have opted to run after the Lord. Happiness and joy filled their lives. Amazing peace and incredible serenity permeated their existence. They are no longer touched by the worldly desires that beget misery, gloom, wretchedness and unhappiness.

Rather, they become *glad and rejoice* in the Lord by virtue of the love that binds them to the Lord. They rejoice in this kind of communion and no one can ever deprive them of such happiness, for His love is better than wine, *we will remember your love more than wine*. It is as though we have become mesmerized and spellbound by Your love. It has completely transformed us. It has caused us to become disenchanted with worldly matters. The world's riches are reduced to nothing. Now we are enchanted by Your love *more than wine*. This love has become to us a source of everlasting joy and a spring of true happiness. That is enough for today. Let us pray.

May God have mercy upon us and bless us, and make His face shine with His Countenance upon us and have compassion upon us. With the prayers and intercessions that are raised on our behalf by the Mother of God, the Pure Saint Mary, and all the angels and apostles, and the prophets, and the martyrs, and the confessors, and the anchorites, and the saints who we ask to pray for us for peace at all times, and the blessings of the saint of this blessed day, and the blessing of Saint Mary first and last, may their holy blessings and the prayers and intercessions be with us all. Amen.

Peace be with you all.

May God make us worthy to say, Our Father…

Have You Seen the One I Love

Draw Me Away

Song of Solomon 1:3-4

In the Name of the Father, the Son, and the Holy Spirit, One God. Amen.

Let us read some verses from Chapter One in the Song of Solomon:

> *Your name is ointment poured forth;*
> *Therefore the virgins love you.*
> *Draw me away!*
> *We will run after you.*
> *The King has brought me into his chambers.*
> *We will be glad and rejoice in you.*
> *We will remember your love more than wine.*
> *Rightly do they love you.*
>
> *Song 1:3-4*

During the Holy Liturgy, we say *Your name is like perfume poured forth.* The Lord's name smells like perfume, sweet-scented fragrances and aromatic ointments. We say, *Your name is sweet and blessed in the mouths of Your saints,* and also *The name of the Lord is a strong tower; the righteous runs to it and are safe,* (Pro 118:10). *In God we boast all day long, and praise Your name forever,* (Ps 44:8).

When someone likes someone else, the mere mentioning of the beloved's name delights them. When their beloved's name is mentioned, it brings joy and happiness. So, when we say, *Your name is poured perfume,* it is an indication of the spreading out of that sweet, aromatic fragrance typically experienced at the pouring forth of perfume. A person who loves the name of the Lord delights when the Lord's name is often mentioned in his presence. Such a person would praise and exalt the Lord's name all day long.

He will constantly sing His name in his heart and praise it with his lips. He will repeatedly talk about that name in the presence of people. When someone loves someone else, every time this person meets other people, he will constantly talk about that person. He always mentions them because it gives him joy and fills his heart with delight. The mere remembrance of the beloved's name is a source of joy and happiness. The name of the Lord is pleasant and sweet, *Your name is sweet and blessed in the mouths of Your saints.*

Some people will, therefore, always contemplate the different names of the Lord, or what we call His characteristics. Try to repeat the Name of the Lord constantly. Keep His name in your heart and in your mind, and it will grant you the spirit of righteousness and love. Repeating His name constantly is an indication of love, and when you love Him, you will constantly ponder and mull over His name. The name of the Lord will always be your song.

At the beginning of the Lord's Prayer we say, *Hallowed be thy Name.* May Your name be always blessed and hallowed.

Your name is ointment poured forth; therefore the virgins love you. The virgin in *Song of Songs* is proud to say to God that the virgins love Him. The phrase, *therefore the virgins love you,* is a sure proof that the *Song of Songs* is not a love story between a man and a woman or between Solomon and one of his lovers, as the adversaries of the Bible and those who lack understanding would like to believe. It will be impossible for a woman who is in love with a man to feel happy and tell him that, *the virgins love you...we will be glad and rejoice in you,* or, *draw us away.* When a woman in love feels that there are other women in her lover's life, she will be extremely distraught and utterly devastated. She may not even have a reason to go on with her life. She will hardly feel happy; neither will she ever think of saying, *therefore the virgins love you.* How could she? What kind of person is she?

> **The name of the Lord will always be your song**

Even the two sisters, Leah and Rachel, who had the same father and mother, could not stand dwelling together with Jacob. They used to tease each other. Rachel even said, *With great wrestlings I have wrestled with my sister,* (Gen 30:8). She had to wrestle with her own sister over their man! Leah even went so far as to hire Jacob to lie with her in return for her son's mandrakes (Gen 30:14-16). They hated each other bitterly. It is, therefore, inconceivable that a woman who loved Solomon would tell him, *Your name is ointment poured forth; Therefore the virgins love you. Draw me away! We will run after you...We will be glad and rejoice in you. We will remember your love more than wine. Rightly do they love you.*

How could a woman in love ever say, *Rightly do*

they love you? Had this been one of the usual love stories, it would have been impossible to experience this happiness and say, *Rightly do they love you!* She would rather break their necks!

Love, as depicted and portrayed in *Song of Songs*, is heavenly; it is celestial. When man loves God, he wants and desires that all others would love Him as well. It is a singularly unique quality of spiritual love that the one you love would also be loved by all. When you love the Lord, you want all the people to love Him too. When you love one of the saints, you want all other people to love that saint as well. You never tire of talking about the qualities and virtues of that saint, and you experience pleasure and happiness when you find new people love him. This is because this spiritual and celestial love is devoid of jealousy, does not seek possession or ownership, and is free from selfishness and egotism.

Consider it a spiritual exercise to ponder on how the saints loved God

In this kind of love, there is no such thing as one being owned by another, the exclusive possession of a particular person and beyond others' reach. On the contrary, one desires that the beloved be the target of love of everyone else. One feels happy to declare, *Rightly do they love you, therefore the virgins love you*, and, *We will be glad and rejoice in you.* This is heavenly, divine love that is devoid of both jealousy, possession or ownership. Rather, it is a never-ending, sacrificial love that finds gratification and contentment when everyone else loves You.

The statement, *Your name is ointment poured forth; therefore the virgins love you*, indicates that those who love You have every reason to do so, O Lord. David ceaselessly praised and extolled the Lord, *Among the gods there is none like You, O Lord,* (Ps 86:8). Everyone has a god that they worship, but I have never found anyone like You, *You are fairer than the sons of men,* (Ps 45:2). There is none like You, for You are, *a God full of compassion, and gracious, longsuffering and abundant in mercy and truth,* (Ps 86:15). You are a God who hates evil. There is none like You. No wonder, *The virgins love you...Rightly do they love you.*

It would be great if you would contemplate why people love the Lord. Consider it a spiritual exercise to ponder on how the saints loved God, why they loved Him, and how they steadfastly abided in this loving relationship with Him. Consider how their love for Him had prompted them to forsake and abandon family, relatives and friends. How they followed Him anywhere He led them, and how emotionally and mentally they had become inexorably attached to Him. Think about how He had become to them the source of nourishment and the means of sustenance, and how He had become their family and friend and everything else. *Therefore the virgins love you.*

Whenever you ponder and meditate on the name of the Lord, you will sing, *Your name is ointment poured forth.* When you adopt Christ's gentle attitude and abide by His kind words, *I am gentle and lowly in heart,* (Mat 11:29), you will understand why, *the virgins love you.*

What is the meaning of *virgins*? It is a reference to those who have consecrated and dedicated themselves to You and no one else. What is the difference between a virgin and a married woman? A married woman has already given herself to someone else, while a virgin has committed herself to no one. This is the difference between a virgin and a married woman from a purely physical perspective. From a spiritual perspective, however, a virgin soul is one that is completely dedicated and thoroughly consecrated to God alone. Such a virgin soul would commit to no one else. In this sense, the word *virgin* would apply to married and unmarried, men and women alike.

The whole Church has been likened to a virgin. St. Paul says, *I have betrothed you to one husband that I may present you as a chaste virgin to Christ,* (2Cor 11:2). Reflect upon this concept. The words *a chaste virgin* is a reference to the whole Church; its men and its women, the married as well as the celibates. All are considered *a chaste virgin* for Christ. This indicates that they have no one else to give themselves to except for the Lord God. This is the virgin soul, one that has not given her love to anyone else but is completely devoted and dedicated to God. The focus of such a soul is the Lord.

All the people who will attain salvation in the Last Day, whether they are married or unmarried, single, celibate, or widowed, have been likened to five wise virgins. These are people who have committed their lives to God, and they have no one else to whom they have given themselves. *Therefore the virgins love you.*

These virgins are people who have not given their love to anyone. Their love has, therefore, been focused purely on God. You, too, should ask yourself, is your soul a virgin soul? Leave the physical perspective out of this. Is your soul a virgin soul irrespective of your physical state; virgin , married, or widowed? Or is it a soul that has other attachments such as worldly lusts, the desires of the flesh, the love of ownership and possession, the hunger for money, power and position? Has your soul become attached to other things, or is it still a virgin soul that has no one else but the Lord?

What does the statement, *Therefore the virgins love you,* mean? It means that the soul that is attached to or preoccupied with another cannot love the Lord. The "other" is bound to come in between God and the soul. The "other" here is not an exclusive reference to another person; it may be the very self, the ego. A self-centered, egotistical person will not be able to love the Lord; there is something that stands in the way. *No one can serve two masters; for either he will hate the one and love the other, or else he will be loyal to the one and despise the other,* (Mat 6:24). There can only be one master, one God.

So, is your heart completely dedicated to the Lord, or are there other things in it that are battling for supremacy? Whatever these things are, whether they are exemplified in another human being or the ego, some kind of worldly pleasure or the desires of the flesh, the love of money, power or the yearning for position, rank and fame- there is something else. If you have given yourself to this "other" thing, then your soul is not a virgin, the "other" thing has taken possession of it. The "other" thing has occupied your soul.

Irrespective of marriage, a virgin soul is the one that has devoted itself to Christ. The important thing is that such a soul has dedicated itself to Christ; it has not given its heart to someone else; it has not given its love to another; and it has not given its thoughts and feelings to anyone else. For such a virgin soul, God is everything, and there is no one else. *Therefore the virgins love you.*

A self-centered, egotistical person will not be able to love the Lord

The reason for this love can be attributed to the fact that there are no obstacles to prevent them from loving you. If there were any obstacles or hindrances, they would not be able to love the Lord. He who smokes is attached to something else. He who covets money has another love, another attachment. For this reason, St. Isaac the Syrian aptly said that the life of monasticism is one of detachment from everything in order to be attached to the One. Therefore, leading a secluded, isolated life is a way of severing oneself from everything to be attached to the One, God. Yet, not everyone is capable of doing that. Not everyone can lead the life of a hermit or recluse. Leading a secluded, isolated life can be hard. It is difficult to abandon everything and adhere to the One. That is exactly what it is: it is the complete disentanglement from all other kinds of love to be steadfastly and firmly attached to God.

Even if I do not want to, I ask You to pull and drag me to You.

That is why the Bible warns that, *Do you not know that friendship with the world is enmity with God?* (Jam 4:4). And, *If anyone loves the world, the love of the Father is not in him,* (1John 2:15), because, simply stated, this indicates that there is "another" thing to which you have become attached. Therefore, ask yourself, is my soul a virgin soul or not? Has it become attached to "another" or is it solely attached to the Lord alone?

He whose eyes are open to the beauty of the Lord will soon find out that everything else is nothing but garbage, trash and grasping for the wind. Until now, we have not discovered the beauty of the Lord. If we become aware of His beauty, if we come to know how sweet He is, we will passionately seek Him. We will wholeheartedly run after Him.

Yet, there are many things that we still find pleasing to us and which still occupy and concern us. That is why we fail to think about and contemplate the beauty of the Lord. There are many things that we love. Our souls are not thoroughly dedicated to the Lord; they are not like that of a virgin.

A virgin's emotional and spiritual energy remains pure and untainted. Her loving power has not been touched yet. It is an energy that has not been squandered or misspent.

However, I have not reached that stage. I am overwhelmed and laboring under many yokes that weigh me down, pull me to the world and what is earthly, and drive me away from You. Every time I try to draw close to You, something pulls me back, and I find myself unable to come closer to You. Some desire by which I am controlled and subjugated prevents me from drawing closer to You. Therefore, I have only one hope in You, now that I am not one of those virgins. *Draw me away*, and I will run after You. Draw me away for I am unable to come to You on my own.

When Jesus saw Peter and Andrew, He called them saying, *Follow Me, and I will make you fishers of men,* (Mat 4:19). It was Jesus who took the initiative, they did not. It was Jesus who saw Mathew, the tax collector. He said to him, *Follow Me*, whereupon St. Mathew followed Him. Likewise, it was Jesus who looked at Zacchaeus and said to him, *Zacchaeus, make haste... for today I must stay at your house,* (Luke 19:5).

On many occasions, the Lord has taken the initiative. That is why I implore the Lord to do the same thing with me, to draw me away, to pull and even force me in Your direction. Even if I do not want to, I ask You to pull and drag me to You. Take me to You, if even by force. I need this kind of external power that will pull and snatch me from the world. I am like someone who has fallen into a pit and is unable to get out of it, someone who feels the need for a certain power larger than what he has at his disposal to lift him out of that pit.

It is like a small piece of metal that has fallen on a magnet and is unable to extricate itself from its magnetic field, its magnetic power. When the magnet moves right, the piece of metal moves right also. When the magnet moves left, it moves left as well. How can it free itself from that magnetic power? It has become powerless to do so. It simply cannot. It is no longer a virgin; it has, as it were, become attached to this magnet and has been rendered powerless to free itself from its grip. Herein lies the plea to, *Draw me away; we will run after you.* For if no external power comes to my aid, I will not be able to free myself on my own. How can I? What a dilemma! What a difficult situation!

A lot of people ask the Lord to, *Draw me away.* I am helpless, O Lord. I want You to intervene on my behalf, for without You I can do nothing. I will be lost if Your hand does not stretch out to me. Just imagine a piece of wood that has fallen into a fire. The fire will burn and consume it as long as that piece of wood cannot remove itself from the fire. That piece of wood would call upon a helping hand to, *draw me away,* to pull and snatch it away from the fire. For if this piece of wood is left in the fire, it will never come out. Likewise, I want You, O Lord, to snatch me from this fire; I want You to bring me out of this Yourself for without You, I simply cannot.

When Isaiah saw the Lord and spoke with Him, he said, *Woe is me, for I am undone! Because I am a man of unclean lips,* (Isaiah 6:5). Because of his unclean lips, he would be annihilated, undone. Thereupon one of the Seraphim took a live coal from the altar and touched his lips saying, *Behold, this has touched your lips; your inequity is taken away, and your sin purged,* (Isaiah 6:7). O Lord, I was unable to do that on my own. I was unable to reach for the altar to take a piece of live coal to touch therewith my lips. How wonderful it was that You sent me one of the

Seraphim to take a live coal from the altar to purify my lips with it.

Sir, I have no man to put me into the pool, (John 5:7). Draw me towards You for I have no one. I have no one. Neither can I control myself. You ask me to be righteous and do the right thing, but I cannot on my own. If I had the ability, I would have done so. Therefore, *Draw me away,* is a cry seeking Divine help and heavenly intervention in man's life to pull him towards God.

I want You to intervene on my behalf, for without You I can do nothing.

Believe me when I say, the biggest obstacle in our ability to repent is the lack of prayer. We fail to ask the Lord to intervene in our lives and give us true repentance. We depend on ourselves and our abilities when we seek repentance. We do not seek God's help when we try to repent. This is impossible! St. Isaac the Syrian aptly says, *He who thinks that there is another door that leads unto repentance other than prayer is blinded and mislead by the devils.* If you truly want to repent, you ought to pour your heart in the presence of the Lord and ask and beseech Him to draw you away to run after Him. Attract me to You, O Lord. Pull me. Draw me. Take me. Help me. Snatch me as a flame out of the fire.

Do not leave me to my own will, my frail determination, or my weak humanity. Do not leave me to trust in my own human abilities for I am no match to the challenges of the world. Only *Draw me away! We will run after you.*

Someone was once held, tied up and placed on top of a pile of wood. The knife was ready and he was about to be presented as an offering. It was Isaac, son of Abraham. How could he possibly save himself? Nothing could help except, *Draw me away! We will run after you.* That was what took place. The Lord pulled him from the top of the altar. Had the Lord not drawn him away, it would have been virtually impossible for him to be saved.

Great are the number of people who are tied up, placed on a pile of wood and about to be consumed and devoured by the fire. Nothing can save them. Nothing can redeem them except, *Draw me away! We will run after you.* Allow the Lord to enter into your life. Do not rely on your hard work, determination, power, strength, or wisdom. *Draw me away! We will run after you.*

God has attracted many unto Him. Saul of Tarsus was on his way from Jerusalem to Damascus, carrying messages by which he would have
There are sins that stand as an obstacle in the way
thrown many men and women in jail. He was at the peak of his anger and revolt against the Church, and with unthinkable cruelty and brutality he was planning to imprison many. However, Jesus appeared to him on the road. *Lord, what do You want me to do?* (Acts 9:6). *Draw me away! We will run after you.*

The Lord said to him, *It is hard for you to kick against the goads.* Come! I will draw you away. *For I will show him how many things he must suffer for My name's sake,* (Acts 9:16). Who could have stood up against Saul of Tarsus? No one! None but the Lord, and Him alone. No one else could have stood up against him. Similarly, it was said that Job the righteous could be beaten by no man. Only God could.

Likewise, there are sins that stand as an obstacle in the way. While man can find himself powerless and incapable of overcoming them, God can beat, defeat and vanquish them. *Draw me away! We will run after you.* Pull me towards You, O Lord. Send me might and power from above. Let me be confident that those who are with us far exceed those who stand against us. I need Your magnetic power to pull me closer to You. This is what Jesus said about His ability to draw and pull others unto Himself, *And I, if I am lifted up from the earth, will draw all peoples to Myself,* (John 12:32). Yes, indeed, O Lord, *Draw me away! We will run after you.*

Lift us up unto You above the clouds that we may walk with You in joy and happiness. Jesus promised to draw us unto Him. He said, *I go to prepare a place for you. And if I go and prepare a place for you, I will come again and receive you to Myself; that where I am, there you may be also,* (John 14:3-4). That is perfect, O Lord. Make us to walk on Your path, behind You. It is noteworthy to mention that the verse does not say, Lead us behind You. Rather, it says, *Draw.* There is this urgency to draw and pull. Force and power are needed.

Someone may be walking in sin unaware of his unrighteousness. God confronts and slaps him to bring him back to his senses. The Lord would call him, Where are you heading? Come back? Where are you going? This lost person starts to realize and become aware of his condition. This slap upon their face may take the form of a difficult situation that might have confronted him at a certain time, a certain predicament or shock, falling sick, death of a family member, or any such difficulties. Upon encountering such difficulties, the stray person would call upon the name of the Lord, *Blessed be Your name, O Lord… Draw me away! We will run after you.*

Draw me anyway You want. Draw me by means of a sermon, or through a word that moves my heart, or even by some difficulty or tribulation. Draw me with Your love or any way You see fit. Draw me by any means You want.

The important thing is that You Yourself draw me towards you. *Draw me away! We will run after you.*

There are those who are lazy and slothful. They can hardly walk along the right path, and they need to be pushed. How could such people run when they cannot even walk? I will tell you about someone who constantly needed to be pushed, and who was finally drawn into the Lord. It was Lot. Lot was reluctant to leave Sodom. Neither he nor his children were willing to depart from there. Yet, the angels kept on pulling and pushing him out of there until he finally departed. He was saved as if by fire. Lot did not even say, *Draw me away! I will run after you.* Rather, it was the Lord Himself who drew him in spite of himself. He was so attached to the land to the extent that he was about to perish.

Now, who knows? I may be just like Lot; I may be in his shoes! After all, the city was beautiful and well watered, *like the garden of the Lord, like the land of Egypt,* (Gen13:10). Green pastures and rich fields were everywhere; blessings and pleasures seemed abundant. I would be unable to leave Sodom unless You have drawn me away and pulled me to You. And when You draw me away, we will run after You.

Many people are just like that. I call upon the Lord to draw me away. I ask Him to become a part of my life, to manage and control it. *O You who has created this heart, fill it with Your love. O You who has formed in me these emotions and feelings, kindle these feelings with Your love. I need You to work actively with me. Be with me. Do not depart from me. Teach me Your way and show me Your paths. Draw me away.*

In both the Old and the New Testaments God has, through a variety of different means, drawn many unto Him. For example, St. Anthony was drawn to the Lord by a verse, he heard a verse that moved his heart. St. Paul the Simple was drawn through difficulties and hardships, a family problem caused his heart to change. St. Paul the First Anchorite was moved when he witnessed a funeral procession, the funeral touched and moved his heart. In addition, there is an example of someone whose heart was touched by a good example and righteous conduct. St. Bachomious the Great provides us with one such example. O Lord, regardless of the manner and irrespective of the means attract me to You. *Draw me away! We will run after you.*

What is the meaning of *we will run?* It means what it says, I will run. In his Epistle to the Corinthians, St. Paul the Apostle says, *Do you not know that those who run in a race all run, but one receives the prize? Run in such a way that you may obtain it,* (1Cor 9:24). This brings to mind a picture of someone who is not satisfied by merely walking in the Lord's path. Rather, he runs, and he runs fast to win the prize. The Lord's path is not for the

O You, Who has created this heart, fill it with Your love

slothful. His ways escape the sluggish and indolent. That is why, we run after You with all that we have. We run with all our might and all our strength.

Nor will I run alone. Hardly! I will run with all the members of my family. *Today salvation has come to this house,* (Luke 19:9). *But as for me and my house, we will serve the Lord,* (Josh 24:15). I, alongside those whom God has given me, will worship the Lord. We will all run along Your path. I will not run alone. I will bring all my friends along. I will bring all my loved ones with me. We will all run along Your path. *Draw me away! We will run after you.*

Many people are lost because of me, O my God.

Perhaps they will be able to find their way if I find mine. Therefore, draw us all unto you that we may run after you. I will run alongside all those around me. I will run with all those who are related to me. As soon as I start running along Your path, they are sure to follow.

Along the Lord's path, there are people who sit at their "Information Desk," as it were. People come and enquire about the way of the Lord. The man at the desk may show them the way, *Go straight, then take a right and you will find the way*. All the while he is still sitting at the information desk. People come and go, while he remains motionless and inactive. Someone will come to him and ask about the Lord's way. He gives them the directions the other person seeks. Another person asks him about the way, and he points out the way, all the while he is still sitting at his information desk. People beat him to their destination while he is inactively sitting in his office.

Another person may be running along the path of the Lord. While so doing, this person may be approached by someone asking about the way. He prompts the seeker to run along, *Come with me... Run with me. We cannot waste time. We cannot stand still. Hurry up!* We will all run after You. However, what is the use if you stand on the road showing people the way while you yourself are not actively involved in running after the Lord? Be active. Move. Run. *Draw me away! We will run after you.*

The Lord's path is not for the slothful

I see St. Anthony entering paradise followed by thousands upon thousands and ten thousands upon ten thousands. I can also visualize St. Athanasius going into the heavens with millions following behind him. I picture a great deal of saints, each followed by great multitudes of people, saying, *Draw me away! We will run after you.*

Paradise is for the zealous runner. It is not for the indolent or the sluggish. When God saved the man sitting by the pool, He did not encourage him to remain seated beside the pool. Rather, He prompted him to carry his bed and go. Walk along the way. Do not remain standing still. The healing that took place beside the pool is merely the beginning of the road. Therefore, you have to run because the road is very long.

If you start running now until the end of your life, you may merely cover a short distance. How so? Perfection is what is expected and required from you. Who can attain perfection? If you are going to slack off, you will never attain it. Therefore, run, for only then may you attain it. Even then, there is a possibility that you may not attain it. At least you have sought and walked in the right path. At least, you have tried. Somewhere along the way, the Lord will meet you. *Draw me away! We will run after you.*

St. Augustine provides us with one of the most striking examples of one running along the Lord's path with sincere zeal. He did just like the rabbit that was able with merely one hop to accomplish what the turtle had done in a number of days. St. Augustine was very far from God. He did not know the Lord for thirty long years, and many people had already surpassed him to the way of righteousness and godliness. Yet the minute he came to his senses and was drawn by the Lord, he was able reach the first ranks with merely a few hops. With a few more, he became a spiritual counselor. With some more hops, he became one of the saints. Now, we all chant the name of St. Augustine until today. How so? He would run. He ran along the paths of the Lord, unlike those who are merely satisfied with their information desks and only content to point the way. Rather, St. Augustine was a man serious in his pursuit. *Draw me away! We will run after you.*

The Lord's path is for those who are filled with enthusiasm and zeal. It is for the fervent, the ardent and the passionate. It is for those who resolutely and determinedly run without stopping or wavering. It is similar to the water of the Nile as it rushes powerfully from the high altitudes of the south along the path until it reaches Egypt. It never stops along the way. For if it did, it would rot. It would become stagnant and change into swamps and marshes. Yet the water is running and gushing forth; it runs through the fields, across the land and in its track. *Draw me away! We will run after you.* I will run along with those around me.

That is enough for tonight.

Let us pray.

May God have mercy upon us and bless us, and make His face shine with His Countenance upon us and have compassion upon us. With the prayers and intercessions that are raised on our behalf by the Mother of God, the Pure Saint Mary, and all the angels and apostles, and the prophets, and the martyrs, and the confessors, and the anchorites, and the saints who we ask to pray for us for peace at all times, and the blessings of the saint of this blessed day, and the blessing of Saint Mary first and last, may their holy blessings and the prayers and intercessions be with us all. Amen.

Peace be with you all.

May God make us worthy to say, Our Father…

Tell Me, O Whom I Love, Where You Feed Your Flock

Song of Solomon 1:7-9

In the Name of the Father, the Son, and the Holy Spirit, One God. Amen.

Let us contemplate some of the verses in chapter one in Song of Songs:

> *Tell me, O you whom I love,*
> *Where you feed your flock,*
> *Where you make it rest at noon.*
> *For why should I be as one who veils herself*
> *By the flocks of your companions?*
> *If you do not know, O fairest among women,*
> *Follow in the footsteps of the flock,*
> *And feed your little goats*
> *Beside the shepherds' tents*
>
> Song 1:7-9

In *Tell me, O whom I love, Where you feed your flock, where you make it rest at noon,* we encounter the human soul in its search for God and His ways, wondering where He is. These words depict a soul that looks for the Lord, seeks and loves Him, and saves no effort to find Him.

What is amazing here is *the one whom I love*. This reminds me of what David the Prophet, whose soul has also been seeking the Shepherd, has said, *Show me Your ways, O Lord, Teach me Your paths*, (Ps 25:4).

The same idea resonates in his psalm, *Your face, Lord, I will seek, Do not hide Your face from me*, (Ps 27:8). His is an example of a soul that loves the Lord and seeks Him everywhere. *Where you feed your flock, Where you make it rest at noon*. These words also remind me of the saintly Mary Magdalene and Mary the wife of Cleopas, who went to Jesus' grave. St. Mary Magdalene would go to the grave every time she knew that someone was going there. *Where you feed your flock, Where you make it rest at noon*. Hers is another example of a souls that seeks the Lord.

Countless people have been seeking the Lord. They would ask the Lord to reveal Himself to them. They want to see Him and enjoy His presence. They want to live with Him, *Tell me, O whom I love, Where you feed your flock, where you make it rest at noon*. How can I find You, O Lord? Will I find You in fasting, in prayers, in praising and singing? Or will I find you in the Holy Liturgy, in Communion, in the Church, in the monastery, or during a quiet retreat of seclusion with You? *Tell me, O whom I love, Where you feed your flock, where you make it rest at noon*.

Such is the nature of souls that are eager to see the Lord, souls that long for and seek Him. David also expressed his desire to seek the Lord in his psalm, *My soul has hungered for You*, an indication of the soul's hunger and thirst for the Lord, its vehement desire to seek and find Him.

St. Augustine had no relationship with God. However, he employed all means possible to find Him. He used logic, philosophy and a number of other means. He wanted to see the Lord and have a relationship with Him.

He desired His companionship and longed to enjoy His fellowship. Finally, he found God "within" him. He exclaimed, *You were with me, but,* because of the abundance of my resistance, *I was not with You* (*Confessions,* 10:38). You were there all along, but I did not feel Your presence. I was wondering, *Where you feed your flock, Where you make it rest,* while You were resting inside of me, in my heart.

Nonetheless, I was unaware of Your presence in me. How touching and heartrending. This reminds me of St. John the Evangelist's, *And the light shines in the darkness, and the darkness did not comprehend it,* (John 1:5). *He came to His own, and His own did not receive Him,* (John 1:11), reiterates the same theme. They did not see or know Him. Though He came to His own, His own did not know or receive or understand Him.

You were there all along, but I did not feel Your presence

Many people who ask the Lord, *Tell me, O whom I love, Where you feed your flock, where you make it rest at noon,* are unaware that the Lord is with them, amongst them and in their midst. They simply do not experience His presence. This also brings to mind what Jesus said to St. Philip, *Have I been with you so long, and yet you have not known Me, Philip,* (John 14:9).

The man born blind also provides us with another example. When Jesus found him again, He said to him, *Do you believe in the Son of God?* The man answered and said, *Who is He, Lord, that I may believe in Him?* To which Jesus responded, *you have both seen Him and it is He who is talking with you,* (John 9:35-37). You are with Him, but you do not see Him. *Tell me, O whom I love, Where you feed your flock, where you make it rest at noon.* This is a call for the Lord, an earnest appeal to see the Lord and a sincere, solemn request to know Him and enjoy His companionship. It is a reflection of an overwhelming desire to join the few followers of the Shepherd in the wilderness, *Where you feed your flock, where you make it rest at noon.*

At a time in which the heat is most severe and spiritual warfare is most intense, a time in which everyone is seeking shelter from the oppressive heat and trying to find comfort for their hearts and their souls, my sole concern and my one desire is to find shelter underneath Your shade. I am seeking You at noon, a time of labor and hard work, toiling under the scorching sun that has beleaguered and stressed me with its excessive heat. Exhausted and worn out I seek You, *Where you feed your flock, where you make it rest at noon.*

What a worthy request! What a beautiful call. A great number of people seek the Lord and reverberate the same request. Saul of Tarsus asked the Lord, *Lord, what do You want me to do?* (Acts 9:6). He expresses his desire to do whatever the Lord pleases, whatever is requested of him. The rich young man also asks Jesus, *Good teacher, what good thing shall I do that I may have eternal life?* (Matt 19:16).

Tell me, O Lord, about Your Divine plan for my life

Tell me, O whom I love, Where you feed your flock, where you make it rest at noon.
I love You, O Lord, from the depths of my heart and with all my being. I long to do whatever is pleasing for You. Sometimes, however, I do not know what to do. I would like to live with You and enjoy Your fellowship, but I do not know how. There are many different paths that lie ahead of me, so which one shall I choose? I would like to know Your holy blessed will and plan for my life. Tell me, O Lord, about Your Divine plan

for my life. *Tell me, O whom I love, Where you feed your flock, where you make it rest at noon.* Let me know what You want me to do.

People oftentimes ask the Lord to make known His plans for their lives. They ask what kind of life the Lord wants them to lead. Is it a life of service or one of seclusion? Is it in matrimony or in celibacy? Is it a life of meditation or one of work? Where do You want me, Lord? Is it in speech or in silence? In utter devotion and consecration or is it something else? *Tell me, O whom I love, Where you feed your flock, where you make it rest at noon.*

This is an example of a human soul that is confronted with many paths. It asks the Lord for help in finding His way among the many paths that lie ahead. The Lord assures you that whatever path you choose, He will walk alongside with you. The important thing for God is your adoring, loving heart. The Lord is not concerned with the "path" you choose. Rather, His main concern is the "way" you choose to lead your life. What kind of life you opt to lead is the important thing for the Lord.

Lot did not show much faith in *Tell me, O whom I love, Where you feed your flock, where you make it rest at noon.* Rather, he chose for himself. He saw that the land of Sodom was green, well watered and ready for pasture. To him, it was like paradise, *like the land of Egypt,* (Gen 13:10-11). He did not care to seek advice from the Lord. Neither did he wish to inquire, *where you feed your flock, where you make it rest at noon.* On the other hand, Abraham the Righteous, did not choose for himself. Rather, he utterly trusted the Lord to lead him into green pastures. Wherever the Lord would lead him, he would follow.

He willingly succumbed to the Lord's command. Abraham's life is guided by his desire to follow in the footsteps of the Lord. *Tell me, O whom I love, Where you feed your flock, where you make it rest at noon.* It is no wonder, then, that when the Lord commanded him to abandon his family and his relatives and to go to a certain mountain that the Lord showed him, Abraham obeyed willingly and wholeheartedly. There, the Lord blessed him and promised, *I will bless those who bless you, And I will curse him who curses you, And in you all the families of the earth shall be blessed,* (Gen 12:3).

Tell me, O whom I love, Where you feed your flock, where you make it rest at noon. I will follow you wherever you go. God informs St. John the beloved that if he wants to know His whereabouts, he should meet Him in exile, on the island of Patmos. And to St. John, if the Lord is to be found in exile, then exile would be the most beautiful place on earth. In fact, St. John does go to exile on the island of Patmos where he sees heaven, the throne of God, and the heavenly hosts. He witnesses an open door leading unto heaven. His is an obedient, willing heart that yearns to seek the Lord wherever He is.

The three young men, Shadrach, Meshach, and Abed-Nego, also sought the Lord and asked Him, *Tell me, O whom I love, Where you feed your flock, where you make it rest at noon.* To which the Lord promised to protect them even in the furnace. When they were finally thrown into the furnace, they were not hurt. *I see four men loose, walking in the midst of the fire... and the form of the fourth is like the Son of God,* (Dan 3:25). Daniel also sought the Lord until he was cast into the den of lions. Nonetheless, Daniel's God sent His angel and shut the lions' mouths (Dan 6:21). God protected Daniel in the lions' den, the three young men in the furnace, Jonah in the belly of the fish, and St. John in exile. The important thing is to find the place where you feel that God will provide for and protect you.

We remember when Abraham, the father of fathers, forgot the Lord's commandment to leave his people and relatives and head towards the mountain that the Lord would show him. In order to avoid the famine, Abraham journeyed to Egypt without consulting with the Lord whether the land he was heading to was an appropriate place where he could secure God's protection and shelter.

The important thing is to find the place where you feel that God will provide for, and protect you.

In Egypt, he encountered many problems. They took Sarah, his wife, to Pharaoh's house because she was a woman of *beautiful countenance*. He faced many afflictions because he had failed to ask the Lord for guidance. Egypt was not the place which the Lord intended for him. It was not there that He would grant Abraham His protection and provide him with His guidance. So, if the Lord was not going to protect him in Egypt, where would he have protected and provided for him? He would rather have protected him in the wilderness with the tent and the altar.

Closely related to this theme are the pertinent verses that also occur in Song of Songs:

Come, my beloved,
Let us go forth to the field;
Let us lodge in the villages.
Let us get up early to the vineyards;
Let us see if the vine has budded,
Whether the grapes blossoms are open,
And the pomegranates are in bloom.
There I will give you my love.

Song 7:11-12

Let us consider the last phrase *There I will give you my love.* What is meant by the word *there*? If You want us to go to the fields, that is fine. If You want us to go to the villages, that is all right. I will go with You to the end of the world as long as I have Your promise that *There (You) will give (me Your) love,* because there is, *Where you feed your flock, where you make it rest at noon.* Wherever You want me, I will go. Whatever the place You lead me to, I will follow. If You want me to relinquish my family and relatives, I will. If You want me to go into exile, I will be there. If it is martyrdom, so be it. If it is the furnace, I will not be shaken.

Whatever the place You lead me to, I will follow

As long as You are with me, I will fear nothing as long as You, *Tell me, O whom I love, Where you feed your flock, where you make it rest at noon.* Show me the way, and I will be there with You. All I want is the assurance that You are there in that place, and that You will protect and provide for me. With this promise and this assurance, I will follow You even to the end of the world.

Rebecca left her father's house. She left her brother, Laban, and followed Isaac wherever he went. Wherever Isaac was, there she would be even if she had to leave her house. In this instance we hear the Lord addressing the human soul saying,

Listen, O daughter,
Consider and incline your ear;
Forget your own people also, and your father's house;
So the king will greatly desire your beauty;
Because he is your Lord, worship Him.
Ps 44:10-12

Whereupon the human soul responds indicating its willingness to forget its people and its father's house as long as it follows in God's footsteps and His paths unto His *green pastures.* The human soul implores the Lord, *Tell me where you feed your flock,* because only He has the assurance of the Good Shepherd who, *...makes me to lie down in green pastures; He leads me beside the still waters.*

He restores my soul; He leads me in the paths of righteousness, (Ps 23:2).

What, however, if the Lord's path leads to death as in the case with the martyrs? How would you feel then? The human soul would respond saying, *...though I walk through the valley of the shadow of death; I will fear no evil; For You are with me; Your rod and Your staff, they comfort me,* (Ps 23:4).

Thereby the human soul indicates its readiness for anything as long as the Lord is going to watch over it even in *the valley of the shadow of death.* The important thing is to, *Tell me, O whom I love, Where you feed your flock, where you make it rest at noon.* My soul longs to be where the Lord is. It yearns to go wherever God leads and follow Him in whichever way He goes, *My soul follows close behind You,* (Ps. 63: 8).

Like Lot, the Prodigal Son journeys into a far off land to no avail. He encounters problems and hardships and decides to return. When he finally comes to himself, he says, *I will rise and go to my father,* (Luke 15:18). He decides to ask him, *Tell me, O whom I love, Where you feed your flock, where you make it rest at noon.*

It would be to your great advantage if you are always preoccupied with the Lord. It is to your benefit and goodness if you keep looking for and seeking Him. Before you go anywhere, you should ask yourself whether you will be able to see the Lord in this place or not. If in doubt, do not go that way for it will avail you nothing. This is not where the Lord wants you. Rather, seek the Lord somewhere else, *Tell me, O whom I love, Where you feed your flock, where you make it rest at noon.*

Occasionally, some young men who desire a life of consecration may be lured into seeking a big, magnificent, and splendid church, one that has authority and influence. This may be running counter to the Lord's desire and plan for them. The Lord may want them to go to a far off village or one of those distant, out-of-the-way, least popular places that are not known to many. These may be the places where people may feel forgotten or even neglected. These may be the places where help is most scant and, therefore, direly needed. For this reason, the children of the Lord refrain from choosing for themselves. Rather, they trust the Lord to choose for them. To them, the important thing is to, *Tell me, O whom I love, Where you feed your flock, where you make it rest at noon.* Their one desire is, *Under Your shadow, I long to rest.*

At times of spiritual weakness and frailty, one may sometimes call the Lord saying, *Tell me, O whom I love, Where you feed your flock, where you make it rest at noon.* At such times one may feel abandoned, bereft of the sustaining power of Divine Providence and experiencing feelings utterly alien and at odds with those to which one has been accustomed. At moments such as these, one feels extremely different. *I am not myself. This cannot be the same person who used to love the Lord and experience true happiness in His presence.*

This is by no means the same person that has once proclaimed, *His left hand is under my head, And His right hand embraces me.* One starts to feel that the words of the Lord are no longer pleasant and sweet, that one's prayers are devoid of their former ardor and zeal, and that one's quiet time with the Lord has lost its former lucidity and beauty. A feeling of apathy overwhelms the human soul as it indecisively and irresolutely searches for the Lord. *Tell me, O whom I love, Where you feed your flock, where you make it rest at noon.*

One longs to return to the Lord. It is true that one

feels driven away from the Lord, yet they still acknowledge their love for the Lord. The human soul has not completely forsaken its first love. One may indeed have forsaken their spiritual activities, practices and prayers, but they remain intricately attached and intrinsically drawn to the overpowering love of the Lord. One's love for the Lord is unmistakably there even though one may err. But how could that be?

It is to your benefit and goodness if you keep looking for and seeking Him

We all know how St. Peter the Apostle cursed and denied the Lord. Yet when Jesus confronted and censured him saying, *Simon, son of Jonah, do you love Me more than these?* Simon replied saying, *Yes, Lord; you know that I love you,* (John 21:15). The human soul desperately longs to return. It silently expresses its eagerness to return to the Lord. *Tell me, O whom I love, Where you feed your flock, where you make it rest at noon.* It is bewildered and puzzled. Yet, it searches for ways to come back to Him and become the person it once was. A lot of people go through similar experiences.

Some people who have succumbed to sin say:
By the rivers of Babylon,
There we sat down, yea, we wept
When we remembered Zion.
We hung our harps
Upon the willows in the midst of it...
How shall we sing the Lord's song
In a foreign land?"

Ps. 137: 1-4

The human soul is eagerly seeking the Lord's dwelling place and passionately desires to enter His Holy Tabernacle. *Tell me, O whom I love, Where you feed your flock, where you make it rest at noon.* This is a call to the Lord. The human soul anxiously seeks the Lord, bewildered and yet eager, exhausted yet determined. It cries out for help having experienced the bitterness of sin and the confusion, bewilderment and uncertainty of going astray. It is desperately seeking help, even the deliverance, of the Lord.

God loves every human soul that seeks Him

This is exactly the case of that human being who is made to taste of the bitterness, anguish and distress of sin. *The plowers plowed on my back; they made their furrows long,* (Ps. 129:3). The same feeling of the human soul in distress is also expressed in, *They surrounded me like bees; they were quenched like a fire of thorns,* (Ps.118:12). It is also expressed, *In the way in which I walk, They have secretly set a snare for me. Look on my right hand and see, For there is no one who acknowledges me,* (Ps 124:3-4).

However, even in the midst of this confusion and perplexity, I do acknowledge that, *You are my help and my refuge in this foreign land.* Hence, I call unto You, *Tell me, O whom I love, Where you feed your flock, where you make it rest at noon.* I wonder how I can repent, how I can return to You, how we can become the way we were and return to my first love. I wonder how we may reconcile, *Tell me, O whom I love,* because I do not know the way.

Even though I have gone astray like sheep, I am desperately seeking your countenance and Your deliverance. *Deliver Your son for I have not forgotten Your commandments.* This same sentiment is reflected in the human soul's call to the Lord, *Open my eyes, that I may see wondrous things from Your law,* (Ps. 119:18), and in, *Show me Your ways, O Lord; Teach me Your paths* (Ps. 25:4). *Tell me, O whom I love, Where you feed your flock, where you make it rest at noon.*

God loves every human soul that seeks Him. He opens His arms to everyone who longs for Him. *He who seeks Me will not be sent away.* Even if you were weeping by the rivers of Babylon, you will not be forsaken nor abandoned. However, while the Lord confirms that He will show you His ways, the human soul wonders in bewilderment how that could be possible. *Where is the way?* But the Lord soon reaffirms, *If you do not know, O fairest among women,* whereupon the human soul again looks inwardly at its weaknesses and filth and questions the *fairness* that the Lord sees in it. *How can I be seen as "fair?"* I do not even know Your way. I have gone astray and ended upon the rivers of Babylon.

However, the Lord again confirms that it is enough for Him that you love Him enough to call His Name. The Lord is happy that you call Him and that makes you *fairest among women.* To that *fair* human soul the Lord is now ready to show the way:

> *If you don't know , O fairest among women,*
> *Follow in the footsteps of the flock,*
> *And feed your little goats*
> *Beside the shepherds' tents.*
>
> *Song 1:8*

Follow in the footsteps of the flock. Many have trodden along that path before and have left their marks along the way. Follow these *footsteps* and you will get there. *Footsteps* is a reference to the life history of the saints. Those are the people who followed the path of righteousness and completed their missions. A monk, for example, who decides to go to the wilderness but finds himself at a loss and confused without a spiritual guide to point the way to him, will surely find the way the minute he resorts to the Lord and asks, *Tell me, O whom I love, Where you feed your flock, where you make it rest at noon.* The Lord will instruct him to *follow in the footsteps* of the saints in this wilderness.

St. Anthony, St. Macarious, and St. Paul the Anchorite were here before and left their marks. All you need to do is to keep an eye on their path and you will accomplish your mission. Follow *in the footsteps of the flock* and you will not go astray. We thank the Lord our God that in every virtue known to mankind saints have attained great altitudes and remarkable heights and have left us unprecedented ideals and unparalleled values. It is enough that we follow in the footsteps of the flock and we will reach our destination and accomplish our mission. Anchorites have followed and tracked these *footsteps of the flock* and have documented them in *The Paradise of the Desert Fathers* and in other books.

There are other saints who have chosen a different path. *Footsteps* is a reference to many paths, not just one. There is the path of devout service as exemplified by St. Athanasius, St. Cyril and our teacher St. Dioscorous. Another path is that of Martyrdom as exemplified by St. George, St. Mina and St. Demiana. Yet another path is offered by priests or ministers who save no effort in serving the multitudes and filling the world with their celestial aroma. Anba Abraham the Bishop of El-Fayyoum offers us an example of a true shepherd in his kindness and compassion towards the poor.

Abba Sarabamoun Abu-Tarha offers us another example in the endless mercy and love he had exhibited towards needy families. Abba Rewies offers us a third example by his self-denial and by leading a life of asceticism and austerity. *Follow in the footsteps of the flock* and you will know the way. This is how the Lord explains that the life history of saints can guide all those who want to walk in the paths of righteousness. Saints have left us myriad of examples that we may follow in their footsteps.

Moreover, these examples abound with the most

minute details of how they have conducted themselves during their daily lives with whatever they had to face or encounter. Therefore, if you are concerned that anger is afflicting you and weighing you down, you are instructed to *follow in the footsteps of the flock* and examine how the fathers have handled anger in their lives. If you are concerned that your sexual desire is troubling and disheartening you, *follow in the footsteps of the flock* and examine what the fathers had done to subdue these desires. If it is self-importance, pride, and conceit, look at and contemplate the examples that the fathers have left for us. Study and examine how they conquered all these weaknesses.

However, the mere examination or study of these examples is not sufficient. The Lord instructs us to *follow*, not merely study, examine or contemplate. The Lord instructs us to *follow in the footsteps*, not to sit still and be content with contemplating the splendor and beauty of the examples given. You cannot be content with

All you need to do is to keep an eye on their path and you will accomplish your mission

merely admiring the great stories that the saints have left. Rather, you need to *follow in (their) footsteps*. You need to stop weeping, crying and feeling sorry for yourselves and take action and *follow* them. You need to stop complaining that you have nobody to guide you and that you do not know the way and start following in the footsteps of those great saints.

Yes, this is the way. You need to follow in their footsteps and if a sin is lurking in your heart, you need to *feed your little goats, Besides the shepherd's tents*. There is a reference to sin in the expression *little goats*. It is a reference to the dark, ugly and filthy sinful desires that we entertain. If we take these infirmities and weaknesses and lay them at the feet of the shepherds, we will find a solution and attain an absolution.

By doing this the human soul that longs for the Lord will attain its goal and objective. Only by following in the footsteps of the fathers and of the saints will this be possible. The human soul has to walk along the same path, *Follow in the footsteps of the flock.*

Herein the Bible shows us that God does not look favorably on heretics and fads, those who seek novel and unorthodox ways. This is not the path unto righteousness and godliness. Someone may adopt a novel attitude to Christian life and thought. The Lord will direct this person to *follow in the footsteps of the flock*, to adopt the fathers' and saints' methods and ways, and to *feed (their) little goats, Besides the shepherds' tents*, if they are to attain righteousness. The

Do not trust in yourself, and do not rely on your own counsel

Lord will instruct this person not to adopt strange ways or follow novel paths but to follow the straightforward path that had been trodden by the fathers before. They had shown the way and even described it step by step. They had tried it and it was proven that it leads unto righteousness. *If you do not know, O fairest among women, Follow in the footsteps of the flock, And feed your little goats Beside the shepherds' tents,* (Song 1:8).

The *shepherds' tents* is a reference to spiritual guides and the dwelling places of the fathers. The Bible says, *He who is without a guide will fall like the leaves of the tree.* Be watchful! There are a lot of goats that have mixed with your sheep. You should feed these little goats *beside the shepherds' tents*. These shepherds will instruct you as to how to get rid of every sin. Do not trust in yourself, and do not rely on your own counsel. *Follow in the footsteps of the flock.*

Walk along the same road. I sincerely wish that some of you will research and study the life histories of the fathers and divide it into different topics and categories and examine how they had treated every subject. St. Isaac says, *Pleasant and delightful are the life histories of the saints; they are like fresh water to tiny, newly born buds.* We need to learn from the life histories of the fathers to nourish our spirituality, just as sprouts and buds need water to blossom. *Follow in the footsteps of the flock.* Do not adopt new fads or follow untried, untested ways.

If you do not know, O fairest among women, follow in the footsteps of the flock, is a reflection of the possible lack of knowledge at times. Many people are proud and conceited and look at themselves as *fair*. The Lord instructs those and shows them the way. The phrase *If you do not know, O fairest among women*, indicates that there are many levels or ranks. Someone may reach the first level; however, many more levels lie ahead. A person may attain higher levels.

Still, there are worthier levels or ranks that are left unknown and unattained. The Lord will instruct that person saying, *If you do not know, O fairest among women, follow in the footsteps of the flock.* That person will then ask the Lord saying, *Tell me, O you whom I love, Where you feed your flock, Where you make it rest at noon.* The Lord will then confirm that many sheep, Godly and righteous people, have been able to reach Him. They have followed the right path until they have attained godliness.

The Lord can easily reveal or manifest Himself in very direct ways. However, He would rather have us follow the old, known and tested rituals of following in the *footsteps of the flock.* Some people claim that all they want is a direct relationship with God. They go far enough to undermine the importance of the spiritual guidance provided by the fathers, the shepherds. They even maintain that confession is needless and unnecessary. However, the Lord's path is different.

While the Lord is capable of revealing Himself directly to those who seek Him, He clearly instructs them who *do not know* to follow *in the footsteps of the flock*, and to *feed (their) little goats at the shepherds' tents* because the Lord Himself has anointed those shepherds. Moreover, those people who have attained godliness and righteousness have pursued and followed His path and sought and hungered for the instructions of His anointed. If we *Follow in the footsteps of the flock*, we will get there.

May the Lord grant us the wisdom to understand His ways and come to know and *follow in the footsteps of the flock*. Glory be unto His name for ever. Amen.

Let us pray.

May God have mercy upon us and bless us, and make His face shine with His Countenance upon us and have compassion upon us. With the prayers and intercessions that are raised on our behalf by the Mother of God, the Pure Saint Mary, and all the angels and apostles, and the prophets, and the martyrs, and the confessors, and the anchorites, and the saints who we ask to pray for us for peace at all times, and the blessings of the saint of this blessed day, and the blessing of Saint Mary first and last, may their holy blessings and the prayers and intercessions be with us all. Amen.

Peace be with you all.

May God make us worthy to say, Our Father...

I Sought Him,
But I Did Not Find Him

Song of Solomon 3:1

By night on my bed I sought the one I love; I sought him, but I did not find him.

Song 3:1

In the Name of the Father, the Son, and the Holy Spirit, One God. Amen.

Our spiritual life is not all about the pleasures that we experience in the presence of the Lord. There are wars to be expected and fought. As the Bible warns us, *a righteous man may fall seven times and rise again*, (Prov 24:16). Satan envies the children of God and tries to hinder their spiritual growth. There are also times in which we manifest signs of weakness and abandonment. Therefore, throughout our spiritual life, it would be

There are times in which we manifest signs of weakness and abandonment

virtually impossible to feel that, *His left hand is under my head, and his right hand embraces me*, (Song 2:6). It will also be difficult to claim that you have constantly been able to abide in the Father because of the intervals in which failures, weaknesses, confusion, uncertainty, and abandonment are likely, even inevitable.

By night on my bed I sought the one I love. I would like to contemplate on the word *night*. There are two meanings for the word *night*. One is physical or literal, and the other is spiritual. The literal meaning for the word *night* could be taken to reflect that the night is a favorable time to exist in the presence of the Lord. The *night* is the time when nature is most serene and peaceful, and when we are far from the hustle and bustle of the never-ending burdens, toils and responsibilities of the day.

It is at night that man can finally recoil and retreat from all of these burdens to ponder and contemplate. It is then that man can enjoy the Lord in solitude and in seclusion. In this regard, it is worth mentioning that one of the fathers has most aptly described the night as a time that should be dedicated to prayer. Our Lord Jesus Christ used to spend the night praying on Mount Olive. It was as though He was enjoying the night on Mount Olive. In Psalm 134, we read, *Praise the Lord, all you servants of the Lord who minister by night in the house of the Lord. Lift up your hands in the sanctuary and praise the Lord*, (Ps. 134:2).

Many saints have experienced the joy of praying in the peace and tranquility of the night. A great deal of saints were in the habit of sleeping for a short while during the day in order to spend the whole night in prayers. We know the story of St. Arsanius who used to put his back to the sunset and stand praying until the sun would rise in front of him. He used to spend the whole night praying. The same thing was said about our Lord Jesus Christ who used to spend the whole night praying. One of our holy fathers has aptly said, *Gain the friendship of the night in order to have a victorious spiritual life during the day*. The spiritual funds that you have been able to store and accumulate during the night will prove useful during the day.

The night belongs to the Lord. He has, thus, established the stars and the planets that shine and give light till the end of time to govern it. It is a sad and deplorable thing that currently the night has acquired a bad reputation. We oftentimes hear about night clubs, nightly gatherings and parties, and all manners of wasteful and unavailing "fun." The night seems to have lost its dignified and venerable spiritual position. However, the fact remains that the night belongs to the Lord. Jesus spent the night praying. To Him belongs the night and the day.

The night is a favorable time to exist in the presence of the Lord

At the present time, the word *night* is associated in the minds of many with amusement, diversion, and distraction. It is not surprising, then, that when they sing, they use the word *night* to reminisce and evoke their shameful and reprehensible deeds at night.

The spiritual person, by ridding oneself from the hustle and bustle and the many wearisome responsibilities of the day, is capable of finding oneself in the seclusion and solitude offered by the night. The night offers the best time to meditate and give an account for your day. Likewise, it also presents the most opportune time to pray in serenity and tranquility. Imagine that while the whole world is asleep, you alone are enjoying the presence of the Lord. You feel as though the Lord is there just for you.

By night on my bed I sought the one I love. I came to

the Lord to tell Him that I have spent the long hours of the day to no avail. I have wasted my time in speeches, debates, discussions, quarrels, reading, writing, etc., in this vain, worthless world. *For what profit is it to a man if he gains the whole world and loses his own soul?* (Matt. 16:26). I have spent the whole morning with people, but I want to spend the night with You. I have spent the day speaking, and now I would like to spend the night in silence and peace. I have spent the day working

Sin is not necessarily a reflection of hatred or antipathy

and toiling, and now I would like to spend the night pondering and meditating. *All you servants of the Lord, who by night stand in the house of the Lord! Lift up your hands in the sanctuary, and bless the Lord,* (Ps. 134:1, 2).

By night on my bed I sought the one I love. Even your bed can be made holy. It could be consecrated to the Lord. Your prayers, your meditations and all your righteous deeds sanctify your bed. This is what is usually referred to as *bedroom prayers.* In the Psalms, David says, *When I remember You on my bed, I meditate on You in the night watches,* (Ps. 63:6).

O, Lord, my God, I am Yours. Everything that I have is Yours. When I stand, I do it for You. When I kneel down to worship, I kneel and worship You. Even when I am on my bed, I am Yours. I am Yours wherever I am and in whatever I do. I belong to You whether I am standing, sitting or sleeping. *By night on my bed I sought the one I love.* This seeking is prompted by love, *I sought the one I love.* Overwhelmed, as I am, by the endless burdens and responsibilities of life, estranged and virtually cut off from the One I love all day long, I have finally come to my bed to seek Him.

Let us now consider another point. The *night* may

also be a symbol of sin and disgraceful, our unrighteous deeds. The *bed* may also be a symbol of laziness and idleness. This may portray a picture in which one finds oneself lying slothfully and indolently. Therefore, even during dark, turbulent times, when one is being indolent and slothful, I remember the Lord, my God. *By night on my bed I sought the one I love; I sought him, but I did not find him.*

The apostles say that you are the sons of light and in the Midnight Praise it says, *Rise up, sons of light, and let us sing to the Lord of Hosts.* The night may sometimes be a symbol of darkness and sin. Yet even then, *I sought the one I love.* What does this mean?

There are those to whom sin is external rather than internal. Those who may commit sin even though they actually love the Lord. They may even feel that no matter what they do, they still love the Lord. St. Peter denied Jesus three times. When Jesus asked Simon Peter, *Simon, son of Jonah, do you love Me more than these?* (John 21:15), Simon answered, *You know all things; You know that I love You,* (John 21:17).

Sin is not necessarily a reflection of hatred or antipathy. It could very well be a reflection of some weakness and infirmity on our part, or strength or might on the part of the enemy. It might also be a reflection of ignorance or a number of other reasons. Regardless of the cause, man ultimately turns to God, *By night I sought the one I love.* The Prodigal Son who, *wasted his possessions with prodigal living,* (Luke 15:13), turned to the one he loved and, fortunately enough, found him. At night in that far-off country, living with the swine, he turned to the Lord.

Jonah the Prophet is another person who also turned to and remembered God at night. Jonah ran away from God in rebellion and defiance. He was thrown into the sea, and a great fish swallowed him. However, in the middle of this darkness, and there in the belly of the whale, he sought the one he loved.

Do not think, O Lord, that I do not love You. I may escape from You, and still love You. And I may sin, and still love You. And I may deny You three times and still love You. Yet, *By night on my bed I sought the one I love.*

There are those who, when targeted and pressured by sin, completely succumb to it until they feel lost and lose their faith. Still, there are those who have inner beauty and a good moral fiber. When these are tempted by sin they *seek the one they love.* Nevertheless, there are times in which man may seek the Lord but fails to find Him, *I sought him, but I did not find him.*

By night on my bed, feeling worn out and exhausted, *I sought the one I love; I sought him, but I did not find him.* The verse, *I sought him, but I did not find him,* is a painfully moving and disconcerting one. What is the meaning of, *I sought him, but I did not find him?*

Lord, You have promised, *Seek, and you will find; knock and it will be opened to you,* (Luke 11:9). Why then do I now seek and cannot find?

The answer to this question lies in what is known in the spiritual world as *intervals of abandonment or forsaking.* During such intervals, Grace forsakes, or abandons, man. When man seeks the Lord, he will not find Him. Man finds himself tiresomely searching for a gleam of hope, a trace of shimmering light in the middle of overwhelming and overpowering darkness. He seeks the Lord, but he does not find Him. *I will make your heavens like iron and your earth like bronze,* (Lev 26:18-20). This person prays and does not find an answer. The special bond and the distinctive, unique ties between man and God are no more. They are gone.

That exclusive, exceptional relationship of old, that peculiar feeling distinctive of God's existence in the heart, and that overwhelming joy characteristic of the unity with the Lord seem to have gone. *I sought him, but I did not find him. And because lawlessness will abound, the love of many will grow cold*, (Matt 24:12-13).

Many people have undergone this stage and experienced this feeling. *Not too long ago, O my Lord, I was a sweeping undercurrent of love. My love was like fire. Now, when I look for that former fire, I cannot feel it. When I look for that former zeal and passion in prayer, I do not find it. When I search for that fervent love, I do not experience it anymore. There is no solace or comfort in reading. Even Your very existence is nothing but an ever-fleeing phantom in my life.* What has happened? *I sought him, but I could not find him; I called him, but he gave me no answer*, (Song 5:6). How saddening and disconcerting it is to experience such a feeling.

A great number of people undergo this experience nonetheless. You seek the Lord, but you do not find Him. You remember a time when the Lord was so near and so close. Whenever you called Him, He would listen. It is no exaggeration to say that the Lord would listen to the heart's desire, even before a prayer has been said. Just looking to the Heights without uttering a word would have been acceptable before the Lord.

Man finds himself tiresomely searching for a gleam of hope

You may have found yourself filled with blessed thoughts and reflections by just opening the Bible and reading only one verse. That one verse may have brought about such a surge of comfort and such an abundance of solace that you may have not found the time to read another verse. Where have all of these feelings gone now? *I sought him, but I could not find him; I called him, but he gave me no answer.* Such is the nature of these intervals in which Grace abandons the human heart.

The Lord persists and keeps on knocking and asking man to open the door

Why do some people undergo these intervals of abandonment and forsaking? Some experience these intervals at times of pride and conceit. When a human being becomes heedless or neglectful, signs of self-importance, vanity and arrogance start trickling into the heart. When this happens, God becomes alarmed about man's spiritual well-being and abandons him out of concern. Then man falls and becomes aware of his weaknesses. Man will then call the Lord, and he will say, *I am weak, O Lord, and I am not able to stand.* The Lord would answer, *I want to restore you to your former humility and meekness. The Lord is near to those who have a broken heart, and saves such as have a contrite spirit*, (Ps 34:18). It is no exaggeration to suggest that if you keep a remorseful, repentant and contrite heart, you will not experience this interval of forsaking or abandonment.

There is another reason that may bring about these intervals of abandonment. Man may show no interest in the Lord. He or she neglects to have a relation with the Lord because they love the world more than God. They have no time for the Lord. When the Lord knocks at the door, they do not have the time for Him. Where do we read that something like this happens? In Chapter 5 in the *Song of Songs*, we read something to that effect, *I sleep, but my heart is awake; It is the voice of my beloved! He knocks,* (Song 5:2). *The voice of my Beloved! Behold, He comes* leaping upon the mountains, skipping upon the hills, (Song 2:8). He knocks, saying, "Open for me, my sister, my love, my dove, my perfect one," (Song 5:2). However, no one has the time to open the door for the Lord. We have many claims upon our time. We are simply busy, Go away for now; when I have a convenient time, I will call for you, (Acts 24: 25).

The Lord persists and keeps on knocking and asking her to open the door, For my head is covered with dew, my locks with the drops of the night, (Song 5:2). The Lord has been waiting for a long time. He has been waiting until His head is covered with dew and His locks with the drops of the night. Still He asks, Open for me, my sister, my love, my dove, my perfect one. In response, He receives, I have taken off my robe; how can I put it on again? I have washed my feet; how can I defile them? (Song 5:3). What a response! How inappropriate! How unbecoming!

It is amazing how human beings seek and even hunt for excuses to stay away from the Lord. I, O Lord, am not free for You right now. I have so many projects going on right now. I am in the middle of writing a book right now. I am busy with service in the Church right now.

We claim that we are busy right now. The time is inconvenient. You may have huge projects and activities that require a lot of attention at the present time. Or you may be currently writing some books. Or the Church service with which you are involved claims all your time. You may have to make important social visits and phone calls. You may even cherish the existence of a sin which is most desirable to your heart. There is no time for the Lord now. What then? The Lord still knocks on the door. We leave Him there standing and waiting. Well! We will see the result of this.

God does not force man to love Him. If a person wants to leave the Lord, God allows them to do whatever they please. In time we will see how this person's life proceeds and ends. The Lord will abandon such a person who is not willing to have a relation with Him. *My beloved put his hand by the latch of the door, and my heart yearned for him,* (Song 5:4). The Lord has but touched the heart and left. Alarmed, the bride declares, *I opened for my beloved, but my beloved had turned away and was gone,* (Song 5:6). In sorrow she continues, *My heart went out to him when he spoke. I sought him, but I could not find him; I called him, but he gave me no answer,* (Song 5:6). Alas! Now is the time for feeling sorry.

The Lord was there. He was within your reach. He was within your grasp. Unfortunately, you left Him. You showed no interest. You did not appreciate the value of life with the Lord. You did not experience the pleasure and the joy of being with Him. In vain I sought things that were of no avail. I have tried to dig up wells in a, *dry and thirsty land where there is no water,* (Ps. 63:1). *I sought him, but I could not find him; I called him, but He gave me no answer.* The Lord is patiently waiting for man to return from his evil ways. However, He will not force him to do so. An interval of abandonment follows. Such intervals are brought about because of man's neglect of and lack of interest in the Lord. The Lord respects man's freedom to choose.

Man does not fully appreciate the work of Grace within the human soul. Conversely, the human soul disdainfully shows signs of rebellion and does not give way for the power of Divine Grace to work. That *first love* (Rev. 2:4) and that exquisite bond that tied the human soul to the Lord seems to have become a thing of the past, a distant memory. Now is the time for suffering and affliction. *I sought him, but I could not find him; I called him, but he gave me no answer.*

Egoism is one of the causes of these intervals of abandonment. Self-centeredness or self-interest oftentimes takes God's place in the heart. When man's attention is solely and wholeheartedly focused on the self, there is hardly a place left for the Lord in the heart. Man's main concern is limited to his work, deeds, position, future, and accomplishments. There is nothing in man's heart or mind except how to advance in life, how to build the self, and how to obtain, get and amass things. Man's world is devoid of God.

> **Self-centeredness or self-interest oftentimes takes God's place in the heart**

The only concern is to advance in life. The sole goal is to build the self, which, ironically enough, cannot be accomplished except with a real relationship with the Lord. But man is solely preoccupied with the self, *I will pull down my barns and build greater... And I will say to my soul, 'Soul, you have many goods laid up for many years; take your ease; eat, drink, and be merry,* (Luke 12:18-19). The self is the focus. What will I do? When can I do and attain this? At such intervals when man is motivated by that insatiable desire to satisfy the needs of the ego, man would, in vain, look for the Lord.

An example of such a person whose main concern is his ego is one who, when entrusted with a certain service in the Church, may neglect and even forget that special bond that ties him to God. He may start to act with self-importance and superiority, ostensibly assuming all the major responsibilities, and trying to become the most important figure in that particular service. To do so, this person may even oppose and fight others until he becomes isolated from them. When he looks for the Lord, he will not find Him.

That is strikingly similar to what has happened with the bride. She also was looking for the Lord. However, she was preoccupied with her clothes, with her recently washed feet, and other concerns, *I have taken off my robe; how can I put it on again? I have washed my feet; how can I defile them?* (Song 5:3). In the midst of all these concerns and preoccupations, the Lord has disappeared, vanished. He has simply gone.

God may sometimes allow us to taste the bitterness and experience the anguish of separating from Him in order to yearn and earnestly seek Him. It seems to me that when the Lord lavishly bestows upon us His tenderness and loving-kindness, we tend to forget His rights, His love, and we *wash our feet* and *take off our robes*. In short, we become spoiled and irresponsible. At such times, the Lord may sometimes withdraw and abandon us. He will not force anyone to love Him. Love is a sensitive issue and a special bond. If it does not flow naturally from the heart, it is useless. No one can be forced to love. God does not compel man to love Him. Never.

Even though God "appears" to abandon us, He cares deeply about us

What, then, is the meaning of *I sought him, but I could not find him?* Since God is omnipresent, what could that sentence possibly mean? It means that I cannot find that special bond, that tie, those all too familiar feelings, that love of times of yore, and that certain joy I used to experience; I cannot find these in the heart.

Rather, I feel such a distance between the Lord and myself. He is way up there in the skies, and I am down here. We have become worlds apart. How deplorable and saddening. There was a time in which You were not just with me; You were in me. We were together; You abided in me and I in You. Where have these days gone? *I sought him, but I could not find him; I called him, but he gave me no answer.*

To suggest that *I could not find Him* is an indication of the Lord's cruelty or unkindness could not be further from the truth. God perceives and senses that by allowing such a distance and such a gap, He may bring us back unto Him. It is when He is at a distance that we start yearning for Him. When we are left and abandoned, we start seeking Him.

God is never harsh or unkind. Even His punishment is but a means to lure us back unto Him. For this reason we oftentimes see that once God moves away, the human soul starts yearning for Him. *I will rise now, and go about the city; in the streets and in the squares I will seek the one I love,* (Song 3:2). Even though God "appears" to abandon us, He cares deeply about us. This distancing on the part of the Lord is only superficial. This is similar to a mother who teaches her infant how to walk. The infant may crawl some, walk some and even fall in the process. The mother watchfully observes her infant at a distance.

Abandoning the infant temporarily is not an expression of lack of love. Rather, as the infant falls and tries to stand up again, its nerves and muscles become stronger. When the infant finally gathers enough strength to stand upright, the mother reaches for them to provide more support, thereby assuring the infant that this abandonment is but for a short while. She is there diligently watching the situation, ready to intervene at the most opportune moment to help the infant to its feet the second it shows inability to do it on its own. The Lord deals with us in a similar fashion.

Sometimes we wonder if the feeling associated

with abandonment entailed in the phrase *I sought him, but I could not find him* would be a permanent one. However, the Lord assures us that it is temporary. We hear His assuring voice, *It is not going to last, my beloved. Even if you forsake me, I cannot forsake you. Even if you leave me, I cannot leave you.* The Lord confirms, *For a mere moment I have forsaken you, but with great mercies I will gather you,* (Is. 54:7). The Lord may have forsaken me, but only for a moment. He cannot stand forsaking us forever.

The human soul exclaims, *The watchmen who go about the city saw me; I said, 'Have you seen the one I love?' Scarcely had I passed by them, when I found the one I love. I held him and would not let him go,* (Song 3:3-4). Now, I will not let him go. I will hold firmly to Him. This is a natural feeling because of the abandonment and the subsequent state of confusion and loss that the human soul experiences without the Lord. Oftentimes, we entreat the Lord to deliver us from a particular hardship and promise that we will never forsake Him again. We even vehemently declare that if the whole world comes against us, our love would remain unfaltering and steadfast, *I held him and would not let him go.*

Have you ever gone through these intervals of abandonment? Imagine your inner recesses, examine and explore why such intervals have occurred. Look at and scrutinize the kind of relationship that you have with God. Reconcile with Him. The time will come in which the Lord will manifest Himself unto you. Then you will declare, *I held him and would not let him go.* This is how you can make sense of the way you lead your life.

Do not despair if you experience intervals of abandonment. Do not give up. Do not fret. Do not think that these intervals of abandonment will last forever. Nor should you think that the Lord has permanently forsaken you. The Lord is still at the door, knocking. He may conceal Himself for a while, but He will not completely disappear. Even though Mary Magdalene thought that she would not see Jesus again, He was there, right in front of her, talking to her. However, she took Him for the gardener. She thought that she was far from Him, ...*they have taken my Lord, and I do not know where they have laid Him*, (John 20:13). She did not realize that it was Jesus Himself who was talking to her.

Sometimes the Lord conceals Himself for awhile so as to spark our interest in Him, sharpen our yearning for Him, and make us seek Him more diligently. Meanwhile, the Lord is always close to us. A similar thing happened with the two disciples who were traveling to the village of Emmaus. Jesus talked to them, *but their eyes were restrained, so that they did not know Him*, (Luke 24:16). Though they were wondering where Jesus was, He was right there talking to them. Intervals of abandonment are, assuredly, superficial and temporary. They are not irrevocable. Neither are they permanent.

This is how Divine Providence works to enhance the human soul's desire to know and seek God. Try to reestablish the relationship that you had with the Lord in the past, *remember ...from where you have fallen and repent*, and return to your *first love*, (Rev 2:5). Instead of saying *I sought him, but I did not find him*, be sure that you will find Him in a little while and that you will hold Him and will *not let him go*. Glory be to His Name forever and ever, Amen.

Let us pray.

May God have mercy upon us and bless us, and make His face shine with His Countenance upon us and have compassion upon us. With the prayers and intercessions that are raised on our behalf by the Mother of God, the Pure Saint Mary, and all the angels and apostles, and the prophets, and the martyrs, and the confessors, and the anchorites, and the saints who we ask to pray for us for peace at all times, and the blessings of the saint of this blessed day, and the blessing of Saint Mary first and last, may their holy blessings and the prayers and intercessions be with us all. Amen.

Peace be with you all.

May God make us worthy to say, Our Father…

PART ONE

By Night On My Bed I Sought the One I Love

Song of Solomon 3:1-4

In the Name of the Father, the Son, and the Holy Spirit, One God. Amen.

In the Song of Songs, Chapter 3, we read the following verses:

> *By night on my bed I sought the one I love; I sought him, but I did not find him. 'I will rise now,' I said, 'and go about the city; in the streets and in the squares I will seek the one I love.' I sought him, but I did not find him. The watchmen who go about the city found me; I said, 'Have you seen the one I love?' Scarcely had I passed by them, when I found the one I love. I held him and would not let him go,*
>
> *Song 3:1-4*

Even though we have explored the various meanings of these verses in the Song of Songs, I would like to approach today's topic from another perspective. We read, *By night on my bed I sought the one I love; I sought him, but I did not find him, (Song 3:1).* The phrase, *By night,* has two meanings. It may be taken either in its literal sense as opposite to the morning, or it may refer to the darkness that one may experience because of sin and the subsequent confusion and spiritual darkness it entails.

The phrase, *on my bed,* refers to the state of slothfulness, laziness, and alienation from the Lord. *By night on my bed I sought the one I love; I sought him, but I did not find him.* The speaker is a black, sinful woman. She exclaims, *I am black and beautiful, O daughters of Jerusalem.* She is also a gentile. She is not one of the people of the Lord (an Israelite). Thus we have this picture of a black, gentile person who is above all else slothful and lazy, sitting on her bed, unwilling to open the door for the Lord. Therefore he *had turned away and was gone,* (Song 5:6).

This is the condition of the human soul that experiences abandonment from the Lord. *I sought him, but I did not find him.* Many seek the Lord and find Him. He promised, *Ask and it will be given unto you,* (Matt 7:7). Furthermore, it is the Lord Himself who seeks us. He looks for us, *Behold, I stand at the door and knock,* (Rev 3:20). However, in the verses under discussion, we see this human soul seeking, but not finding; asking, yet not receiving. What can be the reason for this?

This abandonment can be attributed to two reasons: either the will of man or heavenly Providence. A human being may experience this abandonment because of their own choice. They may be defiant and stubborn and refuse to relinquish their sins and evil deeds. They may utterly reject or deride the work of grace in them and show little or no interest in the work of the Holy Spirit. They may even turn a deaf ear to the Lord's invitation and refuse to heed their own conscience. They will ultimately reach this stage of abandonment and the Lord will forsake them, as well.

On the other hand, God may choose to abandon someone because of their pride and feelings of self importance. These people may be holy and righteous indeed; however, because of this holiness and this righteousness, they may become conceited and proud and even believe that they have reached great ranks of holiness. God may abandon them in order to alert them to their inherent weaknesses.

God may abandon them in order to alert them to their inherent weaknesses

In other words, it is not only bad or evil people that may feel abandoned. Even holy people may be abandoned and forsaken because of their self importance and conceit, their pride and arrogance. The root cause of these outward manifestations may have been, paradoxically enough, their boastful celebration of their own righteousness. The Lord abandons such people that they may become aware of their limitations. *I sought him, but I did not find him.* We also read, *I sought Him, but I could not find Him; I called Him, but He gave me no answer,* (Song 5:6).

The phrase, *the one I love,* has been repeated many times. It first occurs in, *I sought the one I love, but I did not find Him.* Then, *I go about the city; in the streets and in the squares I will seek the one I love.* Third, when, *the watchmen who go about the city found me; I said, 'Have you seen the one I love?'* Finally, *scarcely had I passed by them, when I found the one I love.* These are four different verses that revolve around the theme, *the one I love.*

These verses indicate that even though this human

soul is being slothful, sinful, and lazily wasting time in bed rather than in prayers, the love of the Lord is manifest, nonetheless. Despite the distance, there is love. The many shortcomings, misdeeds, and faults do not extinguish this love. Love exists. That is a surety. As St. Paul the Apostle says, *for to will is present with me, but how to perform what is good I do not find,* (Rom 7:18). So even though I may love the Lord from the depths of the heart, I may oftentimes commit sins because of my inherent weaknesses or addiction to certain habits, not because love is non-existent.

There are those who lead a life of sin and still seek the Lord

O Lord, there are obstacles that prevent me from coming closer to You. But, You, O Lord, know that I love You. It is true that I am asleep, but I love You. It is true that I err and commit sins, yet I still love You. Even though I do not do the things that reflect this love to You, yet love exists.

Do you know to what we can liken this? It is similar to a seed that has in it all the various elements of life. However, in order for this seed to give forth fruit and blossom with life, certain conditions ought to exist. Life exists in this seed, albeit dormant. There is life, but proper conditions must be present in order for this life to spring forth.

I am similar to this seed. My love for You, O Lord, is dormant like a seed waiting for the right moment and the propitious circumstances; the fertile soul, the right nutrition, and a wise farmer to care for it. I will be able to bring forth fruit once You bestow Your grace upon me. Then I will be able to bring forth leaves, branches, flowers, fruits and everything.

By night on my bed I sought the one I love. I sought Him in the dark of night. Zacchaeus, the tax collector, also sought God at night in bed, in sheer darkness. He did not resign from his job to seek the Lord. Rather, he sought the Lord while he was still in the midst of darkness as a tax collector. The thief on the right also called Jesus at night and on his bed. St. Augustine also sought the Lord in the midst of the darkness of the night and on his bed. St. Moses the Black, St. Pellagia, St. Mary the Egyptian; all sought the Lord in the pitch dark of the night, in the midst of the darkness of sin.

These people sought the Lord and found Him. However, this virgin did not. There are those who lead a life of sin and still seek the Lord. They do not wait until they become pure and sanctified. On the contrary, they seek the Lord to become pure and sanctified. Rather than trying to become sanctified in order to seek the Lord, they seek the Lord in the condition in which they are in order for the Lord to help them become pure, holy, and sanctified. They do not wait until they have the spiritual zeal and are active in worship; rather, they seek the Lord while they are still slothful and lazy so that the Lord may rid them of this laziness and grant them this sought after spiritual zeal and fervor.

I am seeking the Lord while I am in bed, lazy and slothful. I seek You while I am lazy so that You may wake me up. I seek You while I am in bed to help me get out of it. I seek You in the midst of my sins so that You may rid me of my sins; and I seek You now that I am distant and far so that You may draw me closer to You. There is a desire, a willingness, but the path is yet untrodden, novel and new. As of yet, I have not started the race. *By night on my bed I sought the one I love.*

Also, the prodigal son sought the Lord while he was on his bed, in a far off country amongst the swine. What profound darkness! What unfathomable pit. He said, *I will rise and go to my father,* (Luke 15:18). This is the condition in which God wants you to come to Him: in dirt, in filth, just the way you are.

Some people may opt to wait until they can attain a pure state and then pray. However, we urge such people to start to pray while they are still lost, lacking in understanding, lukewarm and lacking in spiritual zeal. Even when your thoughts are uncontrollable, you should pray. We urge you to pray and God will grant you the means to purity and cleanliness. Pray while you are in the night and on your bed. *By night on my bed I sought the one I love.*

If seeking You, O Lord, is the exclusive privilege of saints, then we all would have perished and become lost. It is our hope that sinners would also call upon You and seek You. We find hope and encouragement to see the tax collector and the Pharisee seek and call You. Everyone seeks You. *By night on my bed I sought the one I love.*

It is encouraging to know that God has created stars and planets that shine and send forth light in the midst of darkness. Likewise, in the midst of the darkness of sin there are some lights that shine, an indication of the love that still exists in the heart for the Lord, as well as the desire to seek Him. Despite the darkness and the laziness, I called. Not merely have I called, but *I sought the one I love.* The Lord is aware that even though this person is a lazy sinner leading an unrighteous life, quite unlike the children of light, yet there is love and there is a desire in the heart. This is sufficient, despite the limitations and the wrongdoings. The person still seeks the Lord and loves Him. *By night on my bed I sought the one I love.*

I want to be with You, O Lord, all the time, in sin and in righteousness. And even though sin may ruin certain aspects of my life, it can hardly touch my inner feelings toward You. For example, a defiant son may refuse to listen to his father's command not to go out to party, but he still loves his father. The son may later regret his own decision and come to his father and ask for his forgiveness, and explain that even though he has failed to listen to him, he still loves him.

The phrase, *By night on my bed,* could be taken in its literal sense as a reference to the peace and tranquility of the night, its detachment from the hustle and bustle of the day's burdens, the unity one finds with God at night. *I sought the one I love*. During responsibilities and burdens of the day, its problems and the many obligations that one has to fill, such as meetings, work, and the many claims upon one's time, one is bound to feel at a loss, hardly attentive to one's own self.

Pray and God will grant you the means to purity and cleanliness

But *by night on my bed* I have been able to once again be with God seeking the one I love. That is why Jesus advises us saying, *go into your room,* (Matt 6:6). In Psalm 4, we also read, *Meditate within your heart on your bed, and be still,* (Ps 4:4). When you are alone with the Lord in the privacy of your own bedroom, you can ask the *one you love* concerning those ideas and evil thoughts that haunt you during the day and offer an account for them.

By night on my bed. The night offers an appropriate means to seek the Lord. It is during this time that I can shed off the filth and dirt of the daytime; I can free my hands and my feet from its shackles and bonds; I can be in oneness with You. *Who by night stand in the house of the Lord. Lift up your hands in the sanctuary, and bless the Lord,* (Ps 134:2).

When we contemplate on, *By night on my bed I*

sought the one I love, we realize that such a request does not take place in a church or a monastery or in any other place of worship. Rather, it is a request that takes place *at night* and *on my bed.* It is a call for us not to look down upon those who do not go to church. Maybe they seek the Lord, the one they love, in their beds. Our measures and standards are not always accurate and correct. We lack knowledge and, at best, our standards are superficial. We often times think of those who enter their rooms are going to sleep, but they may be, contrary to our beliefs, seeking the one they love and our *Father who sees in secret will Himself reward you openly,* (Matt 6:4).

By night on my bed I sought the one I love. This sister, however, says I *sought him, but I did not find him.* I seek You, O Lord, but You are not there; I call upon Your name, and You do not respond. There is a big barrier that stands between You and I. One is reminded of that awesome and fearsome verse, *When you spread out your hands, I will hide My eyes from you; even though you make many prayers, I will not hear. Your hands are full of blood,* (Isa 1:15).

It is my heart's desire to reconcile with You, O Lord

There are barriers. That former love is gone and that special bond that used to bind us together has vanished. I have been dishonest and unfaithful. That is the reason for the loss of this special bond. This reflects itself upon the way I talk to You now. In the past I used to show You true love, closeness, and warmth. There was that certain nearness and unquestionable proximity. However, when I approach You now, when I talk to You, my words are void and empty. They lack the power to enter into Your presence, Your Holy Tabernacle. There is now this feeling of a great void, a vast distance that separates us. I call upon You, and You do not respond; I seek, and I do not find; I ask, and I do not receive. It is as if You are not my God, and I am not Your son anymore.

Why is there this abandonment? It is my heart's desire to reconcile with You, O Lord. I wish that this fog that hangs over our relationship would dissipate, and this animosity come to an end. How I long to return to our first love, our former relation. I would like to express my sorrow, fix our broken relationship, and cause Your heart to rejoice on my behalf. I yearn to return to Your bosom, the way we were, when You would manifest Yourself to me in the Garden and we would talk face to face, before the serpent drew a wedge between us, before I ate the fruit and the consequent feeling of being shut out from Your presence.

The virgin in the *Song of Songs* is in a better position than Adam. When Adam sinned, he did not call upon the Lord, but hid behind a tree and disappeared from the face of God. In the case of this virgin, however, there is a breach in the relationship, but there is also a bridge, a channel of communication. The worst scenario occurs when there is a gap or a breach of communication in a relationship alongside animosity and hard-feelings. In such a situation, the relationship is likely to worsen. However, there is always the possibility for things to get better if there is an open channel for communication alongside those times that are overshadowed with misunderstanding, discontentment or even animosity.

There is a feeling of anger and displeasure between this virgin and God. Yet, there is also a desire to communicate and approach Him. *'I will rise now,' I said, 'and go about the city; in the streets and in the squares I will seek the one I love.'* There is an eternal quest as exemplified in the desire to ask people and roam the streets seeking the one I love. There is an attempt to bridge the gap. There are those who are not reconciled with the Lord and who do not heed their own salvation. They do not seek it, neither do they try to communicate with the Lord or talk to Him. They do not seek the Lord. If God happens to abandon them, they too will abandon God, and the relationship is severed. It comes to an end.

The virgin, however, is different. For even though I am currently experiencing a period of abandonment, and I feel forsaken; even though I seek You and cannot find You, and I call Your name and You do not answer, yet I will still seek and look for You. I will ask people about You and I will save no effort to restore our former relationship.

When you find your relationship with God undergoing certain hurdles and difficulties, beware not to sever the relationship with God altogether. Never cut off the relationship under the pretext that God does not love you or that He is not responsive to your prayers. Do not try to persuade yourself that since God does not respond to you that you are justified in deciding not to go to church or practice the mystery of confession, etc.. That will end the relationship with God altogether.

Even if you feel that God does not listen to you, or He is abandoning you, you ought not abandon Him. Reason with Him. Talk to Him. Tell Him that if He abandons you, He is not going to lose a thing. Who am I? A trifle and worthless person, one amongst millions upon millions. Who am I? Nothing. However, if I abandon You, O Lord, I am completely lost. It is only my relation with You that ties me to life.

You are the source of life. You are everything to me. You are existence itself. You are my destiny and my eternity. You are my Beginning and End. You are my *Alpha and Omega,* the first and the foremost. If I were to let You go, I am finished, I am lost. Actually, if You were to abandon me, I will run after You in the streets and in the squares, in the cities and in the villages, for without You I cannot do anything. You are everything.

I will tirelessly look for and run after You. I will look for You anywhere and everywhere. Should You be angry with me, I will seek You to reconcile our crisis. I will offer a true and sincere apology, and I would never dare run away from You. How can I? St. Paul the Apostle said, *For in Him we live and move and have our being,* (Act 17:28). We exist through the Lord; we live because of Him and we move by Him. Has St. Paul not also said, *For to me, to live is Christ, and to die is gain,* (Phi 1:21). The same theme reverberates in these words. My life is in Christ. I dwell in Him, and He dwells in me.

Therefore, even if my soul is in a state of slumber and slothfulness, wallowing in the darkness of inequity, it still yearns for You; my soul will not forget You, nor will it ever abandon You. It is but a temporary, transitory and passing phase, one which does not change or touch the heart or my affection for you. It is but a brief period of sickness from which I will be soon healed. It is a hurdle along the way that will shortly be overcome and surmounted. It is but short-lived darkness that will presently give way to light. Count it not, O Lord, nor look upon it as a perpetual, eternal attribute, or an everlasting, unending trait. It is nothing but a transitory phase that will soon be over. Reconciliation and reunion is at hand.

Even if you feel that God does not listen to you, or is abandoning you, you ought not abandon Him

By night on my bed I sought the one I love. What is the meaning of, *I sought the one I love?* It is an admission, a

127

confession of sort. It is true, O Lord, that I coveted worldly things and succumbed to material and carnal desires. It is true that I have been lustful, boastful and discontent. However, all of these are related to the satisfaction of sensual pleasures. They have nothing to do with love. Pleasure is only a superficial, a fleeting desire. Love, on the other hand, is an intensely profound, eternal feeling that resides in the inner depths of the heart.

If I do not find Him today, I will find Him tomorrow or the next day or even next year

In short, the world and all its desires, physical, sensual, social, were to me nothing but a form of pleasure. I indulged in physical and sensual pleasures. I sought to satisfy all my carnal desires. I was proud and conceited, arrogant and haughty. All these were temporary, transient pleasures, nonetheless. They are very different from love. True love is exclusively Yours, *Love the Lord your God with all your heart.*

The heart is completely dedicated to You. These worldly desires are not a reflection of the inclinations of my heart. My lust, my desires, and my indulgence in various worldly pleasures should not be taken as manifestations of love. They were done thoughtlessly and heedlessly, in foolishness and ignorance. They are not a reflection of love. My love is only for You. I do seek *the one I love.*

In the midst of the night, I reason with myself. I reflect on what I may have possibly gained in this world. I consider what I have accomplished. I find, to my chagrin, that I have accomplished nothing. I am in no better position than the Prodigal Son. Like him, I look for the pods *to fill my stomach,* and, also like him, I cannot find it.

I will rise now and seek *the one I love.*

I sought him, but I did not find him seems to indicate that the chance has vanished, it is gone. But has it? Is it gone forever? Hardly! *I did not find him* does not mean that this is a lasting condition, one that is likely to last for ever. This is impossible, even unthinkable. Had this been truly the case, I would have ceased to be. It would be better for me to die. Thankfully, the phrase *I did not find him* only means that I did not find Him yet. It is a temporary, momentary phase. There is reason to believe that I will find Him a little later. If I do not find Him today, I will find Him tomorrow or the next day or even next year.

What is really strikingly amazing about the virgin in the *Song of Songs* is the tenacity and determination she demonstrates. She never despairs. She will never give up. If I cannot find Him, that is okay. I will try again. If I lack spiritual zeal now and if my spiritual fervor is not where it should be, that is okay. Be patient. *By your patience possess your souls,* (Luke 21:19). I will find Him later. If I am not inclined to reading or praying, I should not lose heart. I will feel inclined later. If I do not have the desire to go to church and worship and draw closer to God, or if I am not prepared to partake of the Holy Communion or observe the mystery of confession, I ought to be patient.

These desires will come in time. I should not despair just because I tried to seek Him, and I could not find Him. I should not give up or conclude that God does not exist and that is that. End of story. No. The Lord is there, present and very near. If I cannot find Him now, I will in a little while. Even if I *go about in the city, in the streets and in the squares* and fail to find Him now, I will find Him later. If the watchmen who *go about the city* fail to respond to my inquiries now, they will not later. But never will I abandon Him.

Do not despair. No matter how long this phase of abandonment may seem to you, never give up. If you ever sought the Lord and could not find Him, do not give up. You will definitely find Him, if even after a while.

The wisdom of the Lord is at play in this apparent abandonment on His part. We ought to understand that when the virgin asks for, but fails to find him, she is in bed, asleep and slothful. Were he to come to her in such a state of laziness, she would continue in this state of nonchalance and indifference. She would take things for granted, without appreciation, and with little or no concern. It would appear easy and simple. Now she has him; she enjoys his company. End of story!

However, when she fails to find him while in bed, she decides to *rise and go about in the city, and in the streets and the squares* to seek *the one I love*. This mobility and activity on her part is made possible by the abandonment that has preceded and that she has experienced. Now, she realizes, it is time to rise, move, and go out into the streets, to the marketplace and the squares. It is time to ask for him everywhere.

It oftentimes happens that when God lavishly bestows His blessings and His Grace upon us, we do not feel appreciative or thankful enough. We tend to take things for granted. We even become rather frivolous and spoiled. We may then expect God to do everything for us while we lazily wait in anticipation for His abundant, copious Graces. We do nothing. His Grace is sufficient.

If I want to become pure, I may opt to do nothing to reach this state of purity but rather lazily wait for the Lord's Grace to grant me this desired purity. If I am reluctant to pray, I may deceive myself into believing that such a practice can be attained through His Grace alone. If I desire to lead a fruitful spiritual life that I do not currently enjoy, I may mistakenly do nothing and only ask for the Lord's grace to grant it to me, *Being justified freely by His Grace,* (Rom 3:24).

But what role are you playing in all of this? You are *on* your *bed* seeking Him *at night.* You are doing nothing other than slothfully awaiting God's Grace to be abundantly bestowed upon you. Therefore, if you are going to adopt this lazy attitude, if you are going to ignore the role of hard work and become fully dependant on Grace, then abandonment is in order. The Lord is going to abandon you for some time. You will seek Him, but you will not find Him.

No matter how long this phase of abandonment may seem to you, never give up

If you ask the Lord for the reason, you will come to understand that you cannot attain these virtues solely through grace or the Holy Spirit. How about fellowship with the Holy Spirit? You ought to take an active part and work hard with the Holy Spirit. But to adopt an attitude of laziness and inactivity, to lie *on* your *bed at night* and show dissatisfaction and annoyance that you cannot find Him is absurd and meaningless. You ought to rise and work. You must actively participate with the Holy Spirit and with Grace. Make a pledge with the Lord and promise as Sts. Paul and Silas did, *We are working with the Lord.* Arise and be active. Arise and go about in the city, the streets and the squares and look for the Lord.

Indeed this abandonment has given this bride a motivation and momentum. It has kindled her spiritual fervor. She has become mobile, active and dynamic. She has started to be active and work ever since she became aware of the danger lurking in her former state of idleness and inactivity.

Love can never be one-sided. It has to be reciprocal and mutual. Otherwise, we cannot call it love. God loves you. He grants you His blessings and Grace, and He lavishly bestows His Holy Spirit upon you. In return, you also ought to return His love and show your zeal and enthusiasm through hard work and travail. The *bed* and the *night* will avail you nothing. Rise up and roll up your sleeves and get ready to work. Rise! *Rise up, O children of light, and praise the Lord of Powers to grace us with the salvation of our souls.*

It will avail me nothing if I stay lazy and slothful. It is no use to invite Him to come to me while I do not show the desire to actively participate in this process. I cannot use the *night* and the *bed* as a pretext, a peg on which to hang my excuses. This is simply preposterous and counterproductive. Work is needed. You have to work with the Spirit. Work *while it is day,* (John 4:9). The Bible instructs us to, *walk while you have the light lest darkness overtake you,* (John 12:35).

You cannot just wait in the darkness and ask Him to come while you are lazily staying in *bed*. There is no mixture between darkness and light; there is no partnership between them.

I have to rise and go about in the city, and in the streets and seek the one that I love. I cannot do that in *bed* or in the darkness of the *night*. Rather, I can only seek Him through strenuous hard work and arduous labor and toil. I can seek Him by sweat and blood. This is how I can seek the Lord, the one I love. I ought to understand and realize the gravity of my situation, the enormity of the task at hand and the urgent need to work for the salvation of my soul.

If the Lord is angry or upset with me, this will be my earnest pledge, *Surely I will not go into the chamber of* my house, or go up to the comfort of my bed; I will not give sleep to my eyes or slumber to my eyelids until I have found a place for the Lord, a dwelling place for the Mighty One of Jacob, (Ps 132:3-5). This is it; it is the right attitude. But to go to *bed* at *night* and try to *seek the one I love* in this slothful attitude signifies love that is not productive.

God wants true love, one that translates itself into spiritual warfare and expresses itself in spiritual mobility and activity. God wants love that will manifest itself in honest labor and productive, sincere toil. Many have spiritual yearnings but lack spiritual activity and spiritual work.

O Lord, I love You. I know that You love me. And yet, *If you love Me, keep My commandments,* (Jn 14:15). Those who love Me, their love is productive and evident to Me. It is an active love.

Let us pray.

May God have mercy upon us and bless us, and make His face shine with His Countenance upon us and have compassion upon us. With the prayers and intercessions that are raised on our behalf by the Mother of God, the Pure Saint Mary, and all the angels and apostles, and the prophets, and the martyrs, and the confessors, and the anchorites, and the saints who we ask to pray for us for peace at all times, and the blessings of the saint of this blessed day, and the blessing of Saint Mary first and last, may their holy blessings and the prayers and intercessions be with us all. Amen.

Peace be with you all.

May God make us worthy to say, Our Father...

PART TWO

By Night On My Bed I Sought the One I Love

Song of Solomon 3:1-4

In the Name of the Father, the Son, and the Holy Spirit, One God. Amen.

    I would like to continue speaking on last week's topic so we can have a complete picture. In the Third Chapter in the *Song of Songs* we read:

> *By night on my bed I sought the one I love; I sought him, but I did not find him. 'I will rise now,' I said, 'and go about the city; in the streets and in the squares I will seek the one I love.' I sought him, but I did not find him. The watchmen who go about the city found me; I said, 'Have you seen the one I love?' Scarcely had I passed by them, when I found the one I love. I held him and would not let him go,*
>
> *SS 3:1-4*

By night on my bed I sought the one I love. As I have previously mentioned to you, the *night* may be taken to symbolize sin and darkness or it may be a symbol of peace and tranquility. The *bed* may represent a state of laziness, inactivity and slothfulness, an attitude of nonchalance. However, the statement *by night on my bed I sought the one I love* indicates that no matter how far astray man may depart from God, man's heart still yearns for God. Regardless of the *night* and the *bed*, there is still that longing in man's heart; there is a burning desire to seek God.

This should not come as a surprise. The Spirit of God dwells in us. We are created in God's image and likeness. Accordingly, man is equipped with a natural inclination and an inherent proclivity to yearn and long for God. This yearning is part and parcel of man's nature. We are born with this longing. It is innate. We often maintain that children will naturally and instinctively love their parents because of the natural bond and the blood connection that exist between them. It is even more natural and logical for man to love God and long for Him.

The love of the world is, in fact, foreign to mankind. It is not part of man's nature. Rather, man's true nature is geared to the love of God. For this reason, no matter how far man may stray away from God, there is always the chance for man to return to Him. Let us take the indicator of the compass as an example. It always points north. It may change directions if you move it and point east or west, north or south. However, it will finally correct itself and point north.

Likewise, regardless of the different directions that you may look at, your eyes are bound to finally settle on that single direction leading unto Jerusalem, the city of the Great King. You are bound to finally return to God.

Therefore, no man should lose heart or despair. Man has a natural attraction towards God.

By night on my bed I sought the one I love. As I lie in bed, my thoughts, my longing, and my love take me back to God. I wonder what has separated us. This is similar to the Prodigal Son who goes astray. Eventually, he remembers his father's house and starts to yearn and long for it.

St. Augustine also attempted various ways and tried many roads. He unavailingly indulged in sensual, physical pleasures. He fruitlessly pursued knowledge and erudition. In vain he sought philosophical reasoning and cognition. He eventually realized the futility of all his endeavors. Finally, he came back to God and said, *Late have I loved You, O Beauty so ancient and so new, late have I loved You.*

However lost man is and no matter how far man has strayed away, God's love runs deep in his heart. Never imagine that preachers, shepherds, counselors, fathers of confession, apostles, prophets, priests, etc. introduce the love of God and plant it in your hearts. That is not true. The love of the Lord is already there. It exists in your hearts. All they do is uncover what already exists. They dig and expose the love that is hidden beneath and that runs in your veins. The love of God exists in your inner being because you are created in God's image and likeness.

The love of God exists in your inner being because you are created in God's image and likeness

At certain unexpected moments man may experience that yearning for the Lord. When, how and where these feelings may arise and materialize is beyond our knowledge. We can neither specify nor determine when these moments are likely to occur. The Bible explains this most fittingly, *The Kingdom of God does not come with observation,* (Luke 17:20). So, we cannot with any degree of precision anticipate that you will be graced with the Holy Spirit at a specific hour or time: today or tomorrow, in the morning or at night. However, unexpectedly and without any prior warning, you will experience this yearning for God and your feelings move in His direction.

Something inexplicable may direct you to God and lead you to Him. Everyone, no matter how sinful, how distant and lost, and how corrupt, will at a particular moment experience this feeling of **He was right there in their midst, but they were unaware of His presence** yearning for the Lord. As for the exact time, no one knows for sure. Such moments are often referred to as *visitations of Grace* which, once experienced, move man from the inside. They rekindle a man's yearning and reawaken man's old love for the Lord.

Incidentally, one may find it difficult to precisely account for the bride's *by night on my bed I sought the one I love*. This is not uncommon. Human nature is difficult to fathom and understand at times. The bride here maintains that she is seeking him even though it was he who has moved her feelings and ignited her passion to seek him in the first place. There is no doubt that he is deeply ingrained in her heart and mind. It was he who has unquestionably moved those feelings to call upon and seek him.

Without God's work inside her being, she would not have been able to say *I sought him*. Undoubtedly it is he who has taken the initiative and moved your feelings. It is he who is actually yearning for you. It is he who *put his hand by the latch of the door, and your heart yearned for him,* (Song 5:4). Do we not say, *We love Him because He first loved us?* (1John 4:19). Therefore, it stands to reason that the statement, *I sought him, but I did not find him,* has its root cause in the fact that it is God Himself who has stirred these feelings.

The question that now arises is how is it possible that the bride says, *I sought him, but I did not find him?* There are times in which you do not feel the presence of God even though He is in you. The story of the two disciples of Emmaus offer us an example. Jesus talked to them, but they did not know Him. They even told Jesus, *Are You the only stranger in Jerusalem, and have You not known the things which happened there these days?* (Luke 24:18). Paradoxically enough, they were referring to incidents concerning Jesus unaware that it was Jesus Himself to whom they were talking. He was right there in their midst, but they were unaware of His presence, *their eyes were restrained... they did not know Him,* (Luke 24:16).

Another example that shows us that we may fail to recognize the presence of God is offered when the Lord and two of His angels called upon Abraham. Abraham was hospitable to his guests, offering them cheese, the fatted calf...etc. Obviously, he was not aware that God Himself was there. Otherwise, he would not have presented the Lord with cheese, meat and such things as people ordinarily offer their guests on such occasions. That would have never come to pass had Abraham known that it was God Himself who was visiting him. The Bible says, *Do not forget to entertain strangers, for by so doing some have unwittingly entertained angels,* (Heb 13:2).

Thus, God may be right there and you may fail to perceive His presence. St. Augustine expresses this feeling most aptly. He addresses the Lord saying, *You were with me. However, due to the extent of my complaints I was not with You.* So, You, O Lord, may be right there with me, but I, unfortunately, fail to perceive Your presence. I am not with You. *The light shines in the darkness, and the darkness did not comprehend it,* (John 1:5).

It so happens sometimes that God is there with you, but you fail to feel His presence. You wonder, *I sought him, but I did not find him.* Is it true that God has abandoned you. Or, could it be that you do not feel His presence! Or maybe you lack that spiritual vigilance and awareness that would alert you to the presence of God with you! Sometimes you plead with the Lord, *How long, O Lord? Will You forget me forever?* (Ps 13:1). However, the Lord ascertains that even if a *woman forgets her nursing child and* (does) *not have compassion on the son of her womb, I will not forget you,* (Is 49:15). It is you, David, My dear, who fail to perceive My presence and keep on complaining that I have forgotten you.

This is, unfortunately, the case. The Lord is always present at our side, but we hardly take notice of His presence. We may even express our dissatisfaction and discontent and plead with Him, *Where are You, O Lord? Why are You distant? 'I sought him, but I did not find him.'* The Lord, however, will confirm that He is there, in and with you. By faith you can to discern the presence of the Lord with you. This is what David the prophet says, *My heart also instructs me in the night season. I have set the Lord always before me; because He is at my right hand I shall not be moved,* (Ps 16:7-8). The Lord is before me; He is at my right hand and I feel His presence. The Lord is present all around.

Elijah expresses the same feeling, *As the Lord God of Israel lives, before whom I stand,* (1 Kings 17:1).

Consequently, before you claim that God is not there, *I sought him, but I did not find him*, you ought to examine yourself. It is not that God is not there. It is just you who fail to realize, comprehend and feel His presence.

By night on my bed I sought the one I love; I sought him, but I did not find him. Occasionally, God will conceal Himself from you in order to urge you to seek Him. He will not allow you to see Him so as to kindle your yearning for Him. Like the star that appeared to the Wise Men, He

He will not allow you to see Him so as to kindle your yearning for Him

may appear and manifest Himself for a while only to disappear and conceal Himself for another while. Then, you are bound to look for and seek Him.

God does not want love to be one-sided. It would be unreasonable and illogical if He loves you and you slothfully and lazily sleep on your bed. The Lord is looking for reciprocal, mutual relationship. You too ought to love Him as He loves you. You ought to seek Him as He Himself seeks you.

That is why the bride says, *I will rise now... And go about the city; in the streets and in the squares I will seek the one I love*. The statement *I will rise* is poignant and significant. It indicates the willpower and determination to take action. It is good that now the bride is expressing her resolve to abandon her former attitude characterized by slothfulness and represented by *the bed*. She is now becoming active. Former slothfulness is giving way to activity and action. *I will rise*. The bride is now looking for the Lord, roaming the streets and the squares, and seeking *the one I love*.

It would be a great blessing if everyone among you here would leave this meeting with the resolve to *rise now, and go about the city... to seek the one I love.* Go look everywhere. Look in the city, look in the marketplace, where you may buy the Word of God, *He who has no sword, let him sell his garment and buy one,* (Luke 22:37). It is an invitation to go to the marketplace to buy a sword with which to fight. The Bible instructs us to buy *white garments, that you may be clothed, that the shame of your nakedness may not be revealed,* (Rev 3:18).

Go to the marketplace and look for the Word of God. Whenever you need something for your home, you go to the market and look for it there. Likewise, if the Lord is missing in your life, look for Him. Seek Him wherever He is to be found. He is there in the Church, in a monastery, in a shrine, and in the many places of worship. You may find Him in the altar, in icons and even in your very heart. Just look for those places where the Lord exists. Look for Him in secluded, quiet places. Just keep looking for the Lord; keep on seeking Him.

You ought to fight the slothful, sluggish attitude and adopt an active, dynamic one

The statement *I will rise and go about the city* portrays the human being in an earnest quest to attain salvation. The former state of laziness and slumber is over. There is now a serious attempt to look for the Lord and restore the beauty I experienced in my former relationship with the Lord. It is an attempt to look for a life of purity and chastity, prayer and contemplation. It is an earnest quest to search for the means to salvation.

I go about looking for ways that may lead unto the Lord. Such roads as prayer, contemplation, penitence, reading the Word of God, confession, communion, and fasting; all these are roads that can lead one to the Lord.

All that I need to do is to *go about in the streets* looking for ways that lead unto salvation and seeking *the one I love*. It is useless and futile to lead a life of laziness, inactivity and nonchalance lacking purpose and a sense of direction. I have to *rise, roam,* and *seek* with diligence and earnestness.

The word *rise* is significant and meaningful. Even though salvation is the work of God, you ought to take an active role in it. You need to participate with God to complete it. The prodigal son's declaration *I will rise and go to my father, and will say to him 'Father, I have sinned against heaven and against you... Make me like one of your hired servants,'* (Luke 1418-19), echoes the same sentiment expressed by Zacchaeus. Zacchaeus also decided to *rise* and *give half of my goods to the poor; and if I have taken anything from anyone by false accusation, I restore fourfold,* (Luke 19:8). He refused to sit still, inactive and lethargic. You too should also resolve to *rise* and do something. You ought to fight the slothful, sluggish attitude and adopt an active, dynamic one.

It is true that we beseech the Lord to *rise* on our behalf, *Arise, O Lord God; may all Your enemies be scattered and dispersed, and may those who hate Your Holy Name flee before Your face.* We also say, *'For the sake of the poor and the wretched, I will now rise' says the Lord 'and openly cause salvation to come.'* We also entreat the Lord, saying, *Arise, O Lord, save me, O My God.* Yet, while it is true that the Lord does indeed *rise* to save us, we also have a role to play; we should arise with our Lord Jesus. We should do something.

We ought to shed off the slumber of death and arise from the grave. The Lord asked them to *take away the stone,* (John 11:39), in order to raise Lazarus from the dead. Likewise, you ought to do something to save your soul. This is an invitation to be an active participant in the process of salvation. *I will rise* indicates the responsibility that I personally have to attain this salvation.

I do have a duty to do something. I may just as well bring nothing but dust to the Lord, and He will imbue it with life. I may but present the Lord with the two fishes and five loaves of bread, and He will use that to feed the multitude. Even though the fish and bread may seem insignificant, they underlie the importance of offering something, taking an action and playing a role. My task may be to only cast the net into the sea, and it is God's responsibility to fill it with fish. It is imperative that *I rise* and cast the net. I must do something.

Doing something is evidence of my love for the Lord, a token that I am not forced to love Him, coerced into this relationship with Him, or pushed to walk in His way. No! I also rise. It is a reciprocal relationship; my heart also is ready and eager for this relationship. Jesus says, *If anyone hears My voice and opens the door, I will come in to him and dine with him, and he with Me,* (Rev 3:20).

The Lord will not break the door or force Himself in. It is simply not His way. Even if you plead with the Lord to break the door and force Himself in, He will not do that. Love is not wrestled out of people. That might have worked had we been living in the Old Testament under the Law. According to the Law, people could face different types of sentencing depending on their deeds. The Law would decree that whosoever did a certain thing would be granted life and whosoever did not do such and such will certainly die. It would dictate that certain criminals be stoned to death while others would be sentenced by other means. That was in olden times. Thankfully, however, we live in a different era. It is the age of grace, *Behold, I stand at the door and knock,* (Rev 3:20). So, it is your responsibility to *rise* and open the door for Him. If you do not rise, it is your loss. You have the choice.

'I will rise now, and go about the city; in the streets and in the squares, I will seek the one I love.' I can assure you that the heavenly hosts rejoice as they witness this loving soul roaming the city, the streets, the squares, and the marketplaces *seeking the one I love*. She is now being diligent about seeking the salvation of her soul.

Here I am, eagerly and avidly reading the Word of God, looking for a verse that may rekindle my love for the Lord. Here I am, vehemently and enthusiastically singing a hymn hoping that I may come across something in it that may touch my heart and stir my feelings for the Lord. I am searching. I am searching for all the roads that may lead unto salvation.

There are those who reject the notion of *roads that lead to salvation* and contend that there exists but one way unto salvation. While it is true that there is only one Way unto salvation and redemption as far as Jesus is concerned, to you, as a human being, there are many roads that can lead you there.

Chastity can lead you unto salvation. Monasticism can lead to salvation. Wedlock can lead to salvation. Serving others can lead to salvation. Contemplation can lead to salvation. All these and many others can lead unto salvation. So, there are many roads

There are many roads and all that you have to do is to choose the road that suits you best

and all that you have to do is to choose the road that suits you best. Spiritual fervor and zeal is a road that can lead unto salvation, but so is the road of meekness, humility and kindness. All that you ought to do is seek and roam the streets looking for that particular way that will lead you to find God.

This idea was most aptly expounded by Mar Isaac, *God, knowledgeable as He is with the diverse natures of human beings, has allowed a number of ways to lead unto Him.* The Lord has made possible a number of ways for humans to choose from according to what suits them. Man is mistaken in claiming that there is but one road. Those who lead a monastic, ascetic life are wrong if they claim that only monasticism and asceticism can lead to salvation. What may they possibly mean by such a claim? How about those who ceaselessly labor and toil in the world? Do they not find the Lord?

I will tirelessly explore and meticulously investigate all those roads that lead unto salvation.

Therefore, just as monasticism can lead unto the Lord, so can laboring, toiling and working in the world. Celibacy and chastity lead unto the Lord. Dedication and consecration also lead unto God. Wedlock can lead unto the Lord. Those who have jobs and toil and labor day in and day out in this world can find the Lord.

Nor should we be surprised by this. The Lord Himself has chosen apostles and prophets from all walks of life. They had various characteristics and widely marked traits. We have the scholarly, knowledgeable, mighty and wise St. Paul who graduated from the university of Tarsus. With his wisdom, philosophy, and knowledge St. Paul was able to reach the Lord. Doctors and physicians such as St. Luke, St. Cozman and St. Demian also found God. Simple fishermen like St. Peter, and naive inexperienced tent makers also found the Lord. Even tax collectors were able to find God. There are many roads that can lead unto salvation.

I go about in the streets...I will seek the one I love, brings to mind the image of someone walking and roaming the streets searching and looking. It is a portrayal of those who walk in the road of monasticism attempting to find the Lord through that particular road. It portrays those who march in the road of mercy and compassion seeking the Lord through a different path. It also portrays those who lead a life of prayer seeking the Lord through yet another road. They all can reach their destination, their final goal.

Therefore, suppose you are experiencing a certain lack of spiritual zeal and fervor, and you try to *go about* and *seek* a way out of this languid spiritual condition. Reading may not be as profitable as you may have originally anticipated and may cause boredom to seep into your life, so you put the Bible aside. You turn to prayers only to realize that it is not availing you much either and you are still bored, so you stop praying. You start chanting and singing spiritual songs, but you discover that these are not helping you much, so you stop chanting and singing. You start worshipping and prostrating but find no comfort or solace. You decide to go back to the Bible. You should keep on trying until you find the road to the, *one you love*. You persevere until the right road is spotted.

It is futile and counter-productive to claim that there is but one road unto salvation. What could possibly happen, one might ask, had this been truly the case? What could possibly happen if one tries one road and finds that it does not lead to the *one I love?* You should search diligently as the virgin does, *I will rise...go about the city, in the streets and in the squares...I will seek the one I love.* I will tirelessly explore and meticulously investigate all those roads that lead unto salvation. I will not rest until I attain it.

What might stir and move your feelings will not necessarily move and affect others. It is, therefore, not advisable for a father of confession to attempt to mold his children into his likeness. In fact, even his own children may find a different path other than his, more profitable and suitable for them. Therefore, if you find your way, be careful not to push others to walk that same way. Everyone will find their own special way. The important thing is to attain our goal and reach our ultimate objective.

I will rise now...and go about the city; in the streets and in the squares I will seek the one I love. I sought him, but I did not find him. Here lies the problem. I have fruitlessly tried all the roads and ways, and I have unavailingly searched all the streets and marketplaces. It was all in vain. *The watchmen who go about the city found me; I said, 'Have you found the one I love?'* I found myself all alone, wretched, miserable and helpless. I have looked here and there to no avail. I searched for the Lord in various places, but my efforts are futile and useless. I found the watchmen *who go about the city*.

Those are the watchmen whom God has appointed to guard values and principles, and who are entrusted with His commandments, instructions and Holy statutes. I found those *watchmen*, those who keep the peace, save the lost souls, and guide others in the right path. Seeing them, I asked, *Have you seen the one I love?* I consulted those guards, the guides and counselors who have trodden these paths before. They have found the Lord and discovered His ways. They have lived with the Lord and experienced His love first hand. So, I asked them, *Have you seen the one I love?"*

Yet, even though these *watchmen* have undoubtedly seen Him a great number of times, they choose not to respond. This reluctance to respond should not, however, mislead us into thinking that they are indifferent or nonchalant. They may have been praying for this soul, *Scarcely had I passed them, when I found the one I love.* It is amazing that even though the watchmen do not respond verbally to her inquiry, she finds Him immediately after she passes them.

Having lost my way, God sends His people to find me

At times, it may be sufficient to just go to certain people and talk to them about your problems in order to find a solution to these problems. They may not even offer any suggestions or propose any solutions. It is enough to go to these people and talk to them about a certain issue. They may not even respond to your particular inquiries or concerns, but you may find that your problem has been miraculously solved later on:

The watchmen who go about the city found me; I said, 'Have you found the one I love?' Scarcely had I passed them, When I found the one I love. It is indeed wonderful to have people to whom we can talk about certain issues even if they do not respond to our concerns. Later on we may find that the problem has been resolved.

Even more noteworthy here is the fact that the human soul has not initiated that search for the *watchmen.* Rather, it is the watchmen *who go about the city* that *found me.* Having lost my way, God sends His people to find me. Lost, puzzled and confused I ask, *Have you seen the one I love?* To my surprise, I look and He is right there in front of me.

What this implies is that God may vanish for a while and then reappear. Or maybe you fail to see Him for sometime and recognize His presence later. These periods of abandonment do not last for a long time. God will never permit that you keep on looking for Him for a prolonged period of time. He may only entice you a little in order to urge you to become more zealous and enthusiastic. He may conceal Himself for a little while in order to create in you this feeling of longing for Him. He may make Himself scarce so as to prompt you to ardently look for Him, to make you aware of your weaknesses and limitations, and to call upon His name.

He will, however, never desert or abandon you for ever *He will not always strive with us; nor will He keep His anger for ever,* (Ps 103:9). The Lord's abandonment may last but for a brief moment, but He ascertains that, *I have loved you with an everlasting love; therefore with loving kindness I have drawn you,* (Jer 31:3). However, it is during that brief moment that those feelings of dejection and loss have engulfed me. How can I live without You, O Lord, even for a brief moment? That is impossible.

How can I live without You, O Lord, even for a brief moment?

The Lord is all around you. If you do not feel His presence, if but for a brief moment; it is only for a short time, you are bound to find Him later. When you do, you will realize through past hardships a lesson.

This virgin who has encountered multiple hardships and various difficulties while she has been seeking the Lord, has learned a valuable lesson. Now that she has finally found Him, she is determined to *hold him and would not let him go,* (Song 3:4). Now that I have finally found You, O Lord, I will never let You go. I am determined to cling unto You with all my power and strength, tightly and vehemently. How can I let You go again after all that I have been through?

St. Basil the Great states that *things that come with ease, pass with ease.* This is very relevant to us today. It so happens that sometimes when you pray, the Lord does not hasten to grant you your desire or request.

You are not appreciative and thankful enough when your desires or requests are answered speedily. You do not truly value and appreciate what you get. That is why God chooses not to grant your wishes speedily so as to prompt you to keep on praying for long periods of time, pleading and beseeching, imploring and persevering, calling upon Him again and again, *Lord! Lord! Lord!*

An example of this is offered by Elijah. Elijah prayed for rain six times, but his request was not heard. The seventh time, he saw a cloud in the shape of a fist. One may be tempted to ask why the Lord delays His response in granting requests. The answer lies in the fact that one does not usually appreciate those things that come easily. Also, before Elijah could raise up the widow's son from the dead, he had to stretch himself out on the child many times before the soul of the child finally came back to him. It was not easy. Had it come to pass easily, the true value of such a magnificent deed would not have been fully appreciated.

Sometimes God refrains from granting us our requests speedily and easily. The value of something or a person increases in accordance with the difficulty, the time and the effort it takes to get this thing or person. Hence St. John the Baptist who was to prepare the way for the Lord was the fruit of long years of prayers. That was also the case with Isaac the Great. Similarly, had the Lord given Hannah her heart's desire speedily and without difficulties, it might have never turned out to be Samuel the great whose life was to be consecrated for the Lord.

There are things that should not come easily to you. You have to fight and struggle, plead and entreat. Then God will grant you your requests. This is human nature. This is also a law in Economics, when supply increases, demand decreases. It is a law that is also applicable to Grace. When you experience the abundance of God's grace, you are likely to feel bored, lacking in zeal and enthusiasm, and showing little gratitude. Moreover, you are even likely to feel less inclined to seek the Lord.

However, when the Lord keeps things from you and does not heed your requests, you are more likely to hold more tightly unto Him. You are even more likely to show sincere feelings of gratitude when God grants you a request after having entreated for it for long.

If, for example, there is a certain sin that overpowers you and you want to rid yourself of it, and you try many ways to do so. You resort to prayers only to find that you are still unable to shun this particular sin. Then you try to talk to counselors and spiritual guides, only to find that this is not helping either. You resort to reading to no avail, and you fruitlessly try many different tools of spiritual warfare. All your endeavors are useless and futile, and all your attempts are doomed to failure. You feel overwhelmed and you call upon the Lord to help you rid yourself of that sin. You are still incapable and helpless.

When the Lord finally helps you get rid of that sin, you are bound to bless the name of the Lord and earnestly vow and solemnly pledge not to return to it ever again. You are even likely to pledge never to come close to anything, any place, or anyone that might instigate the remembrance of this sin.

If this house at the end of that street is your stumbling block, you will not even come close to the street itself, nor the neighborhood, nor even the whole city. You will keep as far away as possible. This earnest pledge is the result of a long struggle and stubborn patience. You thank the Lord you are free at last. You feel extremely grateful and thankful. You will always be on your guard. You will always be watchful, alert and vigilant. It has been a long, difficult and arduous road.

Jacob toiled and cared for Rachel for a period of fourteen years. He loved her dearly. He did not take real delight in Leah. She was someone thrown his way. He was not infatuated with Leah, nor was she the object of his affection. Leah is, in fact, a symbol of such things that are easily acquired and which are therefore not fully appreciated. Even though Leah bore him such children as Levi, who later brought forth priesthood, and Judah, through whose descendants Jesus came, Jacob was not really in love with her.

It was Rachel who was the object of his love, respect and admiration. It was Rachel for whom he toiled for a period totaling fourteen years, seven years followed by another seven years. Even though Rachel bore him no children, he was fascinated and mesmerized by her. Rachel was everything to him; he had to work hard for her.

You may think that God does not care for you or show mercy and compassion. You may feel that He does not heed your prayers and entreaties and that He does not want to grant you your desires. This is God's wisdom and holy will. He knows that you will not appreciate the things that come easily to you. You will even soon lose whatever comes easily to you. That is why the Lord will make sure that you completely understand the value and appreciate the worth of anything before you receive it. He wants you to appreciate, cherish and keep those things that you receive.

Now, you plead with the Lord. I have been through a great deal: I rose and went about the city; I roamed the streets and the squares; I looked and searched for You here and there, and I asked the watchmen that go about the city. I sought You but I could not find You. The Lord will respond to this plea saying, Enough. Now that you have found Me, you can say, *I held him and would not let him go.*

That is enough for tonight.

Let us pray.

May God have mercy upon us and bless us, and make His face shine with His Countenance upon us and have compassion upon us. With the prayers and intercessions that are raised on our behalf by the Mother of God, the Pure Saint Mary, and all the angels and apostles, and the prophets, and the martyrs, and the confessors, and the anchorites, and the saints who we ask to pray for us for peace at all times, and the blessings of the saint of this blessed day, and the blessing of Saint Mary first and last, may their holy blessings and the prayers and intercessions be with us all. Amen.

Peace be with you all.

May God make us worthy to say, Our Father...

PART THREE

By Night On My Bed
I Sought the One I Love

Song of Solomon 3:1-4

In the Name of the Father, the Son, and the Holy Spirit, One God. Amen.

Tonight, we continue contemplating on the *Song of Songs,* and I would like to conclude this topic so as to move on to the following one. In the third Chapter we read, *By night on my bed I sought the one I love; I sought him, but I did not find him,* (Song 3:1).

The soul recounts its spiritual experiences and memoirs with the Lord

It is important to notice that this chapter records the spiritual history and relationship of the human soul with the Lord. The soul recounts its spiritual experiences and memoirs with the Lord. It reminiscences about its past and recollects and lays bare its experiences. In Ecclesiastes, we also have a similar picture. There, Solomon tells about his spiritual

155

experiences, his life and relationship with God. He speaks about the many different states he has to undergo until he has finally found the Lord. It is like some sort of public confession, an open admission and an account of the soul of its experiences in life. Everyone in the world has an experience or a number of experiences with God. I wish that you would spend some time to reflect on your relationship with God and your many different experiences with Him.

The story recounted in the *Song of Songs* is the spiritual life story of the human soul that has experienced life with God, one in which it has tasted the sweet and sour and undergone the good and the bad. This human soul has witnessed Gethsemane. Yet, it has also experienced the Mount of Transfiguration. It has tasted the bitterness of being alienated from God, but it has also experienced the sweetness of His companionship and His nearness. It has undergone many different states and feelings.

This human soul has experienced kindness and thoughtfulness, *It is the voice of my beloved! He knocks, saying, 'Open for me, my love, my dove, my perfect one,'* (Song 5:2). It has also encountered rejection and denial, *I sought him, but I did not find him,* (Song 3:1). It has experienced, *I am my beloved, and my beloved is mine,* (Song 6:3), and, *His left hand is under my head, and his right hand embraces me,* (Song 2:6). However, it has also encountered deprivation and abandonment and has been much afflicted by the guards. It has been depicted as *black,* yet, it has also been portrayed as *beautiful,* (Song 1:5). It has been subjected to humiliation and disgrace from her *mother's sons* who called her *keeper of the vineyards*, (Song 1:6). On the other hand, she has also been exalted and praised by her bridegroom, *Behold, you are fair, my love! Behold, you are fair! You have dove's eyes,* (Song 4:1).

Such is the condition of the human soul as it experiences living with the Lord, as it savors things that may be sweet or sour, and as it goes through difficulties and happiness. It is a long road in which man marches with the Lord. There are failures, difficulties and hardships along the road, but there are also triumphs and successes.

I have told you many times before and I still maintain that one of the most telling verses that reflects spiritual life is the last verse in chapter eight in the book of Genesis. After the Flood, we read, *While the earth remains, seedtime and harvest, cold and heat, winter and summer, and day and night shall not cease,* (Gen 8:22). In your lives, my beloved, there is day and night, cold and heat, summer and winter. No man leads an exclusively happy, easy and comfortable life. Every man is bound to encounter periods of darkness and difficulties, if only temporarily. Even the righteous *children of light* are occasionally subjected to phases of darkness and difficulty.

Love is forever in her heart.

This virgin reminisces and recounts those phases of abandonment, deprivation, and the many attempts made to seek the Lord. Throughout it all, she has always felt the love that has so tightly united her with the Lord. In the midst of those stages of abandonment when she *sought but could not find him*, she would be searching and inquiring, *Have you seen the one I love?* (Song 3:3). She would make an effort to find him, *I will rise now...and go about the city; in the streets and in the squares I will seek the one I love,* (Song 3:2). Even though the relationship with the Lord has been severed, she has not lost that love.

Love is forever in her heart. Love for the Lord is the foundation of this relationship. It is not founded on formalities, false pretenses, mere rituals, commandments, or fear. Rather, it is based on love; it is based on strong foundations and profound feelings.

When she talks with the Lord, she does not call Him *my God*. Rather, she calls Him *my love*. We maintain that God has lavishly bestowed His grace upon us when He called us His children and asked us to pray saying *Our Father*. This soul, however, would not call upon the Lord except by saying *my beloved*. Examples for this abound: *My beloved is mine, and I am his. He feeds his flock among the lilies,* (Song 2:16). *I will go about the city... I will seek the one I love,* (Song 3:2). And, *Like an apple tree among the trees of the woods, so is my beloved among the sons. I sat down in his shade with great delight, and his fruit was sweet to my taste,* (Song 2:3). The more we read, the more examples we encounter that testify to the love that this soul has for God.

Be wary of merely regarding God as a mighty, fear-inspiring God who reigns distantly and impersonally from the heavens. This is not the whole picture. Christianity has given us a new perspective in which commandments, virtues and all manners of spiritual practices spring forth from love. As such, there is no such thing as independent virtues. Rather, there are virtues that arise and originate from love. Love is the root and the source; virtue is merely the outward expression and reflection of

She is totally lost in God's love; she is drunk and inebriated by His love

this love. In other words, virtue is the natural and logical outcome of love, *If anyone loves Me, he will keep My word,* (John 14:23). This means that keeping the commandment is the result of love and that keeping the commandment without love is spiritually unavailing and unchristian.

There are those who adopt a rigorous moral code

and conduct themselves with the utmost propriety and decorum. Their behavior is socially appropriate; they are of good repute. However, this appropriate behavior does not stem from their love for the Lord. We can therefore call or regard this behavior as a "social virtue" or a "behavioral virtue." This behavior should not to be confused with true spiritual conduct that, by necessity, springs from love.

The love of the virgin in the *Song of Songs* is based in God. She finds pleasure and happiness in her love of the Lord, *How much better than wine is your love,* (Song 4:10). She is totally lost in God's love; she is drunk and inebriated by His love. Moreover, she even admits her passion for him, *I am lovesick*, (Song 2:5), an image that indicates God's irresistible love. God's immense and boundless love has rendered her completely powerless that now she is *lovesick*. Her body is weaker than her spirit and that spiritual love has, therefore, completely captivated her and thoroughly engulfed and overwhelmed her entire being.

Those who are physically ill may have a fever and their body would crumble under the yoke of such a high temperature. There are those spiritual highs as well. They are not in need of treatment. They are just intoxicated by their love for the Lord. This is similar to what some people told St. Paul the Apostle as he was talking about the Lord. They told him, *Much learning is driving you mad,* (Acts 26:24). I wish we were all infected with this holy Pauline madness! What a blessing that would be! Because of the abundance of his love to the Lord, St. Paul speaks words that others fail to grasp and understand, and he himself experiences feelings that are alien and incomprehensible to others. He is, in short, *lovesick*.

The bride says, *How much better than wine is your love!* The problem lies in the fact that the love of the world is forever wrestling against the love of God. The love of

God is not our true pleasure and real happiness. It is true that we love the Lord, yet we still find pleasure in worldly matter. These are incompatible and in opposition; they are at odds. They wrestle for supremacy, *The flesh lusts against the Spirit, and the Spirit against the flesh,* (Gal 5:17). These two wrestling desires are contradictory and diametrically opposed. He who truly loves the Lord finds true happiness in his love for Him. Such a person does not fight and struggle to abide by the Lord's commandments and keep His word. It is not difficult for such a man to follow God's statutes.

The Lord's commandment is his true joy and happiness. The Lord's word is his pleasure and delight, *The statutes of the Lord are right, rejoicing the heart; the commandment of the Lord is pure, enlightening the eyes,* (Ps 19:8). *Your word is a lamp to my feet, and a light to my path,* (Ps 119:105). The Lord's words and judgment are *sweeter than honey and the honeycomb,* (Ps 19:10). Man finds joy in the Lord and is exceedingly happy in His commandments, *I have seen the consummation of all perfection, but Your commandment is exceedingly broad,* (Ps 119:96). The very Name of the Lord is a source of pleasure and delight, *Your Name is sweet and glorified in the mouths of Your saints.* This bride has found her true joy and delight in the Lord, and she therefore exclaims *the virgins love you,* (Song 1:3).

Your name is ointment poured forth; therefore the virgins love you. Every one and every soul that is not preoccupied with others loves You. The word *virgin* here refers to all people, married and unmarried alike. They are spiritually *virgins,* which is to say their souls are not concerned or occupied with others. Similarly, all who are saved are represented by the five wise virgins; they represent the righteous whether married or unmarried. They are *virgins* because the heart and the soul are neither concerned nor occupied with another. *You shall love the*

Lord your God with all your heart, with all your soul, and with all your mind, (Matt 22:37).

According to St. Augustine, the five virgins stand for the five senses of human beings. The reference again is to all those who go about their daily lives through the use of their five senses, yet they have dedicated their entire heart and soul to the Lord. The Lord, no one else, has become their goal, their objective. *Therefore the virgins love you.* This is the first reason: the soul has found happiness and delight in the Lord

He who truly loves the Lord finds true happiness in his love for Him

The soul that loves the Lord cannot find any god like Him. David says, *Among the gods there is none like You, O Lord,* (Ps 86:8). If, therefore, there is none like Him, then, *like an apple tree among the trees of the woods, so is my beloved among the sons,* (Song 2:3). If we are to compare the Lord with all the pleasures of the world, or all the beloved in the world, or all other gods, we will find Him, *like an apple tree among the trees of the woods.* For this reason, the bride contends, *My beloved is white and red, chief among ten thousand,* (Song 5:10). The beloved is distinguished even amongst ten thousand. The beloved is eminent and notable, distinguished and prominent, even among ten thousands.

When can the Lord become the desire of your heart, your sole yearning? When can the Lord become the most special, and the most distinguished and the most eminent? When can you love Him above all else? When can you say that *my beloved* is *chief among ten thousand?* And, *among the gods there is none like You, O Lord.* You ought to diligently try to reach that level in which God becomes your sole concern and preoccupation and all your time is dedicated to the Lord. Strive to reach that state in which you experience that you love the Lord with all your heart, and you will find that there is none like Him among either the pleasures of the world or all those that compete with the Lord for your love.

What else does this bride say? She finds a certain exclusively unique beauty in the Lord, *Behold! you are handsome, my beloved! Yes, pleasant,* (Song1:16). What beauty in the Lord! What do we mean when we say that the Lord is handsome or beautiful? Sometimes one walks in the righteous path and finds that the paths of the Lord are dreary and bleak and the gate narrow. Sometimes man finds that the commandment of the Lord is heavy and burdensome. Man may even concede that if it were not for eternity, reward and punishment, fear and trepidation, one would not have chosen to walk in that difficult, dreary road. O Lord! Ever since I have come to know You, Lord, I have encountered trials and hardships; I have walked through difficult roads, seen the cross, been to Gethsemane, and cried and shed many tears.

Never think that God is lonely and isolated and cannot find those who love Him

How can you say that, my beloved? If you know the Lord, you will discover that His paths are lovely. Even if you are to carry the cross, you will discover how sweet it is to be carrying it. Even if you are to encounter trials and hardships, *In this you greatly rejoice, though now for a little while, if need be, you have been grieved by various trials,* (1Pet 1:6). You will delight in the Lord. You will find joy in the cross, and you will rejoice in the thorns and in the nails. You will experience happiness in trials, in difficulties and in hardships. You will experience first hand that life with the Lord is happiness itself. It will always be the source of eternal, never-ending happiness. *Rejoice in the*

Lord always. Again I will say, rejoice, (Phil 4:4).

Thus, this is a call to love the Lord, His paths, His church, His children, His commandments, the trials that He permits, the difficulties He allows, His cross and everything that He brings your way. It is a call to experience His beauty and you will be able to say, *Behold! you are handsome, my beloved! Yes, pleasant,* and you will discover that, *Among the gods there is none like You, O Lord.*

Nor does the bride only see the beauty and splendor of the beloved. She, in addition, sees many other attributes, *His eyes are like doves by the rivers of waters,* (Song 5:12), and, *His countenance is like Lebanon, excellent as the cedars. His mouth is most sweet, yes, he is altogether lovely,* (Song 5:15-16).

Never think that God is lonely and isolated and cannot find those who love Him. Do not think that you will be doing Him a favor and easing His solitude and alleviating His loneliness if you love Him. Far from it. God is our obsession, longing and yearning. He is our passion and desire. This, in fact, brings to mind what was said about holiness, *holiness is the process of substituting one desire for another.* It is replacing the lust for the world with the lust for God.

By necessity, everyone has desires and yearnings. It is natural that one has inclinations and desires, likings and longings. We will not, as Buddhists do, suggest that everyone has to get rid of all desires and discard all proclivities. We are only suggesting that one ought to replace all the lusts for the world with the love of God. Then one is bound to yearn for God and all that is Godly, and one will find in God all joy, happiness and delight. In Him, man will find true fulfillment for all imaginable yearnings and desires, *I shall not want.* Ever since I started living with the Lord, my every need has been fulfilled, and

I do not lack a thing. I feel satisfied and I do not want anything from the world.

Thus chants the bride in the *Song of Songs, His countenance is like Lebanon, excellent as the cedars.* The reference here is to beautiful Lebanon for which we ask the Lord to grant her peace and tranquility. Lebanon is an extremely beautiful country. It is known for its exceeding natural beauty, gorgeous, beautiful mountains, breathtaking scenery, and the great stretches of fine-looking greenery. Likening Him to Lebanon and describing Him as *excellent as the cedars* are apt images that convey beauty and splendor. Like the beautiful cedars, God will likewise be seen as *excellent as the cedars*.

Let us all imagine someone wholeheartedly engulfed and utterly lost in contemplating and exalting the beautiful characteristics of the Lord. Let us attend and listen to such chants and praises of the Lord for His attractive and lovely attributes, *His eyes are like doves.* We should remember that doves are a symbol of the Holy Spirit. Therefore, the eyes of the Lord are the Holy Spirit, symbolizing that spiritually discerning, insightfully piercing gaze that examines and scrutinizes; that holy pristine, spotlessly immaculate look that enters and penetrates the inner recesses of man. They are eyes that are simple and humble, compassionate and kind, serene and profound, lovely and beautiful, *His eyes are like doves by the rivers of waters. His mouth is most sweet, yes, he is altogether lovely.*

Trust me when I tell you that from the *Song of Songs,* it would be sufficient for you to only experience *he is altogether lovely.* When will you come to realize that God is *altogether lovely* and experience delight and joy in living with Him?

The Lord is not a tariff or tax imposed upon you. Nor is He a yoke or a heavy burden upon your shoulders.

To you, God is not an eternal judgment and neither is He that powerful, mighty impersonal ruler. On the contrary, God is your sheer joy and utmost delight; He is *altogether lovely*. When St. Augustine found the Lord, the world and its lust became utterly inconsequential to him. When St. Paul found the Lord, he felt that all the world is but rubbish. *Yet indeed I also count all things loss for the excellence of the knowledge of Christ Jesus my Lord, for whom I have suffered the loss of all things, and count them as rubbish, that I may gain Christ,* (Phil 3:8).

When one loves the Lord, the love of the world withers and dies. Therefore, if there is a certain sin that you find unconquerable, it is only because the love of God has not reigned full supreme. If you love the Lord and long for Him, you will find that sin vanishes and disappears. It will exist no more.

The bride sees in God the Shepherd that tends to her needs. He takes care of her, *He feeds his flock among the lilies,* (Song 2:16). He leads her to *green pastures* and beside the *still waters,* (Ps 23:2). He takes her to his gardens. Let us dwell on this pertinently fitting image, *My beloved has gone to his garden, to the beds of spices, to feed his flock in the garden, and to gather lilies,* (Song 6:2). What an appropriate expression. How melodious! How sweet!

I feel satisfied and I do not want anything from the world

One ought to dwell on every word, *My beloved has gone to his garden, to the beds of spices, to feed his flock in the garden, and to gather lilies. I am my beloved's, and my beloved is mine. He feeds his flock among the lilies,* (Song 6:2 -3). These words attest that the Lord is not a heavy yoke. Rather, gardens, spices, lilies are the Lord's. Life with Him is a delight and a pleasure. I will, therefore, go with Him to the *beds of spices* and enjoy a pleasure-filled life with Him.

One may wonder what I may possibly mean by *beds of spices* when all we see is nothing but fasting, prayers, prostrations, and the like. Where are those *spices*? It is indeed *spices* when you delight and enjoy fasting and experience its effects on your life. Let us consider the example of a man whose only interest is filling his belly with all different kinds of foods. Such a person never seems to have enough; he keeps on eating and eating till he becomes overweight and obese.

Other people would warn such a person about matters related to health. They would suggest such things as losing weight since the heart cannot sustain such a huge mass of flesh and fat. This person may start to fast and lose weight, not out of love for the Lord, but out of self interest and because of health concerns. Well! If fasting can be beneficial for health reasons, why do you not fast for the Lord? Why do you not fast and enjoy it? Enjoy it and refrain from referring to it as a form of punishment, a burden, or a cross.

God is so wonderful and incredibly amazing

The saints used to sing and exalt the Lord even in prisons and along the way to martyrdom. They even experienced pleasure and delight as they were proceeding to their demise. These are the *beds of spices*. When virtues become spices is the subject of another lecture. The important thing here is that this bride regards the Lord as a Shepherd who provides for her needs, leads her to his gardens and his beds of spices and lilies.

In Him the bride does not only find the Shepherd, but she also experiences the quickness and promptness of His response. Once she calls Him, He responds right away, *The voice of my beloved! Behold, he comes leaping upon the mountains, skipping upon the hills. My beloved is like a gazelle or a young stag,* (Song 2:8-9). God is swift. There are people who are inaccessible and unapproachable. You may try very hard to reach them. You tirelessly entreat and plead. You patiently await for their response. You humble yourself before them or you show them a great deal of respect.

Yet, it is very different with the Lord who comes *leaping upon the mountains, skipping upon the hills... like a gazelle or a young stag.* Where can you find a god like that? Where can anyone find a god who once His name is called, He swiftly comes to one's heart, resolves one's problem and eases one's concerns? God is so wonderful and incredibly amazing. He is astoundingly unbelievable in all His characteristics. He is exceedingly swift.

Moreover, God is also omnipotent and all-powerful. The God that you worship is a mighty God. He is capable of providing protection and shelter. My beloved is like a, *filly among Pharaoh's chariots,* (Song 1:9), and around his coach there are, *sixty valiant men, every man has his sword on his thigh, because of fear in the night,* (Song 3:7-8). This is God the invincible, the omnipotent and the all-powerful. It is power that supports and sustains, not one that instills fear in the hearts. The human soul will therefore feel surrounded and shielded with amazing might which is the Lord's.

Within the bosom of the Lord, that human soul feels protected and fortified with the powerful arm of the Lord encompassing it. This is the same powerful arm that struck the rock to bring forth water, and caused the waters of the Red Sea to be divided. It is also the same powerful arm that had sent quails and Manna. It is the Lord, the omnipotent and all-powerful. This omnipotence and power is to protect man, not to threaten or frighten him. This is the Lord who lifted up the heavens and established the earth for my sake. He is our mighty Lord and we love His might.

The Lord has also bestowed His might upon us, *You shall receive power when the Holy Spirit has come upon you; and you shall be witnesses to Me,* (Acts 1:8). The bride in *Song of Songs* finds that everything in her beloved is pleasant and lovely. She sees many beautiful characteristics that we will consider one by one. When she has finished enumerating these characteristics, she says, *This is my beloved, and this is my friend, O daughters of Jerusalem,* (Song 5:16). Have you ever seen anyone like Him? This is He. This is the Lord whom we love.

What a shame it is that one may hide the cross one is wearing for fear of getting into some kind of trouble! This is absolutely wrong. There is none like God in pleasantness and sweetness. There is none as powerful. When you really live with Him, you are sure to experience pleasure and delight. If you have not yet felt this happiness and pleasure, it means that you have not yet really lived with the Lord, loved or experienced Him. He has not yet entered your heart, and you have not entered His. You are still outside. You have not been into the *beds of spices* to *feed in the gardens, and to gather lilies.* You still have a long way to go.

I have taken too much time. That is enough. Let us pray.

May God have mercy upon us and bless us, and make His face shine with His Countenance upon us and have compassion upon us. With the prayers and intercessions that are raised on our behalf by the Mother of God, the Pure Saint Mary, and all the angels and apostles, and the prophets, and the martyrs, and the confessors, and the anchorites, and the saints who we ask to pray for us for peace at all times, and the blessings of the saint of this blessed day, and the blessing of Saint Mary first and last, may their holy blessings and the prayers and intercessions be with us all. Amen.

Peace be with you all.

May God make us worthy to say, Our Father…

Have You Seen the One I Love

I Sleep, But My Heart Is Awake

Song of Solomon 5:2

In the Name of the Father, the Son, and the Holy Spirit, One God. Amen.

There are those who delight in the positive aspects of their lives and rejoice in them, regardless of the existence of negative ones that may be wearisome. In Gethsemane, the disciples were unable to stay with the Lord and watch and pray for even one hour. It was an unpleasant and awkward situation in that difficult hour of warfare. The Lord told them to stay up with Him, and they did not. He could have been angry with them. However, the Lord focused on the positive aspects which were in them, and said, *the spirit indeed is willing, but the flesh is weak...watch and pray,* (Matt. 26:41).

> **Although the flesh is weak, the Lord Jesus found a good virtue, that they have a willing spirit.**

Although the flesh is weak, the Lord Jesus found a good virtue, that they have a willing spirit. We might tell the Lord, since the spirit is willing, should it not be victorious over the weak body and control it, rather than become subjugated and dominated by it. How then do You consider it a willing spirit if it is conquered by the flesh? The Lord tells us to refrain from our harsh judgments. Regarding the weak flesh, I still see that there is a willing spirit. After a while it will carry the flesh with it. It is not necessary for us to begin with full and complete health.

Moreover, this virgin sees herself as asleep. She remains without a spiritual outlook. There is no passion. There is no vigilance. There is no vitality. There is no activity. However, she affirms it is acceptable. *I sleep, but my heart is awake,* (Song 5:2). I have something that encourages me, that my heart is awake. Although I sleep, I am keenly sensitive to the voice of my Beloved. Indeed, I am asleep, but I still can hear the voice of my Beloved knocking and saying, *Open for me, my sister, my love,* (Song 5:2). These are great words. Although I sleep, I can hear His voice. This is not death, only slumber. The Lord told them, *the child is not dead, but sleeping,* (Mark 5:39). She still has the breath of life in her. It maybe that the life in her is concealed and veiled, but there is still life in her. She still has life and that life will definitely bring forth fruit.

The trees do not produce fruits all year long. Yet, I do not cut it down and throw it into the fire. The tree still has life. Plowing around it and enriching it with fertilizers may help it bring forth fruits later. *I sleep, but my heart is awake.*

I sleep, but my heart is awake. It is counter productive to focus on the negatives and admonish and reproach sleep. It would be wonderful, however, if the heart that is awake is beaming gleefully and vivaciously with hope. We should not lose sight of the fact that had God relinquished hope in the state of the Church when it is lukewarm, lacking in zeal and ardor, or had He given up hope in ever awakening our hearts, we would have all perished. Rather, time and again, the Lord has consoled, sustained and encouraged us that even though our bodies are asleep and *the flesh is weak*, our hearts are awake and *the spirit is willing*. It is these alert hearts that the Lord seeks and desires.

One may be asleep like waste land: *The earth was without form, and void; and darkness was on the face of the deep.* However, there is something positive, nonetheless. *The spirit of God (is) hovering over the face of the waters,* (Gen 1:2). Something beautiful is bound to come out of it.

It is these alert hearts that the Lord seeks and desires

Habakkuk the prophet, seems to reiterate the same theme. *Do not rejoice over me, O sin, for even if I fall, I will rise up again.* This is an affirmation, an assertion, that even though one may commit a sin or make a mistake, one will not wallow in the dirt but will brace oneself and rise up again. We have that same conviction that after every Golgotha, there is a resurrection. Therefore, despite my apparent frailty and weakness while being nailed to the cross, in a short while I will resurrect in great glory.

There are positive aspects in everyone's life. Some people, however, give up and resign themselves to despondency and despair. Some people can only see futility, uselessness and hopelessness when they confront difficulties and challenges. *Lord, by this time there is a stench, for he has been dead four days,* (John 11:39).

The Lord, on the other hand, ascertains that this is not true. He sees life in Lazarus. *If you would believe, you would see the glory of God,* (John 11:40). God confirms that the person who is thought of as dead, even with *a stench,* and has been in that condition for a long time will rise up again. It has a heart that is awake, and the minute the Lord's words *Lazarus, come forth* is heard, it will rise, come out of the grave and see and witness the Light.

There is hope. There is hope for everyone. No one can shut the door of hope to anyone regardless of their condition. Even if the human spirit is *without form, and void; and darkness (is) on the face of deep,* even if it has developed a *stench* for lying in the grave for four days, and even if she is *asleep.* The important thing is that the heart is *awake.* There is always hope.

This hope is extended to the servants of the Church. It is by no means limited to the parishioners. A servant should never give up on any human being, however unpromising and discouraging their attitude might be. There is no despondency, hopelessness nor despair in service. St. Paul the Apostle asserts, *Therefore we do not lose heart. Even though our outward man is perishing, yet the inward man is being renewed day by day,* (2 Cor 4:16). If we appear to be outwardly asleep, inwardly we are fully awake. Even though the disciples are asleep in the upper room, afraid for their lives, unable to go out and make their faith public, their hearts are awake and will, one day, like a mighty giant, fill the earth with their message of faith, hope and promise.

There is hope. There is hope for everyone

We even thank the Lord that there are hearts that are fully awake, diligent and watchful over those whose hearts are asleep. Not only have some become asleep, but their hearts have also fallen asleep. Their hearts lack alertness, vigilance and attentiveness. We thank the Lord for there are others who remain awake, vigilant and watchful for their sake.

Though some sheep must have fallen asleep the night Christ was born, there were shepherds who remained watchful and fully alert. They were mindful and vigilant; therefore, none of the sheep perished. Herein lies the role of the Church. Even if the parishioners fall asleep, the Church remains alert, vigilant and watchful. To extend the metaphor, even if the Church becomes less vigilant and alert, the eyes of the Lord will remain wide open to protect His people. There is no need for alarm.

There are some whose conscience may appear to have fallen asleep. Yet, there is that spiritual seed that is bound to give forth fruit even after awhile. God has placed a living seed in the heart of everyone. This seed is waiting for the opportune moment in which it will take root and blossom. However, there are various kinds of seeds. Some seeds come to fruition in a few days, others in a few months.

Those among you who have had experience planting dates know that the seed may be buried for five, six, or even seven months with no sign of life. After many months have elapsed, they may notice that there is something that resembles a small needle coming out of the earth. That needle will continue to come out, and a small greenish color is noticed. The seed, thank God, is coming to fruition. That little seed that was dormant and buried for a few months will, in time, be a palm tree. Throughout, the seed has born life, albeit dormant, inactive, and hidden, awaiting for the Lord's power to flourish and blossom in the fullness of time.

I sleep, but my heart is awake. This sleep may be due to laziness and slothfulness. It may be due to a spiritual weakness or infirmity, a sign of the lack of spiritual ardor and zeal. In other words, this *sleep* may be a consequence to inevitable spiritual warfare which entails the possibility of succumbing to sin and the subsequent undergoing of a potential state of spiritual slumber and slothfulness. There is sleep, but my heart is still awake.

Therefore, every time I commit a sin, the pricks of my conscience alert and pierce me and I realize that something is wrong. I sin again and the voice of conscience forebodingly warns and alerts me to the inappropriateness of the deed. Yet I sin again and the thorns pierce even more sharply than ever before: *It is hard for you to kick against the goads*, (Act 9:5).

These *goads* in the human soul are utterly opposed to sin and urge and spur us to refrain from committing sin and to change our ways. Then we become alert and ask for God's forgiveness. We are equipped with a distinctive feeling, a unique sentiment that even though we may seem asleep, yet our hearts are awake and sensitive. It is because of this unique sentiment, the pricks of the conscience, that we do not fail to feel the inadequacy and inappropriateness of a wrong thing.

It is, therefore, not uncommon that someone may undergo this phase of spiritual slumber, laziness and weakness and the subsequent feeling of being spiritually inept. Nevertheless, the fact that one's heart is still awake will warn us that something is wrong since it is not in the image of the Lord. *Wake up O you who slumber. Rise that Jesus may shine upon you.* That invitation, that urges and spurs us to wake up, resonates relentlessly and persistently. Blessed is he who accepts the invitation without delay. St. Augustine rebuked himself bitterly in the presence of the Lord for putting off that invitation. *I wish I had accepted your love sooner.*

Nor is there any doubt that Saul of Tarsus had had

this spiritual alertness that was bound to manifest itself, albeit later, in the fullness of time. The Lord's invitation, *It is hard for you to kick goads,* is an indication, beyond a doubt, of those *goads*, the pricks, that he had. Saul did indeed have them, and even though he resisted and struggled against them, he could not prevail. Neither could he resist for ever. The day would come in which he would declare that he had

Out of His riches He brings forth gems and pearls

been blatantly wrong. It is impossible to have a life without Him.

Similarly, you would be fooling no one but yourself if you do not heed this invitation. There is this distinct voice in you that declares that you cannot have a life away from the Lord. Even if you can do it this year, you will not be able to do it next year. If you are able to resist Him today, you will not be able to resist Him tomorrow. That distinct inner voice would persist even more. *Wake up O you who slumber. Rise that Jesus may shine upon you.* It is high time to wake up and regain your spiritual alertness.

For this reason, you may talk about the Word of God at anytime. Do not, however, be disheartened if you do not get a response, for the Word of God is living and effective and will remain in the heart of man and will be imbued with life in due time. You may have spoken about the Word of God to someone. You may have thrown the Word in someone's heart or mind. This word may remain dormant for some time.

Yet, it will, in time, assume such an amazing power and such an enormous energy that, when released, no one will be able to resist or shun It. *Out of His riches He brings forth gems and pearls.* No matter how hard one tries to avoid and escape from the beauty of such words, one's attempts are doomed to failure. For how could one escape from words such as these? One feels surrounded, even besieged, by the mighty Word of God. The Word has become alive, and one is utterly helpless to do anything but accept It.

The Word of God was there in your heart all along.

When I state that the Word of God has become alive, I mean that all the means that would help the Word to bring forth fruit are made available. The Word is like a seed waiting for the right circumstances to sprout and blossom. Those of you who may have traveled through the desert may have noticed that some plants come out of the ground. Some people claim that these plants just sprout for no reason. This is not true.

What actually happens is that the wind may blow causing some seeds to fall off some trees. These seeds are then carried by the wind to other soils and may be left buried in these soils for months or even years. One day the rain falls. The water dampens the soil and the seed receives the nutrition that it requires to sprout and blossom. The time has come for that seed to take root and sprout. It is as if grace has now touched and changed one's heart. *I will rise and go to my father...* (Luke 15:18).

That dormant life in the seed has finally become active; it is now time to bloom, sprout and come to bud in the midst of the dust. Likewise, you yourself must have experienced numerous occasions in which the Lord has sown seeds in your heart, seeds that were buried in the dust. The time will come when the rain will fall such as an event that would touch and move you; a time in which you become malleable, ready and compliant. It is at such a time that you hear the Word of God declaring, *I sleep, but my heart is awake.*

The Word of God was there in your heart all along. It has been dormant but alive, nonetheless. Now is the time for the power and the energy of the Word to be released. *I sleep, but my heart is awake. It is the voice of my beloved! He knocks…*

I cannot help wondering about this person whose beloved is knocking at the door only to get no response. When we pray, we have the assurance of a prompt response, *I sought the Lord, and He heard me,* (Ps. 34:4). Even before we finish our prayers, the Lord hears and answers them. However, we turn a deaf ear when the Lord Himself calls. We do not respond. *Behold, I stand at the door and knock. If anyone hears My voice and opens the door, I will come in to him and dine with him, and he with Me,* (Rev 3:20).

His invitation oftentimes goes unheeded. We remain slothful, asleep and we try to find pegs on which to hang our excuses. Why do you not respond? Why do you not answer the door? Rise and open for, *my head is covered with dew, My locks with the drops of the night*, (Song 5:2). The Lord continues, *Open for me, my sister, my love My dove, my perfect one*, and there is still no response. The human soul is in a state of inertia and indolence.

The Lord, however, is tolerantly waiting. He is patient and long-suffering. Those who do not hear His voice today may hear It tomorrow. Those who do not respond this year, may do so next year. The Lord will never give up on any human soul. We cannot but be thankful and grateful for this; we would perish if the Lord was ever to give up on us. We would be similar to, *those who have gone down to the pit*, (Ps. 30:3). We always cling to the Lord's patience and tolerance. The Lord Himself finds excuses for us. He understands the frailty and weakness inherent in the human condition. He patiently awaits by our bed side urging us to wake up, *Wake up, children of light, and praise the Lord of Hosts.* Arise! *I sleep, but my heart is awake. It is the voice of my beloved! He knocks…*

Nor is it astonishing that this slothful and sleepy person tries to come up with various excuses for this state of inertia and indolence. Even though the Bible clearly illustrates that, *you are inexcusable, O man,* (Rom 2:1), people still try to come up with some excuses: *I have taken off my robe; How can I put it on again? I have washed my feet; How can I defile them?* (Song 5:3).

St. Augustine has aptly expounded the meaning of these verses and fittingly linked them to service. He has suggested that even though the Lord is inviting and calling the indolent human soul to service, it has shown little interest and slight willingness to heed that call and accept that invitation. The reason for this state of indolence is clear in the verses, *I have taken off my robe; How can I put it on again? I have washed my feet; How can I defile them?* It is important to understand that the washing of feet is a symbol of cleanliness and purity.

When Jesus says, *If I do not wash you, you have no part with Me,* Simon Peter replies, *Lord, not my feet only, but also my hands and my head.* The Lord, however, said to St. Peter: *He who is bathed needs only to wash his feet, but is completely clean,* (Jn 13:8-10). We oftentimes reason along the same lines and follow the same logic. We may be tempted to claim that having washed our feet, we have become clean and have been experiencing a life of purity.

Now, if we were to commit ourselves to service, we are bound to encounter various challenges, people's varying temperaments and attitudes, the burden of the service itself, what to say and what to withhold, to mention just a few. We may feel reluctant to serve so as not to *defile* our feet. When we serve, we are definitely going to tread on the dust, encounter and even confront different people with different attitudes and dispositions. Therefore, we may become wary and even suspicious of the possibility of defilement.

However, the Lord encourages us and promises to wash our feet again and again. The Lord would be happy to wash our feet. Just like He washed His disciples' feet, He will gladly wash ours. For this reason, our Lord encourages us to rise and serve, to meet the pitfalls and challenges of service and the various stumbles and slips it entails, to face the people's troubles and problems as well as their rejection and denunciation, to encounter the Samaritan woman as she forcibly slams the door, to go to the Pharisee who hypocritically and insincerely invites us to his house, to encounter brothers who bear false witness, and to be exposed and subjected to the many difficulties and hardships that we will inevitably run into. We can always count on the Lord's assurance to wash our feet as He had washed His disciples'. We should not hide behind the pretext that we have *washed (our) feet, How can (we) defile them?* The Lord will wash them again.

If we were to commit ourselves to service, we are bound to encounter various challenges

Similarly, we may *have taken off (our) robe* and feel reluctant to put it on again. Do not be alarmed. The Lord will give us a brilliant white dress in its place. The Lord will clothe and adorn us with beauty and splendor. He will bestow upon us new garments and clothe us with the righteousness of the saints. He will grant us His Grace with bounty and abundance. So, it would be a shame if we are still trying to find excuses and pretexts. We should not say that we *have taken off (our) robe*. The Lord's invitation should be wholeheartedly and joyfully accepted.

If the Lord invites you, arise and let go of any obstacles or pretexts. Some people were invited but had various excuses to reject the invitation. One stated that his father is dead and he has to bury him, another stated that he has just gotten married and he has to attend to his wife's needs, and a third stated that he has just bought cattle and needs to look after them. The Lord rejected all these excuses and pretexts: *Let the dead bury their own dead,* (Mat 8:22).

We should not reject the Lord's invitation; we should not try to find excuses. What was the consequence of the rejection of that bride? What did it avail her? *My beloved had turned away and was gone*, (Song 5:6).

There is hope for us even if we become indolent and slothful The human soul may enjoy that state of slumber and indolence to the extent that excuses and pretexts become readily available. However, just as there are excuses and pretexts, there are *goads* and *pricks*. The Lord would use these to pierce the human soul to come around and awaken. I sleep, but my heart is awake. *It is the voice of my beloved! He knocks.*

My beloved does not knock on the door. Rather, He knocks on the heart. The voice of my beloved is stronger than all my excuses. When I hear his voice, *Open for me, my sister,* I cannot deny that request. The tiniest act of love and kindness on the part of the Lord would render the heart powerless. The heart would melt in adoration. *My beloved put his hand by the latch of the door, and my heart yearned for him*, (Song 5:4). The question that will naturally arise here is why has her *heart yearned for him?* The only feasible answer is that the heart is awake inside of her.

Oftentimes Satan tries to persuade us that it is futile and useless to try. We sometimes feel overwhelmed, weighed down and troubled, *Lord, how they have increased who trouble me?.... Many are they who say of me, "There is no help for him in God."* Nevertheless, we always have hope, *But You, O Lord, are a shield for me, my glory and the one who lifts up my head*, (Ps. 3:1-3). There is hope for us even if we become indolent and slothful. There is no such thing as a human being who is always and incessantly awake. We all experience phases during which spiritual slumber may overtake us. It is important to understand, however, that that slumber should neither last long nor be sound and deep. It is also important not to wait till you hear the voice of the knocker at the door.

The statement *I sleep* may be considered as a confession of the sins and imperfections of the human soul. Unlike the human soul that is asleep and pretends to be awake, the soul that admits that it is indolent and asleep will ultimately wake up. I admit that *I sleep* and that I could have been more energetic, effective and vivacious. I could have exhibited more love and affection, and I could have become more productive and diligent. Unfortunately, *I sleep*.

During sleep and slumber, indolence and slothfulness, Satan works best. He will slyly impart an opinion, furtively encourage a thought, or secretly present an obstacle. He will even covertly manipulate your disillusionments and hopes and find ways to entice and seduce you. Many things could occur during slumber. It is for this reason that our Lord Jesus Christ advises us to *Watch and pray, lest you enter into temptation*, (Matt. 26:41).

It is inappropriate to be asleep and lazy. The children of the Lord are always awake. They are both intellectually alert and spiritually vigilant. Not only should the heart be awake and alert, but rather this alertness should be perpetual and all encompassing. It should not only be confined to themselves, but should also extend to include others. St. Paul the Apostle aptly expresses this notion, *Who is made to stumble, and I do not burn with indignation,* (2 Cor 11:29). I cannot but be vigilant if those around are asleep.

You should stay alert and vigilant and be like the watchers of the night. The darker it may get, the more vigilant you should become. Nor should you use the phrase *I sleep* as a pretext to indulge in a state of laziness. This is completely inappropriate and erroneous. The Bible expounds the infirmities and weaknesses of the saints, but this is not an invitation for you to copy the saints in their weaknesses. Rather, you should emulate them in their righteous endeavors and godly deeds. *Rise, O you who slumber, that Christ may shine upon you.*

It is God's undertaking to awaken those who are asleep. It is also the mission of the children of God to awaken and fend for not only themselves but also for others. Those who wake up and rise will joyously sing, *I was glad when they said to me, "Let us go into the house of the Lord,"* (Ps 122:1). *I sleep, but my heart is awake. It is the voice of my beloved! He knocks saying, Open for me...*

God is not content by merely knocking on the door. Neither does He delight in merely calling the human soul. The Bible states that, *My beloved put his hand by the latch of the door, and my heart yearned for him,* (Song 5:4). When the Lord finds that the human soul is unwilling to heed either His knocking on the door nor His own voice calling *open for me,* He puts his hand by the *latch of the door.* He has obviously been searching for ways to reach that human soul.

Finally, He can find nothing except that little opening, the *latch* in the door. Through this opening He puts His hand. Having done that, *my heart yearned for him*. It is true that He does put His hand by the latch of the door, but He will never force the human soul to open unwillingly. It suffices that He puts His hand. Putting His hand to the latch of the door means squeezing the soul slightly and wringing it softly. It is as if the slothful human soul negotiates with the Lord.

It is also the mission of children of God to awaken and fend for not only them-selves but also for the others

Though you may not be moved to open the door, your conscience has been touched. If that little event has not been able to move the soul, allow that there be a bigger one; if that gentle word has failed to move and touch the heart, use stronger more poignant words. It is as if the human soul is pleading the Lord to put His hand to the latch of the door and do something.

The human soul comes to realize its need. *My heart yearned for him* is an indication of intense longing and a sign of enormous love for the Lord. For such a long time have I neglected Your love, O Lord. For years I have heard Your voice but have failed to respond. Now I feel ashamed because of Your great love. I feel embarrassed to see You waiting at the door. I feel uncomfortable that You are calling me, waiting outside until your, *head is covered with dew, and (your) locks with the drops of the night*. I am ashamed, humiliated and mortified. It is time for me to rise and awake. *I arose to open for my beloved*.

The Lord tries through various means to lure the human soul unto Him. However, the door is shut. The Lord has to knock on the door. He even puts His hand to the latch of the door. Yet, even though the doors are closed, the Lord is patiently standing behind them knocking. Does that not imbue us with more hope? Does it not fill us with promise? For, if the Lord is standing behind closed doors knocking, how much more will He be with those whose doors are already open.

They will surely have a taste of the Kingdom of Heaven. With those the Lord will dine, and they will see the Lord in all His splendor and glory. They will enjoy being in unity with the Lord and *abide* in the Lord just as the Lord will abide in them. They enjoy and experience myriads of blessings as they undergo a transformation into the image of the Lord as they become a *temple* and a dwelling place for Him.

Opening the door is equivalent to repentance, but admitting the Lord into one's heart is the beginning of companionship and fellowship with Him.

Open the door. Opening the door is equivalent to repentance, but admitting the Lord into one's heart is the beginning of companionship and fellowship with Him. In order to enjoy the companionship of the Lord, you should not be content to merely repent or feel penitent, but you should delve into a closer and more intimate relationship with Him. *I opened for my beloved, But my beloved had turned away and was gone,* (Song 5:6).

This is the condition of the human soul that fails to respond promptly. The longer you lead a sinful life, the more wretched will your condition be. If you do not open the door for the Lord quickly, sin will leave its marks and scars upon you, even in your subconscious. You may find certain images haunting you, even later in life. A lot of people have expressed their sorrow for the sins they have committed prior to their opening the door for the Lord. They have regretted experimenting this and trying that, and expressed their disappointment at losing their former simplicity, purity and innocence. They have even expressed profound feelings of grief and sorrow for having tasted of *the tree of the knowledge of good and evil.*

This disillusionment that they have experienced is the outcome of the tardiness and slothfulness they have shown in responding to the Lord's invitation to open the door for Him. Those who respond sooner are unlikely to experience such an anguish or undergo such difficulties. There are many people who have started a relationship with the Lord, but they have been haunted by their past for a long time. They have tried to get rid of their past but found it difficult, if not impossible. The present is not the cause of their dilemma.

The real causes are the images, thoughts, and the evil deeds that have accumulated in the past. These keep torturing and taunting these people. They often feel weighed down and distressed because of this. They implore the Lord to *wash (them) thoroughly* that they may be *whiter than snow,* (Ps. 51:7). It is only then that they can forget about the inequities of the past and all the troubles and problems these inequities have caused. Only then can they live in true harmony and companionship with the Lord. Only then would the Lord have complete dominion.

I sleep. However, she has now opened the door. She is no longer asleep. When the human soul admits its slumber, it acknowledges its past inequities. However, the human soul finally comes to its senses. *I arose to open for my beloved.* Nonetheless, *my beloved had turned away and was gone.* But the human soul is determined. *I sought him* in the streets and in the market place. *I charge you ... If you find my beloved, that you tell him I am lovesick*, (Song 5:8). She has become fully awake now. It is true I was asleep, but now I am different. I have changed. This story is only a recollection of the past. The bride is thoroughly awake now. The time of sleep is gone and now she is *lovesick*.

Unfortunately, she is experiencing that feeling of lovesickness only after her *beloved had turned away and was gone*. There are those who, feeling the toll of deprivation, would hastily seek the Lord. However, when the beloved knocks saying, *open for me*, the response was, *I have taken off my robe, How can I put it on again?* How unfortunate. It is for this reason that the Lord occasionally inflicts some sort of deprivation so that the human soul would seek, pursue, and even ask people about Him declaring, *I am lovesick*. It is a blessing that the Lord leads the human soul into such an admission. Let us pray.

May God have mercy upon us and bless us, and make His face shine with His Countenance upon us and have compassion upon us. With the prayers and intercessions that are raised on our behalf by the Mother of God, the Pure Saint Mary, and all the angels and apostles, and the prophets, and the martyrs, and the confessors, and the anchorites, and the saints who we ask to pray for us for peace at all times, and the blessings of the saint of this blessed day, and the blessing of Saint Mary first and last, may their holy blessings and the prayers and intercessions be with us all. Amen.

Peace be with you all.

May God make us worthy to say, Our Father...

PART ONE

I Am Black and Beautiful, O Daughters of Jerusalem

Song of Solomon 1:5

In the Name of the Father, the Son, and the Holy Spirit, One God. Amen.

Let us address the human soul. The human soul when it is in the state of sin is a black soul, in the eyes of people, a black soul. But it is beautiful by the blood of Jesus that cleanses it from every sin. She says I am black right now, but I am beautiful later. I am black in the state of sin, but I am beautiful in the state of repentance. I am black in my past which is filled with evil and far from God, but I am beautiful in the hope that is placed before me. I do not believe that my state in sin will continue. I do not believe that this blackness will continue forever.

> **I am black in the state of sin, but I am beautiful in the state of repentance.**

I believe that I am beautiful because I was created in the image of God and His likeness. This blackness is new to me. It is not in my nature. I am by nature a holy breath that came out of the mouth of God. A holy breath that came out of the mouth of God and was placed within me. I am beautiful because I am the image and likeness of God. He created me as such.

But the sun has tanned me, (Song 1:6). The one who is black by nature is not darkened by the sun. It is their genes, the characteristics that they have inherited, that make them black. But she says I am by nature white, but the sun has darkened me. Reasons that are from without have made me black. Reasons from without have made me black, and blackness is not of my character. Blackness is not of my nature, blackness is not from my original image, the Godly image. *I am beautiful, O daughters of Jerusalem.*

Beautiful because God will grant me His overwhelming purification and I will become clean. Beautiful because He will wash me and I will become whiter than snow. Beautiful because God will never leave me alone in my state. Grace will touch me one of these days. The Holy Spirit will visit me and work in me on a day which I do not know, but I will wait for Him with hope. I am certain that I will take off my blackness and become beautiful.

I was black with my original sin, and I entered the basin of baptism and became white and beautiful. Then it happens that the sun darkened me, and my skin became darkened once again. But I will enter the basin of repentance, the repentance that they call a second baptism. Then I will become beautiful as I was. I am black, but I do not lack hope. I feel that I will get rid of my blackness one of these days.

It is true that I am black because I asked and did not find, because I am in a state of abandonment. And if God lets go of a soul, it becomes black, but I am certain that I will see God. I will find Him, even after hard work and after some time. God will grant me His beauty and His forgiveness and I will become white as I was. *I am black and beautiful, O daughters of Jerusalem.*

You who are beautiful and live in holiness and purity, those who live in grace, do not mock me, and do not make fun of me, and do not look upon my blackness as if it was a shame. St. Paul would prevent you from your arrogance as he says, *Therefore let him who thinks he stands take heed lest he fall.* (1 Cor. 10:12) Do not be arrogant, but fear the Lord.

I am certain that I will take off my blackness and become beautiful.

Remember those that are in shackles, because you are shackled like them. And remember the disrespected as if you were in their bodies. It is possible for blackness to reach any person in existence. It is possible to be darkened by the sun. Never mock anyone. Do not mock me, because *I am beautiful, O daughters of Jerusalem.*

I had a sister who was black and she became beautiful, and she was the earth in its first day, she was black. The Bible says that in the first day of Creation, *The earth was without form, and void; and darkness was on the face of the deep,* (Gen 1:2). Therefore since there was darkness, there was blackness. But the Spirit of God was hovering over the surface of the water and, *Then God said, 'Let there be light'; and there was light*, (Gen 1:3) and the earth was beautiful. And then God looked at His creation and found it to be good.

I am waiting for that day when God would say, *Let*

there be light. I am waiting for that day when God would say, *Let there be light*, so that I may become beautiful, just like all of you. The earth that was without form and void and on its face darkness, it did not despair. It did not despair at all, because it saw beauty in the eye of hope and in the near and coming future.

I do not live in the present state or I will be suffocated by despair. I do not live in my present darkness. I live in the coming light. I do not live in the present blackness, but I wait until God washes me, and then I become white. It is strange that the Bible would say that I will become whiter than snow. The phrase, whiter than snow, is full of sympathy and hope for people. It is not a standard whiteness, it is not a normal white. Rather, it is a whiteness more than snow. Purity more than snow.

> **I do not live in my present darkness, but I live in the coming light.**

I am certain that the grace of God will find me. The Church of the Believers said *I am black* and it believed surely in the coming Savior, and with the coming sacrifice, with the Lamb that carries the sins of all the world, whose blood cleanses us from every sin, so it said *I am beautiful.*

The prophet David said, *I am pure*, (Psalm 86:2). What does he mean by pure? Is he talking about his purity? No. He is talking about the purity that will come through the blood that is being shed. When God washes the soul, it becomes whiter than snow. He says, those that are pure are enjoying grace. This grace will purify and cleanse and sanctify and wash us, so that we will forget all the dark and we will become whiter than snow.

I have another sister that was on one of these days black and then she became beautiful. She was black in a very frightening way and she became beautiful by the grace of God that was granted to her. Do you know who she is, O daughters of Jerusalem? She is the mother of all Jerusalem herself. The prophet Ezekiel spoke about her in Chapter 16, he says, *Son of man, cause Jerusalem to know her abominations and say.* And what does He say?

> *As for your birth, on the day you were born your navel cord was not cut, nor were you washed with water to cleanse you, nor rubbed with salt, nor wrapped in cloths.*
>
> *No eye pitied you, to do any of these things for you out of compassion for you; but you were thrown out in the open field, for you were abhorred on the day you were born.*
>
> *And when I passed by you, and saw you struggling about in your own blood, I said to you in your own blood. 'Live' Yes, I said to you in your blood, 'Live!'.*
>
> *Ezekiel 16:3-6*

After a period of time He says,

> *'When I passed by you again and looked upon you, indeed your time was the time of love; so I spread My wing over you and covered your nakedness. Yes, I swore an oath to you and entered into a covenant with you, and you became Mine,' says the Lord God.*
>
> *'Then I washed you in water; yes, I thoroughly washed off your blood, and I anointed you with oil.*
>
> *I clothed you in embroidered cloth and gave you sandals of badger skin; I clothed you with fine linen...*
>
> *You were exceedingly beautiful, and succeeded to*

royalty.

Your fame went out among the nations because of your beauty, for it was perfect through My splendor which I had bestowed on you,' says the Lord God.

Ezekiel 16:8-14

This black one was struggling about in her own blood and was thrown on the side of the road. Then the Lord looked upon her and it was the age of love. The age of love He refers to as the time that was defined by the love of God for visiting this soul. The age in which the Godly love works, and this is the age of love.

Therefore I bathed you in water and washed you in baptism and wiped you in oil, the holy Chrismation oil, and you became beautiful, and you became fit to be royalty. Your beauty became famous. However, this beauty was not an innate pureness, not an inherent pureness that is yours. Why?

There is a very important verse here, He says your beauty, *was perfect through My splendor,* your beauty was perfect through My splendor, *which I had bestowed on you.* I bestowed upon you My pureness, I gave you My beauty, so you became beautiful, O black one.

Many souls were once black and became beautiful. St. Moses the Black, his soul was black and became beautiful. St. Mary the Egyptian was black and became beautiful. St. Pelagia. All the repenting saints that started their lives with blackness, their souls were black and became beautiful, because the Lord has bestowed His pureness upon them.

However, this soul does not say I am black, but I became beautiful. She says, *I am black and beautiful.* I am black and what? And beautiful. In that she lives with hope and sees the future as if it was laid out before her. She is sure, sure that the soul, regardless of how fallen she was, take notice of this sentence, the soul, no matter how fallen she was, is a very worthy soul and precious to God. Worthy and precious with God. And its price is very high. The cost of this fallen soul is the blood of our Lord Jesus Christ. Beautiful soul.

There are souls that you may see as black, but God may see it as beautiful. In the eyes of the believers, there was no blacker soul than that of Saul of Tarsus who had once persecuted the Church. God looked into the soul of Saul. I do not say He looked upon his black soul, but I say He looked into his beautiful soul, He looked into his beautiful soul, and said to it, Saul, Saul, how long will you refuse my abundance. I am holding you, My beloved, and I am washing you so that you may become whiter than snow. But you keep kicking and throwing the soap and throwing the sponge and tossing the water. How long will you continue to refuse to be cleansed?

I will bathe you despite your defiance. I will tie you and wash you until your body becomes red. All the persecution and the violence that is inside of you, I will wash. And then Saul you will become whiter than snow. You will become whiter than snow. You will not simply become white. I will let them whip you with rods and stone you. Your blood will flow on My behalf. As your blood flows, I will sing to you and say, *My beloved is white and red,* (Song 5:10). You will not simply become whiter than snow, the redness will flow upon you from persecution and you will become white and red. *I am black and beautiful, O daughters of Jerusalem.*

The soul, regardless of how fallen she was...is a very worthy soul and precious to God.

I am black, but I am not afraid of damnation. I do not believe that I am a lost soul. God will come and will order the Seraphim to take a coal from the altar and with it wipe my lips and say *you are purified*. I am black, but I trust that Jesus will come and wash my feet and say to me, you are completely purified. I am black, but I am standing by the Cross, reaching out my hand for a drop of blood. and this will be enough for me.

I am black, but I am not afraid of damnation

I am black now, but I was not black always. Black and beautiful. I am a black soul, like the soul of the Prodigal Son who was believed to be dead. The father said, My son was dead. He was lost. But I am beautiful. Death has no effect on me. I could be a dead soul like the father said, because truly the father said that my son was dead. I could be a dead soul as the father said, but I put in front of me the saying of Jesus, *He who believes in Me, though he may die, he shall live,* (John 11:25). He who believes in Me, though he may die, he shall live. I am a beautiful soul.

They said to God about me, I may rot. I have been four days in the grave. I may rot. But I trust that I will leave this grave, and I will rise one more time and God will come to my house before the Cross, and I will live again, because I am a beautiful soul. *I am black and beautiful, O daughters of Jerusalem.*

The sin may soil me on the outside. Sin may soil me on the outside, but the love of God is deep within me from the inside. I feel that the sin that soils me is a foreign sin to me, and I am foreign to it. And my soul from the inside is white and beautiful, O daughters of Jerusalem. Just like St. Peter the Apostle who denied Jesus Christ. He denied the Christ.

Moreover he became afraid and claimed that he did not know the Man. He was afraid and swore and said, I do not know the Man. A black soul in front of everyone. But Peter's soul said, *I am black and beautiful, O daughters of Jerusalem*. How could you be beautiful, my beloved, if you deny the Christ and say I do not know the Man? I am beautiful because I will tell the Lord in front of everyone, *Lord, You know all things; You know that I love You,* (John 21:17).

Lord, You know all things; You know that I love You. Okay, but what of the denial and the swearing and the cursing? This is the external soul, the black soul. And the love is the internal soul, the white soul. I am two souls in one. One soul that has been destroyed by evil on the outside and became black. The other, white from the inside, saying, I am beautiful, O daughters of Jerusalem. But I will shed this black soul because it is alien to me. Alien to me. I am not from it, and it is not from me. I am for You, O Lord. I am for You. And from the inside God was worshipped, and the Lord was on the inside.

As the houses of Solomon and the tents of Kedar, the blackness is the blackness of fighting, and the whiteness is the whiteness of victory. The blackness is what was done by the materialism of humans and the world and Satan, and the beauty is what God has done on the inside. According to one of the philosophers, during that time I was fighting within myself, struggling, until I felt like two people in one. One pushes me and the other stops me. Black and beautiful.

This is the struggling souls on earth that falls and rises, sins and repents, fails and confesses, and searches for God and finds Him sometimes and not others. These struggling souls that are being chased by Satan with every possible way may seem black, but they are beautiful souls.

Beautiful in its struggles and its fatigue, even when it falls, God will not look down upon it. It is like the soldier who fights and is struck by the enemy; his blood will flow and he will be dismembered. People look at this soldier that has been injured, whose members have been cut, whose blood has been shed, yet continues to hold his weapon. They look upon his soul as if it was black, and it is saying, I am black and beautiful.

The sun has darkened me, but I have not lost my loyalty to God nor have I not lost my attachment to righteousness. I am black and beautiful. Souls live on grace and live on hope, and live in the love of God whom it misses. Every time a man lives a prodigal life, he finds his soul to be black.

He stands in front of God as a sinner, and cries, *Have mercy upon me, O Lord, for I am weak; O Lord, heal me, for my bones are troubled. My soul also is greatly troubled,* (Psalm 6:2,3). This sinner stands in front of God begging, in repentance, in withdrawal, in feeling that he is worthless. Would you call his soul a black soul or a beautiful soul?

Take for example, out of the Bible, the tax collector that was praying in the Temple during the prayer of the Pharisee, and he said, *God, be merciful to me a sinner!* (Luke 18:13). He felt that his soul is black. He is unable to look upwards. He is unable. He could not raise his eyes upwards. He could not go inside. He stood from a distance. His soul is black. I have a black soul. Please forgive me so that I can be saved. Wash so that I can become whiter than snow.

The Pharisee also saw him as a black soul. He saw a black soul. He pointed to him and said, *God, I thank You that I am not like other men - extortioners, unjust, adulterers, or even as this tax collector,* (Luke 18:11). I thank You I am not like this tax collector who has a black soul. This tax collector had a beautiful soul in front of God and he left purified. It is possible that many of angels were whispering amongst themselves as they were looking upon the soul of the tax collector saying, it is black and beautiful, O daughters of Jerusalem. O Pharisee, this soul is more beautiful than you. You who fast twice a week, and collect all your money, but the soul of the tax collector is black and beautiful, but more beautiful than you. Black and beautiful.

The soul of another was black and beautiful. The soul of the Thief on the Right who was crucified on the Cross. Even the Bible says his was a black soul, because he said regarding Jesus that He was put between sinners. And it says, they crucified Him between two thieves. And despite his repentance and his entrance with Jesus into paradise, as Jesus said, *Today you will be with Me in paradise,* (Luke 23:43), even until now we call

Every time a man lives a prodigal life, he finds his soul to be black.

him the Thief on the Right. Have we stopped calling him a thief? We continue calling him the Right Thief. The word *thief* refers to its blackness, and the word *right* refers to its beauty. The soul of the Right Thief while on a cross looked at all those Jews and sang, *I am black and beautiful, O daughters of Jerusalem.* I am black and beautiful, O daughters of Jerusalem.

Rahab the harlot was also black and beautiful. In the eyes of everyone she was black. She was the sinner woman who was well known in the entire village. In the eyes of God she was more beautiful than all the souls in Jericho. It was the scarlet cord that said she was beautiful, beautiful, beautiful is this Rahab the harlot, more beautiful than all the people of the village of Jericho. *I am black and beautiful, O daughters of Jerusalem.*

Every soul that is black and beautiful says to you, do not judge by appearances. Do not judge by appearances. Appearances never tell the truth. The prophet David, in the eyes of his brothers, was very small and sick, a black soul. He is too small, too young, he has not developed yet. Who said that in the eyes of his brothers he was such? He sang and said, *I was small among my brothers, and I was disrespected among my mother's people,* (Psalm 151:1). What does that mean? My brothers were superior and better than me. But God was not pleased with them. *I am a black and beautiful soul, O daughters of Jerusalem.*

> **I am beautiful. I am weak, but I work with the strength of God.**

There are plenty of black souls, and at the same time beautiful. All repentant souls, all souls that love God from inside and repent due to weakness from the outside are black and beautiful souls. It is not black and beautiful when you commit a sin and remain in it and insist upon it and live in carelessness.

It is a black and beautiful soul that falls and revolts against sin, and rebels against it, and fights the spiritual wars of the Lord against the powers of darkness and against the rulers of this era. The souls of the pure ones are not born pure. The souls of the pure ones were not always pure. Some were born pure and carried on. And some lived black for a period of time and then became beautiful. *I am black and beautiful, O daughters of Jerusalem.*

God took for Himself from every race and from every color. What do they say? They say,

But God has chosen the foolish things of the world to

*put to shame the wise, and God has chosen the weak
things of the world to put to shame the things which
are mighty, and the base things of the world and the
things which are despised God has chosen, and the
things which are not, to bring to nothing the things
that are .*

1 Corinthians 1:27,28

The foolish and the weak and the despised, every one of
their souls screams, *I am black and beautiful, O daughters of
Jerusalem.* Do not think of me as foolish or weak, I am
more knowledgeable and more powerful than you, I am
beautiful. I am weak, but I work with the strength of God. I
am weak, black, but I work with the strength of God. And I
am ignorant, black, but I think in the knowledge of God.
And I am from nothing and nonexistent, but God has given
me existence. He gave me His existence.

Once upon a time, a handful of earth was taken
from the ground by God in His hand and He blew in it, and
suddenly this hand full of earth started singing in front of
the world saying, I am black and beautiful. A hand full of
earth that was trod upon by the animals of the earth, and
was run over by the heifers became beautiful in the image
of God.

How wonderful it is when we say black and
beautiful in a hymn, this coming beautiful verse, what do
they say, *the poor living from the earth and the miserable
rising from the garbage to sit with the leaders of his people.*
The miserable what? Rising from the garbage. This soul
that the Lord has lifted from garbage to sit with the leader
of its people says, *I am black and beautiful, O daughters of
Jerusalem.*

I am black. I was in the garbage. I was one of the
poor ones sitting upon the dirt, and God has bestowed His

beauty upon me. And it shall be always. God never worked on those that had power and were proud of it. So He does not send greatness to people, but in the weak and poor one, the ignorant and non-existent one, in the poor, in the dirt, in the rising from the garbage God works.

The Virgin Mary herself felt that she is an orphan daughter, poor, betrothed to a carpenter who was poor. People looked at her and never paid attention. From a village, small, weak, and disrespected, she is the youngest amongst the daughters of Jerusalem, Bethlehem. Even from the youngest daughters of Bethlehem, she said, I am black and beautiful. Even in Nazareth, the disrespected, they said of it, *Can anything good come out of Nazareth?* (John 1:46). The village of Nazareth stood in front of the daughters of Jerusalem and says to them, *I am black and beautiful, O daughters of Jerusalem.*

My reputation to you is bad, but in the eyes of God it is beautiful. In another place someone was singing this song and that was the manger. What is the reputation of the manger? Or its beauty or brilliance? Or what is its value to people? And the manger stands in front of the whole world and says, *I am black and beautiful, O daughters of Jerusalem.* Is there anything blacker than the manger? How dirty and small is it? Kings, presidents, and leaders come and travel across countries wishing that they could worship in fear in this manger to take blessings. You get blessings from the manger? They say yes because the manger sings and says, *I am black and beautiful, O daughters of Jerusalem.* I am disrespected in the eyes of people, but well respected in the eyes of God. These small places, the manger, Nazareth, Jerusalem, the poor Virgin, orphaned, betrothed to the carpenter. People's judgments are one thing, and the judgments of God are a different thing.

Let us finish here and pray.

May God have mercy upon us and bless us, and make His face shine with His Countenance upon us and have compassion upon us. With the prayers and intercessions that are raised on our behalf by the Mother of God, the Pure Saint Mary, and all the angels and apostles, and the prophets, and the martyrs, and the confessors, and the anchorites, and the saints who we ask to pray for us for peace at all times, and the blessings of the saint of this blessed day, and the blessing of Saint Mary first and last, may their holy blessings and the prayers and intercessions be with us all. Amen.

Peace be with you all.

May God make us worthy to say, Our Father...

PART TWO

I Am Black and Beautiful, O Daughters of Jerusalem

Song of Solomon 1:5

In the Name of the Father, the Son, and the Holy Spirit, One God. Amen.

Last time, I spoke to you about some of the spiritual meanings of the verse *I am black and beautiful*. I would like to point out that rather than applying this expression to humans, we may find it pertinent to certain spiritual aspects.

Many virtues may appear to be trying and tiresome. They may be *black* even though they are *beautiful*. There are those who choose to walk in the narrow way; they enter through the *narrow gate*, and walk through difficult, troublesome paths in which things may at first sight appear *black* and unpleasant, dreary and tiring. Yet, as these people persevere, endure and continue to persist, they are likely to hear these virtues softly whispering in their ears, *I am*

Many virtues may appear to be trying and tiresome

black and beautiful.

All manners of toils and burdens that a man is likely to undergo for righteousness' sake are colored with this dual dye, these two facets. This is by no means exclusively confined to spiritual life. Rather, it extends to encompass all aspects of our everyday, routine life. A student who stays up all night to study is an example of this.

Rather than going out with his friends, this student chooses to stay at home, study, and persist to get ready for exams. The student's choices may appear to be *black*, but they are *black and beautiful*. They will ultimately lead to what is best for the student; these choices will lead to success. Similarly, Golgotha and the Cross may at first sight appear to be *black* in the eyes of people, *He that is hanged is accursed of God*, (Deut. 21:23).

The hardships and the many difficulties that we may face for the sake of the Lord may, in the sight of people, appear to be gloomy, depressing and disheartening; they may appear *black* but they are *beautiful*. Let us contemplate on what St. Paul the Apostle says in his second Epistle to the Corinthians:

But we have this treasure in earthen vessels,
that the excellence of power may be of God and not
of us. We are hard pressed on every side,
yet not crushed; we are perplexed, but not in despair;
persecuted, but not forsaken; struck down,
but not destroyed —always carrying about in the
body the dying of the Lord Jesus, that the life of Jesus
also may be manifested in our body.
For we who live are always delivered to death for
Jesus' sake, that the life of Jesus also may be
manifested in our mortal flesh,

2Cor 4:7-11

We are *delivered to death* everyday. How *black*? There is pressure, perplexity, and persecution. All these seem *black*. Yet, they are *beautiful* since they are the shinning road, the guiding light unto the Lord. The *blackness* associated with *always delivered to death* is strikingly juxtaposed against the *beauty* entailed in *that the life of Jesus also may be manifested in our mortal flesh*.

In chapter 6, St. Paul reiterates the same theme. He says:

> *As deceivers, and yet true; as unknown, and yet well*
> *known; as dying, and behold we live; as chastened,*
> *and yet not killed; as sorrowful, yet always rejoicing;*
> *as poor, yet making many rich; as having nothing,*
> *and yet possessing all things.*

2Cor 6:8-10

To lead our lives with God as *unknown*, *dying*, *sorrowful*, *poor*, and *having nothing* may indeed seem *black*, bleak and dreary. Yet, even then beauty abounds. He who loves the Lord will necessarily love the *narrow gate*, the difficult, dreary, and bleak road. Out of that narrow, difficult path, a song most melodious and tunes most sweet will resonate and resound in the ear of those who love the Lord, chanting, *I am black and beautiful, O daughters of Jerusalem*.

He who loves the Lord will necessarily love the narrow gate

Who are the daughters of Jerusalem? Those are the believers, the children of God. Jerusalem is the city of the Great King. It is the heavenly Jerusalem, the dwelling place of the Lord where He lives with His people. It is the new city, the everlasting joy and happiness. The daughters of Jerusalem are those precious, saintly, and holy souls that are born into, and live in, the city of the Great King. Virtues call upon the daughters of Jerusalem, those that dwell in this saintly city, the children of God, to encourage them not to lose heart or become disillusioned or troubled by reason of the tribulations and hardships they encounter in the world. They ascertain that these tribulations are *black and beautiful*.

Therefore, the phrase *black and beautiful* may refer to difficult commandments on the one hand, or tribulations and hardships on the other. They both can be seen as *black and beautiful*. Such virtues as long-suffering and offering the other cheek offer us an example. It is extremely difficult to *bless those who curse you,* (Matt 5:44). It is, in fact, quite unthinkable. It is also very difficult to turn the other cheek if someone slaps you on the face. Likewise, it is unreasonable to go two miles with *whosoever compels you to go one mile,* (Matt 5:41). It is odd to patiently endure other people's injustices and wrongdoing. It is even more preposterously outlandish and bizarre when you are expected to *love* those who do you an injustice.

All the various trials that confront humanity and appear to be *black* are still beautiful

This evokes what a poet has once said:

Or who have the eyes to witness and see

The slain weeping for him who slew like me!

Unbelievable! The murdered bemoaning the murderer! Tears of compassion and love shed for those who caused the pain!

In our daily lives, we are expected to take a position concerning such commandments as the turning of the other cheek, walking for two miles, loving one' enemies and patiently putting up with and forgiving those who wrong us. All these seem formidable, trying commandments testing as they do our human dignity, our human will, our sense of the self, and our very ego. Yet, even though you may see these commandments as *black* and dreary, they are, nonetheless, *beautiful*. In essence, through them man is uplifted and invigorated. Accordingly, these commandments chant soothingly saying, *I am black and beautiful, O daughters of Jerusalem*.

We do not seek the *wide gate*; we do not look for the rosy, easy roads. Rather, we walk carrying the cross, always reminding ourselves that there is no way to the Resurrection except through the Golgotha. If you do not suffer with Christ, you cannot hope to attain greatness and glory with Him. The tribulations and hardships of the present, though *black* and dreary they may appear to be, pave the way for the eternal glory to come, that unspeakable joy and that unfathomable splendor. For this reason, they are *beautiful*. Every trying situation, every hardship and every cross is *beautiful* as long as we undergo these difficulties for the Lord's sake.

All the various trials that confront humanity and appear to be *black* are still *beautiful*. All the crosses and all the trying situations still declare, *I am black and beautiful, O daughters of Jerusalem*. Peter was frightened by the blackness and the dreariness entailed in the Cross that confronted Christ. When Jesus told him that the Son of Man will be crucified, he vehemently implored the Lord to avoid that dreary death.

St. Peter thought that *beauty* was on the Mount of Transfiguration. There he declared, *Lord, it is good for us to be here*, (Matt 17:4). However, Christ gently turned Peter's attention to the fact that the Cross, the agony, the passion, the nails, the whips and the thorns are *black and beautiful*.

We are not on this planet to enjoy worldly pleasures. The Bible instructs us not to love the world nor the things therein. Denying ourselves the pleasures of the world may seem *black* and harsh; yet, it is also *beautiful*. Asceticism, austerity and dying to the world and denouncing its pleasures are virtues that are at once *black* and *beautiful*. Man may opt to lead a rigorous, rigid, austere life, poor and naked, possessing nothing, like our saintly fathers in the wilderness.

Yet, living in asceticism and hermitage, leading a life of deprivation and austerity, denouncing the world and dying to its pleasures and lusts, committing themselves to solitary confinement and solitude, self-discipline and self imposed dispossession, these saints look at this rigorous life of deprivation and dispossession and try to fathom its depths and delve deep into its meaning. They will hear this life chanting, *I am black and beautiful, O daughters of Jerusalem*.

Trust me, it is no exaggeration to suggest that that spiritual life in its totality can be summed up in this one verse: *I am black and beautiful, O daughters of Jerusalem*. Spiritual life is the narrow gate, the harsh, difficult road, the cross, the Golgotha, suffering patiently for the Lord's sake. Those who lead this kind of life find pleasure in it. The phrase "I am black and beautiful" is strikingly similar to the Lord's *He who finds his life will lose it, and he who loses his life for My sake will find it,* (Matt 10:39).

How can someone lose their life? It is inconceivable. When people learn that someone is being heedless and reckless, without concern for their well being, they are baffled and shocked. They even consider this as a terrible waste, a catastrophe. It is shocking. How can a person lose his life? But in our case, the person calls upon the Lord saying, *Lord, I am finished*. The Lord replies saying, *It is beautiful to lose yourself for My sake.* The phrase *I lose my life for Your sake* is at once *black and beautiful.*

It is for this reason that Christ says, *He who finds his life will lose it, and he who loses his life for My sake will find it,* (Matt 10:39). That is also why we find that the first virtue in Christianity is self-denial, *If anyone desires to come after Me, let him deny himself, and take up his cross daily, and follow Me,* (Luke 9:23). Denying the self and taking up the cross are

Self denial permeates and abounds with beauty

black and beautiful. Self denial permeates and abounds with beauty, for once the self disappears, the Lord will appear and be manifest in him; when the self dies, the Lord will live in him. Only after the ego perishes can one hope to lead a pure, holy life.

True Christian life starts with death. Death is *black* and dreary in the eyes of the world. It is, however, the beginning of true Christian living. How can that be? If we die with Him, we will live with Him, *Buried with Him in baptism,* (Col 2:12). Baptism, the beginning of Christian life, is dying with Christ and resurrecting with Him. We, therefore, start with death, which looks bleak and *black.* However, we end with life, which is *beautiful.* Death to the world is at once *black and beautiful.*

During baptism, once a baby is submerged in the holy water, he starts to cry and scream thinking that he will be drowned. It looks as an unpleasant experience. In contrast, the people around the baby are joyous and happy. The baby is dressed in white clothes and his parents are congratulated because the baby has died with Christ; he has died to the world and was buried in baptism. The old nature in the baby is now dead and a new person is born. It is truly a *black and beautiful* experience, one that is at once dreary and beautiful. Holy baptism encourages the daughters of Jerusalem: *I am black and beautiful, O daughters of Jerusalem.*

Trials and tribulations are at once *black and beautiful.* Just consider the hardships and difficulties that confronted Job. He was denied everything. He lost all his children and his money. He lost all his material possessions: camels, sheep, lambs, oxen, cows and donkeys. Nothing was left for him. However, regardless of all these plights Job says, *Naked I came from my mother's womb, and naked shall I return there.*

All the various trials that confront humanity and appear to be *black* are still *beautiful*

Then, he was tested in his own health; he was stripped of his own skin. We see him not only bereft of his material possession, but also deprived of his own health, plighted with sores and blisters, *Painful boils from the sole of his foot to the crown of his head,* (Job 2:7). Such was his condition to the extent he would use a potsherd to scrape himself and he became the target of people's mockery, *their taunting song... their byword,* (Job 30:9). His stench was such that his own wife could not stand him. She found it offensively repugnant and horribly repulsive.

Job was even deprived of his own dignity. He would call his servant, and he would not answer him, *I call my servant, but he gives no answer; I beg him with my mouth,* (Job 19:16). Furthermore, he was deprived of his friends. They even bitterly mocked and rebuked him. He had nothing left. What a trial! What an ordeal! His health, his money, his children, his dignity were all gone. Nothing was left for him.

Such was his ordeal, yet it was at once *black and beautiful*. How could we say that this plight was *beautiful*? The answer is that it was through this ordeal that Job was able to say, *I have heard of You by the hearing of the ear, but now my eye sees You*, (Job 42:5). The word *now* is a reference to the ordeal that Job undertook. He was able to see the Lord through this plight, this ordeal. Through it he was thoroughly washed and thereby he became *whiter than snow*, (Ps.51:7). He went through that *black and beautiful* ordeal and came out of it richly blessed and lavishly rewarded; his wealth was multiplied many times over. Moreover, he had received virtues, gained knowledge of the Lord and witnessed and saw Him with his own eyes.

Trials and temptations are oftentimes *black and beautiful*. They are *black* to the extent that we ceaselessly and vehemently shout and entreat the Lord to *lead us not unto temptation*. We do so because of our view of temptation as *black* and fearsome. So, how can temptation be regarded as *beautiful*? The Bible says, *My brethren, count it all joy when you fall into various trials*, (James 1:2). So, we call upon our father Job to explain for us the contradiction inherent in these apparently incongruous terms *fall* and *joy*. The concept *fall* seems to be dreary and *black*. Conversely, the phrase *all joy* evokes happiness and beauty. Therefore, these many and various trials into which we fall whisper in our ears, saying, *I am black and beautiful, O daughters of Jerusalem*.

The problem is that some people see only the *black*, bleak aspect of a problem. They passively stop there. That is it. We may be called upon to console somebody who has been afflicted with many trials. We may be tempted to think that when trials abound, hope is vanquished. It is of no use. It is a calamity of overwhelming proportions. It is a difficult time of unprecedented hardships and trials. However, throughout this exceedingly difficult time a voice may be heard saying, *I am black and beautiful, O daughters of Jerusalem.*

It is only *the sun (that) has tanned me,* (Song 1:6). What is meant by sun here? The reference is to God who is called the Sun of Righteousness. The rays of the Lord has touched these many trials, and she is tanned by them and thereby goodness would, in turn, beam out of her. Even though she may seem *black,* she would cause goodness and righteousness to shine forth; they would be manifested in her. *I am black and beautiful, O daughters of Jerusalem.*

Another trial offers us an example that was, at once, also *black and beautiful.* It was a trial that was *black* and, I might add, abounding and booming with beauty and loveliness. God said to Abraham, *Take now your son, your only son Isaac, whom you love...* Whereto Lord? Take him into my arms, kiss and embrace him? Hardly. It was an order to take him, *and offer him as a burnt offering on one of the mountains of which I shall tell you,* (Gen 22:2).

Can there be anything darker or *blacker* than that? What a *black* commandment! What a nightmare! I cannot tell Sarah. She may have a heart attack and die. That is why he rose very early in the morning before Sarah was up and took his son. Had somebody met him along the road, he would have heard about this *black,* bleak news. He would have become aware that I was about to take my only son, the one that I love, whom I received after long years of expectation, promises, and despair, to slit his throat with my own hands. Is there anything more preposterous? Is there anything *blacker*? However, it was *black and beautiful.* The knife that Abraham raised to cut off Isaac's throat was *black and beautiful, O daughters of Jerusalem.* This is one of the most beautiful examples of obedience, love, faith, Divine will and Providence, sacrifice and salvation.

The icon of Isaac about to be sacrificed at the hands of Abraham is found in some of our churches because of the beauty of the message it conveys. It is *black and beautiful*. It could be frightening for little children to look at an icon in which a father is holding a knife to kill his son. Yet as *black* as the image may appear to be, it is still *beautiful*. How?

In fact, there are many layers of meaning entailed in the *beauty,* spiritual depth and wisdom of an experience. The dreariness and *blackness* are but a reflection of our human perception and understanding of that experience. A trial is *beautiful* in God's scheme; it is, however, *black* according to our human perception. Out of any trial that may befall you, some goodness is bound to ensue. And for every difficult commandment something good will surely follow.

For every difficult commandment something good will surely follow

Abraham had experienced trials for a long period of time. Ever since he came to know God, a series of *black and beautiful* events seemed to follow him. No sooner had that heavenly light shone forth upon Abraham, than the Lord said to him, *Get out of your country, from your family, and from your father's house, to a land that I will show you,* (Gen 12:1.) I will leave my country? And my father's house and my family? I will go and live in a strange place?. That must have appeared as *black*. However, the Lord comforted him,

> *I will bless you and make your name great; and you*
> *shall be a blessing. I will bless those who bless you,*
> *and I will curse him who curses you; and in you all*

the families of the earth shall be blessed.

(Gen 12:2-3)

Going to a strange place must have appeared *black*. Yet, the blessing entailed in this seemingly *black* commandment made it *beautiful*.

Obedience to a commandment may appear to be *black and beautiful* for a person who is willing to exercise restraint. Such a person subdues his own personal will and executes the will of another. That is why, obedience may indeed seem *black*. It is normal that everyone wants to execute their own personal desires, wills and wishes. Thus, the difficulty lies in asking them to rid themselves of the will to pursue their own plans and to relinquish their own wishes. For this reason, some of our fathers would regard obedience as equivalent to martyrdom. Rightly so.

It is extremely difficult when you renounce your own desires and subdue your will in order to execute those of another. It is not easy. This is similar to a situation in which a boy boisterously and joyfully plays ball and is asked by his father to relinquish the game and head to his room to sit still and study. It is difficult. It is difficult when the boy surrenders his own desires, subdues his will and abandons what he is doing to obey the commandment of his father. It is difficult, but it is *beautiful* nonetheless. Despite the difficulty inherent in obedience, there are numerous advantages. Without obedience, man cannot live a righteous life. Obedience may occasionally appear to be *black*, but it is also *beautiful*.

Despite the difficulty inherent in obedience, there are numerous advantages

On the other hand, those who follow their own

wishes and desires, may experience comfort and the pleasure that life may offer for awhile. And yet their lives end in blackness. The prodigal son offers us an example. The young son may have reasoned with himself, *What am I doing here under my father's roof? Why should I put up with his orders: "Come here! Go there?" Why do I stay in my father's house as a dependant receiving orders right and left? Why don't I take my part of the inheritance and go out and enjoy the world like other people do? I want to enjoy my freedom, my inheritance and my friends.* To him, this seemed a beautiful life. He ended up encountering nothing but loss, confusion and darkness.

Atheists and existentialists offer us another example. They believe that the existence of God annihilates theirs. They think that the existence of God will necessarily diminish their own enjoyment of life. To make things easier for themselves, they deny the existence of God hoping that they will thus feel better, live without any commandments in complete freedom, and doing as they please. They mistakenly take this kind of life as a *beautiful* life, whereas, in reality, it is indeed *black* and dreary. It is hardly *black and beautiful*. There is only blackness there. They may be under the illusion that their kind of life is beautiful, but they are terribly mistaken. It is only *black*.

Those who obey the commandments, those who restrain and subdue their will offer us the opposite picture. It may at first sight seem *beautiful* to attend gatherings and meetings. It may also appear *black* to stay up late to pray the Compline (Retiring) Hour Prayer and read a little in the Bible. You may be bored, tired, or sleepy. However, you are expected to stay up and pray. Do not be lazy. Rather, keep on praying and increase your prayers. Even after you finish the Compline, go to the Midnight Prayers. That may be too much!

The midnight Prayers contain that long Psalm which contains 22 passages each of which contains 8 verses which brings this one Psalm to 176 verses. That is *black and beautiful, O daughters of Jerusalem*. What is *black and beautiful* about leaving the warmth of your bed and jumping out of it to pray? What is *beautiful* when one is tired and sleepy and in need of rest and relaxation? It is the love of God that impels one to relinquish the warmth and the comfort, the laziness and the idleness of sleep and pushes us to stand in the presence of the Lord like a flame of fire praying ceaselessly with zeal and fervor. That is *black and beautiful, O daughters of Jerusalem*.

We may delude ourselves into thinking that a life of comfort and pleasure is *beautiful*. Nothing can be farther from the truth. Struggling, fighting, and becoming weary, those very things which people may regard as *black*, are *black and beautiful*.

How about fasting? How about the difficulties entailed therein? Fasting means going through a difficult time, one in which we deprive ourselves of certain types of food, thereby lacking the necessary nutrients, proteins, vitamins and other necessary nutritious elements. That is difficult. Indeed, it is *black and beautiful*.

And how about prostrations? They may be taxing to one's physical condition. Still, they are *black and beautiful*. Ask any priest, monk or nun, and they will tell you about the unique spiritual pleasure that they derive from prostrations. In the eyes of the world, prostrations may regarded as *black*, but in the eyes of the children of God, they are *black and beautiful, O daughters of Jerusalem*.

All spiritual practices share this characteristic, this aspect of being *black and beautiful* at one and the same time. Take tithing, for example. We may reason among ourselves about the soundness of such a practice, *Is it* reasonable to practice tithing at these difficult times in which we can hardly make both ends meet? The concept of tithing would appear all the more *black* when we are experiencing a time of scarcity and high priced inflation. Yet, it is *black and beautiful, O daughters of Jerusalem*. It is *black* because you take a portion of your money at a time of need, *but she out of her poverty put in all the livelihood that she had*, (Luke 21:4). It is *beautiful* because it blesses all the rest of the money.

The practice of giving your first earnings to the Lord may even sound harsher than the practice of tithing. After long years of education, you have finally started your professional life. Yet, the first salary, the one you have long been waiting for is to be dedicated to the Lord. It is difficult. It is *black and beautiful*. This virtue of offering the first fruits you get and tithe it to the Lord chants to those who practice it, saying, *I am black and beautiful, O daughters of Jerusalem*. Although it may be difficult to give away money, it is also *beautiful*.

It is the love of God that impels one to relinquish the warmth and the comfort

Does this mean that virtue is forever *black and beautiful?* Hardly. It is only *black and beautiful* in the eyes of humans, those who still dwell in the flesh and whose material and spiritual needs are in eternal contest, competing against each other, those who have not yet attained perfection. To saints, however, there is no such thing as *black and beautiful*. In fact, the Groom would address them saying, *Behold, you are fair, my love! Behold, You are fair! You have dove's eyes*, (Song 1:15).

He does not say *you are black and beautiful*. He only sees beauty and fairness in them, *If you do not know, O fairest among women, follow in the footsteps of the flock,*

(Song 1:8). What could that possibly mean? She does not say, *I am black and beautiful* in the presence of the Heavenly Groom. She does say, *I am black and beautiful, O daughters of Jerusalem,* though. That is to say, the combination of the two sides *black and beautiful* is merely restricted to human beings and human understanding, also in the eyes of the daughters of Jerusalem.

Even when she says *I am black*, she seems to be admonishing and reminding them that it is not fit to regard me as *black* for it is only *the sun (that) has tanned me.* She is warning them, *Do not look at me as 'black' for I am 'beautiful.'* The Lord Himself calls me saying, *rise up, my love, my fair one, and come away,* (Song 2:10).

The last point that I would like to talk to you about concerning this present topic *black and beautiful* is related to reprimands, rebukes and discipline. Human beings generally regard reprimands and discipline as *black*. Spoiled, pleasure-seeking and pampered people can hardly withstand a word of reprimand, criticism, admonishment or other types of punishment and look at these as *black*. These reprimands stand in direct contrast with the verse *For whom the Lord loves He chastens*, (Heb 12:6). These reprimands address the human soul saying, *I am black and beautiful, O daughters of Jerusalem.*

Human beings generally regard reprimands and discipline as *black*.

Spoiled and pampered people like praise; they like to be commended and applauded. Those who seek their salvation see more beauty in admonishment and reprimands than in words of praise and admiration. This is reminiscent of the proverb that says, *He who makes you cry, cries with you; he who makes you laugh, laughs at you.*

The proverb echoes the same meaning expressed in *For whom the Lord loves He chastens*.

For this reason, when St. Peter the Apostle implored the Lord to avoid the death of the cross, *Far be it from You, Lord; this shall not happen to You,* (Mat 16:20), Jesus reproachfully retorted, *Get behind Me, Satan! You are an offense to Me,* (Mat 16:23). Incidentally, I daresay, that if a priest ever said these words to a confessor, they may take offence and decide never to set foot in the church again. The reason is that pampered, spoiled people find it extremely difficult to endure criticism and reproach or tolerate censure and reproof.

In contrast to those spoiled people, the daughters of Jerusalem, those who love and seek the Kingdom of heaven and are keen on exploring all the ways leading unto it, regard these criticisms and reproaches as *black and beautiful*.

God teaches us through words of love and encouragement sometimes and through reproofs and reprimands at other times. Sometimes He sends us good tidings, and at other times He instructs us to take up the cross. Sometimes He lavishly bestows His goodness upon us; He profusely and copiously rains His abundant blessings from His sanctuary until we have more than what we need; at other times, however, He allows trials, hardships and tribulations; He also allows the Golgotha and Gethsemane. This is how the human soul is tested and refined; this is how it gains its resilience and fortitude.

This is the story of the human soul that has endured the sweet and bitter for the Lord's sake; it has gone through the road of the cross, experienced the narrow road, and entered through the narrow gate; it has suffered and was injured for His sake. To people, this soul may look fatigued and emaciated, wasted and withered.

Nothing can be farther from the truth, *If in this life only we have hope in Christ, we are of all men the most pitiable*, (Cor 15:19).

We are people who look as *deceivers*, as *sorrowful*, as *poor*, as *having nothing*; our lives are characterized by prayers, prostrations, fatigue, loneliness, struggle and resistance. This is fit, for only through many tribulations can we hope to enter the Kingdom of Heaven. The soul that has fought the good fight in the world, gone through many hardships and tribulations, and faced humiliation and mortification, will be ushered into the Kingdom of God and will declare to the other souls there, *I am black and beautiful, O daughters of Jerusalem*.

This is the Christian life. It is the *narrow gate*, the hard, difficult road, and the cross, on the one hand. It is happiness and joy, on the other. When we consider His commandments we are relieved because *His commandment is not burdensome or heavy*.

It may only appear to be *black*, but it is *beautiful*.

Glory to His Holy Name.

May God have mercy upon us and bless us, and make His face shine with His Countenance upon us and have compassion upon us. With the prayers and intercessions that are raised on our behalf by the Mother of God, the Pure Saint Mary, and all the angels and apostles, and the prophets, and the martyrs, and the confessors, and the anchorites, and the saints who we ask to pray for us for peace at all times, and the blessings of the saint of this blessed day, and the blessing of Saint Mary first and last, may their holy blessings and the prayers and intercessions be with us all. Amen.

Peace be with you all.

May God make us worthy to say, Our Father...

PART THREE

I Am Black and Beautiful, O Daughters of Jerusalem

Song of Solomon 1:5

In the Name of the Father, the Son, and the Holy Spirit, One God. Amen.

I am black is a uniquely peculiar and extraordinary phrase. It is uttered by the humble, unassuming, and contrite soul that is readily prepared to confess its sins and shortcomings. Such a soul does not feel uneasy or embarrassed to confess its sins and admit its deficiencies or shortcomings. Many people speak of their virtues and fail to mention their deficiencies or vices. A noble, righteous soul that strives to reflect on its true image does not find it humiliating and degrading to say *I am black.*

> **That soul that declares its deficiencies is *beautiful* indeed.**

Those who confess their sins and admit their deficiencies are, in fact, more highly respected and esteemed than those people who are listening to these confessions.

Nothing can be more oppressive and revolting than people who ceaselessly talk about their greatness and virtues. Burdensome and troublesome are those who continuously contend and incessantly argue when their mistakes or shortcomings are mentioned. They try to hide and cover their mistakes, and they may even resort to lies and deception. One may find their crooked ways repulsively hideous and disgusting.

Yet this soul declares its deficiencies *I am black* is *beautiful, beautiful* indeed. *I am black* because of my sins; *I am black* because of my deficiencies. However, I am *beautiful* through Your love that covers every deficiency. I will not cover my shortcomings; I will uncover and reveal them, but Your love will cover me, *Love will cover a multitude of sins,* (1 Pet 4:8).

Why did she say *I am black and beautiful* in confessing her sins and shortcomings? It is because the minute human beings confess their sins, their darkness is erased and their sins are forgotten. God will erase every shortcoming you admit; He will no longer remember the sins you confess. Through confession, your soul will be cleansed, washed and become white. Only when you confess and admit that you are *black* will you be able to attain this state of beauty.

Conversely, those who continuously try to hide their deficiencies and conceal their shortcomings, thinking that they are whiter than snow, may one day be exposed by God for who they really are. Their filth and their blackness may then be made public. They are not beautiful after all. Indeed, it such a commendable thing to see those who confess their sins and say, *I am black and beautiful, O daughters of Jerusalem.*

The human soul may confess its limitations by saying *I am black* in the presence of the Lord: *Against You, You only, have I sinned and done this evil in Your sight*, (Ps 51:4). It may also acknowledge its deficiencies and say *I am black* in the presence of people so as not to become haughty, boastful, or conceited. It may even inwardly acknowledge its blackness and say *I am black* to its own self so as not to become puffed up, arrogant and self-aggrandizing.

> **I am *beautiful* through God whose precious blood blots out every single sin I confess to Him**

By so doing, the soul becomes contrite and humble, and man avoids the conceit of being righteous in his own eyes. Those who are righteous and pure in their own sight will never admit to their deficiencies; it would be impossible for them to say *I am black*. When confronted by the Lord, both Adam and Eve refused to acknowledge their guilt or admit to their wrongdoing. Neither one of them was capable of saying *I am black*.

Therefore, the first lesson that we can learn tonight from *I am black and beautiful* is the admission of deficiencies and the confession of sins. However righteous a person may be, there are bound to be certain deficiencies and dark points that they should confess. I am black by my deeds, my will and my choice. I am *beautiful* through God whose precious blood blots out every single sin I confess to Him. By acknowledging His great love, He forgets every sin I confess to Him.

I am black and beautiful, O daughters of Jerusalem... Because the sun has tanned me, (Song 1:5-6). In what light can we understand these lines? When one considers and contemplates the purity, brilliance and luster of the sun, one is likely to realize the blackness within. In meditating the holiness of God, one would definitely come to the realization of their serious and grievous shortcomings; they would be *lighter than vapor,* (Ps 62:9), for they have done nothing good. For this reason, every time I contemplate this amazingly great brilliance and totally indescribable beauty, I feel that I am in the black of darkness and I have not attained anything yet, ...*the sun has tanned me.*

A person may feel satisfied when he compares himself to other people in matters of righteousness. On the other hand, when he compares himself with the Apostles, the saints and the prophets, the picture will drastically change. Many dark stains and filthy spots will be revealed in his life. When he compares himself with the angels, he will soon discover the darkness and filth within. When he contemplates and considers the purity and righteousness of God, he can only admit *I am black and beautiful, O daughters of Jerusalem... Because the sun has tanned me.*

His blood and His grace will transform me and I will become beautiful

This supreme and ultimate holiness that I see and, this infinite and unbounded perfection which I witness in God, has *tanned me.* Now in the balance I can only be *found wanting,* (Dan 5:27). This can be the only logical conclusion you can come to when you make these comparisons. Even the Bible tells us that, *the heavens are not pure in His sight,* (Job 15:15), and *He charges His angels with error,* (Job 4:18). Therefore, when I contemplate the Lord's holiness to which even the heavens' compare poorly, I can only beseech the Lord to silence every tongue and give ear to my admission *I am black... because the sun has tanned me.*

However, *I am beautiful* through the blood of Jesus

that wipes away every sin. Despite all this blackness, He will clothe me in the *best robe*, grant me a pure, white dress, *transform (my) lowly body that it may be conformed to His glorious body*, and reveal Himself to me as He has done to His disciples on the Mount of Transfiguration. He will grant me that glorious, spiritual, and pure body that will restore unto me the Godly image. His blood and His grace will transform me and I will become beautiful. *I am black and beautiful, O daughters of Jerusalem.*

We may also approach *I am black and beautiful* from another perspective. It is relevant to those saints who have concealed their virtues to the end. Not only that, some have even pretended to be weak, sinful and ignorant in front of people. Their souls were beautiful, nonetheless. You may perhaps be familiar with the life story of Habila, the nun. When all the nuns were asleep and the monastery was quiet, she would stand and lift up her heart in prayers through the night.

No sooner had the morning come and the other nuns awoken, than she would lazily and apathetically move to a corner, show no interest in attending church or taking an active part in the daily life of the convent. She would just sit around indifferently, heedless of the other nuns' warnings and reproofs for her laziness, inactivity and lack of zeal. She ended up gaining a reputation for being lazy and nonchalant. At night, however, she would stand in the presence of the Lord with unmatched passion, zeal and ardor. Even when as she was apparently and seemingly apathetic, she was praying in secret.

In the other nuns' opinion, this woman was black. One day, however, Abba Daniel discovered the truth about her. He had visited the convent and spent the night. In the dark of night, he asked his disciple to accompany him, *I want to show you the great virtues of this nun to whom they refer as Habila*. They saw her standing surrounded by angels. There was a beam of light linking her to the heavens. She prayed all night long, ceaselessly, vehemently, and resolutely. She would consider those nuns sleeping in their cells and say: *I am black and beautiful, O daughters of Jerusalem... Because the sun has tanned me.* The virtue of working in secrecy has tanned me in your eyes.

Many of the stories of the saints tell about those saints who have pretended to be crazy, stupid, and ill. Many saints have had this virtue; namely, hiding their virtues, revealing their sins and limitations, or even assuming the responsibility for sins that were not theirs. Here is another example. The word spread that Abba Shishoy was an extremely virtuous man, living in righteousness and possessing profound wisdom and knowledge. The elders in the village decided to go visit him and take his blessing.

When his disciple knew that the elders of the village were coming to visit his master, he said: *Get ready, father, for the leaders of the city and the elders of the village are coming to get your blessing.* Abba Shishoy said, *Very well, my son, I will get ready.* Whereupon, he took his clothes and put them in a bowl and started to wash them with his feet. When the visitors entered, they were shocked: *Who is this crazy man? There are no monks here! There is only a crazy man!* They left him. His disciple came in and asked: *What are you doing master? Why did you do that? They left saying that you are a crazy man.* The old man turned to his disciple and said: *This is what I wanted to hear.*

Not every one of you is capable of doing this, of course. However, these are examples of people who have thoroughly and unwaveringly refused the vain, transient, and ephemeral glory of the world. They have steadfastly and sincerely shown aversion to people's praise and commendation. They have shown no interest in others' praise and demonstrated complete indifference to their commendations. Moreover, they would, at times, pretend to be at fault when they were not. This is an example of a soul that is at once *black and beautiful*.

The virtue of working in secrecy has tanned me in your eyes

In the eyes of people, you are *daughters of Jerusalem*. Those who see you will say that you are righteous. However, this human soul that has pretended to be amiss and at fault has been *black and beautiful* at the same time.

Abba Macarious the Great was a recluse, a hermit. When the brethren would insist that he drink a cup of wine, he would accept it for fear of hurting their feelings. In return, he would deny himself water for a whole day. So if they insisted that he take two or three cups, it only meant that he would prevent himself from drinking water for two or three days. One day, the brethren tried to persuade him to drink: *Father, you are an elderly man of ninety years. Your body needs warmth. Take some of this wine.* Again they insisted and he drank.

His disciple, however, implored them not to insist on having the old man drink that wine. He explained to them that every time the old man drank wine, he would prohibit himself from drinking water for many days. This is an example that shows us that while in the eyes of people this man would drink wine, he would, in fact, torture himself by denying himself water and by leading a true ascetic and austere life. His is an example in which the expression *black and beautiful* fits most aptly.

Many people refrain from publicly and openly

contributing to charitable organizations. In private, however, they do. In the eyes of other people they may be regarded as stingy, miserly and tightfisted; they do not want to give money away. However, their souls are beautiful because they do not show off.

This is the case for every virtue that is done in secrecy, away from the eyes of others. Others may even have the impression that there is nothing particularly special about a certain person. They may think that he is just an ordinary person, or even less than an ordinary person. To all appearances, such a person's soul may be considered *black* but it is, in fact, *beautiful* because that person does not parade or show off.

Those people who pretend to be uninformed and ignorant, who give the impression that they are ordinary, average and unknown, who refrain from seeking high ranks and sought after positions, and prefer instead to sit in the last row, and may even endure being the object of others' ridicule and disdain, those people's souls will sing, *I am black and beautiful, O daughters of Jerusalem*. The virtue of doing things in secrecy has *tanned me*.

A person who tries to project this unworthy image of the self rather than the real, true image will, in general, be described as *beautiful*. The tax collector's image was *black* in the eyes of the Pharisee, but it was *beautiful* in the sight of the Lord. He stood in shame and disgrace because of his sin. In his humility and meekness, he was unable even to look upward towards the sky, *black and beautiful, O daughters of Jerusalem*.

For His sake, a man may deny himself everything

Such is the contrite spirit that looks inwardly into the self and judges it, honestly admitting and giving a true account of its weaknesses and limitations. It is a *blac* *beautiful* spirit indeed. Even though a person abundant penitent and remorseful tears may appear to *black*, yet such a person is *beautiful*. The Lord addresse such a person, saying, *Turn away your eyes from Me, for they have overcome Me,* (Song 6:5).

Black and beautiful may also be used to refer to the life of austerity and self denial that a man may opt to lead for the Lord's sake. For His sake, a man may deny himself everything. Lazarus the Poor provides us with an example even though he had no choice. He lived as a wretched beggar. The dogs would lick his sores, and he longed to be fed with crumbs that he could not obtain. His was a life of deprivation and grinding poverty.

This is *black and beautiful*. It is *black* here on earth, but it is *beautiful* in the heavens. This *black*, wretched soul, that would sit under the rich man's table longing after the crumbs offered to the dogs, was carried by the angels to Abraham's bosom and was more beautiful than the rich man and his riches and treasures.

Beautiful are also those who have led a life of asceticism, denying themselves everything. *Beautiful* are those who sold all they possessed and gave their money away to the poor, those who led their lives in scarcity and dispossession, in hunger and thirst, in nakedness and in the cold, denying themselves food, comfort and all the pleasures of life, opting to live impoverished and in need for the sake of the Lord. Under such dire circumstances of poverty, degradation and disgrace they may appear ragged, unkempt and *black*. In the sight of the Lord, they are just exquisite and *beautiful*.

To the onlooker, such people as these are poor, miserable and wretched. However, they see themselves in a different light. St. John's words, *Do not love the world nor*

One I Love

(2 John 2:15), resonate in their ears
these words are most relevant.
ҽ denied themselves the love of
ᴗres; they no longer have the desire
ᴗy show no interest in money, food and

ᴉeatness, grandeur, authority, splendor and
ᴧce mean nothing to them. They know that they may
ᴩpear *black* and poor, possessing nothing. Yet, they find
comfort in St. Paul's words, *If in this life only we have
hope...., we are of all men the most pitiable,* (Cor15:19).
Souls that are denied everything and are, thereby, the *most
pitiable*. They indeed appear to be deprived of every
pleasure. They are *black*, but they are *beautiful* at the same
time.

In reference to monks and nuns, some may
sarcastically ask, *How come these people look different?
Some have grown their hair! Others have completely shaved
their heads!* They may even go so far as to say that they
look ugly. Yet, those shaved heads are *black and beautiful*.
Likewise, women who do not follow the latest fashion and
refrain from using all the means of beautification available
to them are described as peasants and old-fashioned.
Nonetheless, they are *black and beautiful, O daughters of
Jerusalem*. This is also the case of everyone who leads a life
of austerity and self-denial, refraining from all the
pleasures of the world and its lusts.

Not only is this limited to those forbidden
pleasures, but it also includes the permissible, allowable
ones. Some people deny themselves even those desires
that are not prohibited or banned, the ones that are
permissible. Others may regard them as *poor, wretched
and miserable.* You ought to tell them, on the contrary,
they are *black and beautiful, O daughters of Jerusalem.* For

even though they appear to be in deprivation and need, they are truly not. Only those who are denied the fulfillment of a certain desire they seek and love would feel this sense of deprivation, disappointment and frustration. On the other hand, those who do not desire or love certain things, those who opt to stay away from the pleasures of the world because they do not love the world in the first place, may be *black* in your view, but in His sight they are *beautiful*.

The virtue of asceticism appears in such a light. It is deprivation, renunciation and the abandonment of the world. It will, therefore, appear *black and beautiful*. Consider the virtue of self-denial. Even the Lord *made Himself of no reputation, taking the form of a bondservant, and coming in the likeness of men...being found in appearance as a man*, (Phil 2:7-8). He was born in a barn and lived as a poor man. In the eyes of people, he was merely the son of a carpenter, a humble, lowly social rank. He even lived as a fugitive in Egypt in His childhood. People must have regarded Him as a weak person. However, the angels would look at this person and regard Him as a paradigm of self-denial. They will therefore chant telling these people that He is *black and beautiful, O daughters of Jerusalem*.

For in that He Himself has suffered, being tempted, He is able to aid those who are tempted, (Heb 2:18). My self-denial and My renunciation have made Me *black* even though *I am beautiful, O daughters of Jerusalem*. This was the humanity of Jesus in the eyes of the people.

This great love of His was manifested upon the Cross. It was whipped 39 times. It was crowned with a crown of thorns. It was mocked in the red robe while He was carrying the Cross. O Lord! What is all this humiliation and disgrace? What is all this dishonor and shame? You had not hidden Your cheeks from the shame of spitting. They would slap You on the face mockingly saying *Prophesy to us, Christ! Who is the one who struck You?*, (Matt 26:68). *He was led as a lamb to the slaughter, and as a sheep before its shearers*, (Is 53:7).

What is all this humiliation and disgrace? Yet this humiliation and disgrace would shout out saying, *I am black and beautiful, O daughters of Jerusalem*. Do not look at Me as *black* for *the sun has tanned Me*. The Sun of Righteousness has sent Me to the world to take the form of a bondservant and sacrifice Myself. *That though He was rich, yet for your sakes He became poor, that you through His poverty might become rich*, (2 Cor 8:9). Should it come to that? You, O Lord, become poor! How *black and beautiful*.

It is the emblem of self sacrifice; it is an example of self-denial

Incarnation and redemption can be summed up in *I am black and beautiful, O daughters of Jerusalem*. People look at the crucified Christ and see the black side. The Cross is, *to the Jews a stumbling block, and to the Greeks foolishness*, (1 Cor 1:23). It was true that, *He that is hanged is accursed of God*, (Deut 21:23). It is a *black* image that some have rejected and refused to acknowledge. It is the emblem of self sacrifice; it is an example of self-denial. It is *black and beautiful, O daughters of Jerusalem*.

The image of the Gethsemane, Golgotha and the crucified Christ is *black and beautiful*. Our Lord Jesus Christ has changed the standards and principles that govern the world. He has transformed the values and ideologies in which people believe. He has offered people a *black* picture in a *beautiful* framework. Or rather, He has offered a *beautiful* perspective to what some people may, unfortunately, perceive from a *black* vantage point.

Many virtues may be labeled as *black and beautiful*. Let us take, for example, the virtue of forgiveness. In the *Paradise of the Holy Fathers*, you are instructed to prostrate and ask for forgiveness regardless of whether you have sinned or not. One may wonder, How can I prostrate and bow down to someone who is wrong? How can I ask someone's forgiveness? This is an extremely difficult situation. *Whosoever slaps you on your right cheek, turn the other one also*, (Matt 5:39). Exceedingly hard! Also: *Repay no one evil for evil,* (Rom 12:17), and *Do not resist an evil person*, (Matt 5:38).

What does this mean, *Do not resist an evil person?* Shall we just sit around with our hands crossed, doing nothing as we are ridiculed and targeted by evil? It is quite preposterous! Its outrageous. However, it is an example of a virtue that is at once *black and beautiful, O daughters of Jerusalem*. It is a paradigm of a noble soul that has been able to rise above the world and its limited sense of pride and glory. It is the image of that noble heart as it surpasses the common infirmities and weaknesses characteristic of human nature. It is an emblem of a noble, gallant and magnanimous heart indeed. What a *beautiful* picture even if it seems *black*!

Forgiveness in Christianity is oftentimes taken as a sign of weakness. Some people may regard a Christian's forgiveness and reluctance to respond to wrongdoing as an indication of powerlessness, a failing and an infirmity. The turning of the other cheek is considered by some as a sign of weakness, humiliation and disgrace. Yet, these are *black and beautiful*. Apologizing for wrongdoing: *I am sorry*, is *black* according to the standards of man, but it is *beautiful* in the sight of the Lord.

This is similar to the muddied water carrying the

soil that comes from the south of Africa and runs in the Nile River. This soil and mud fertilize and enrich the land. Rain falls in the south, runs down the mountains gathering, as it does, dirt, soil and mud along the way. Finally it reaches Egypt almost black. Yet, it is beautiful at the same time. The farmers are exuberant when the water is black and muddy. Although the water appears to be black from the stand point of some people, to the farmers this blackness foreshadows the goodness and abundance that the land will yield.

Likewise, a human being who unwaveringly and ceaselessly toils and labors to abide by such Christian virtues as long suffering, modesty, forgiveness and patience. Patience, for instance, is a *black and beautiful* virtue. To many, patience is excruciatingly bitter and *black* and yet sweet and *beautiful*. For example, those who continuously encounter various types of difficulties and hardships may choose to patiently wait on the Lord and trust that He will resolve whatever problems they are encountering. It appears to be a *black* virtue, but it is *beautiful*.

Let us consider a person who is wrongfully treated and unjustly accused of committing things he has not committed and still chooses not to defend himself, and patiently and silently endures injustices and unfairness. While that person may feel the hurt and the pain of injustice and, more importantly, while people may think that he is in pain and anguish, the experience is at once *black and beautiful*.

Also, let us consider the story of Joseph the righteous. Joseph was his father's favorite. His brothers sold him as a slave. He accepted being called a slave. He patiently endured slavery in silence without defending himself. Who can endure slavery? One of the fathers asked: *Who sold Joseph?* When people among his audience answered saying, *His brothers sold him*, he responded, *No, it was his modesty that had sold him*. Had Joseph revealed that he was their brother, they would not have been able to sell him.

So he accepted slavery and was silent. He was even very loyal in his position as a slave. The house of Potiphar was filled with riches. Later, he was wrongly accused of crime and was thrown in jail. Even then, he did not defend himself. In people's view, Joseph was wrong; he was nothing but a disloyal slave who deserved to be thrown in jail by his master. People regarded him as guilty and accountable, not even entitled to defend himself.

> **To many, patience is excruciatingly bitter and black, and yet sweet and beautiful**

It is a picture that is at once *black and beautiful, O daughters of Jerusalem*. Such is the condition of anyone who refuses to defend himself and patiently accepts injustices. It is *black and beautiful* but only if the root cause is noble, if the motive is not an attempt to seek the vain and transient glory of this world.

St. Macarious the Great was unjustly accused of having had an affair with a woman. He accepted the accusation in silence. He said to himself: *Now you have to toil and work hard, O Macarious, for you have a wife and children*. He patiently and silently endured the injustice. When it was time for that woman to give birth to the child, complications arose during the labor, and she admitted her wrongdoing. People came to apologize to St. Macarious. However, having heard about their intention to apologize to him, he left the neighborhood. He accepted the injustice and refused to accept the attempt to regain his reputation and dignity.

Who can accept injustice? Who can tolerate wrongdoing? It is not easy. A noble soul that endures is *black and beautiful*.

I am black and beautiful, O daughters of Jerusalem is a combination of two viewpoints: the way the world looks at me, on the one hand, and the Lord's view, on the other. It is a reflection of the outward, external appearance versus the inward, internal reality.

I am black and beautiful may be taken to represent the outward appearance as opposed to the inward reality. There are those whose inward lives are purer than their outward appearance. Hypocrites, conversely, have a beautiful facade covering a black, rotten inner reality.

The Pharisees offer a case in point. They are similar to the unmarked graves on the outside, but on the inside they are filled with bones and rottenness (Luke 11:44). In contrast, the children of God are pure on the inside and would not be bothered with the outside. To the children of God, what people say or think of them, or how they lead their lives on earth are inconsequential and insignificant.

The situation may appear black on the outside, but it is beautiful on the inside. Outwardly, there is sickness and difficulties, but inwardly there is peace of mind; outwardly, there are persecutions, but inwardly there is a profound, unfathomable composure and serenity: two diametrically opposed pictures.

Let us pray.

May God have mercy upon us and bless us, and make His face shine with His Countenance upon us and have compassion upon us. With the prayers and intercessions that are raised on our behalf by the Mother of God, the Pure Saint Mary, and all the angels and apostles, and the prophets, and the martyrs, and the confessors, and the anchorites, and the saints who we ask to pray for us for peace at all times, and the blessings of the saint of this blessed day, and the blessing of Saint Mary first and last, may their holy blessings and the prayers and intercessions be with us all. Amen.

Peace be with you all.

May God make us worthy to say, Our Father…

Who is This Coming Out of the Wilderness

Song of Solomon 3:6

In the Name of the Father, the Son, and the Holy Spirit, One God. Amen.

In order to be able to benefit from the *Song of Songs* and understand the verses in their true spiritual sense, we will consider two recurring, though slightly different verses that occur in this book. The first verse occurs in Chapter three: *Who is this coming out of the wilderness like pillars of smoke, perfumed with myrrh and frankincense, with all the merchant's fragrant powders?* (Song 3:6). The second verse is in Chapter eight: *Who is this coming up from the wilderness, leaning upon her beloved?* (Song 8:5).

This human soul is leaning on her beloved during its life span

Who is this coming up from the wilderness, leaning upon her beloved? The words *coming up from the wilderness* may be taken as a reference to any human soul, the whole church or even other things as we will discuss later. What is important here is to realize that this human soul is *leaning on her beloved* during its life span.

The human soul cannot be victorious or successful in life unless it leans on her beloved, our Lord. Some people depend and lean on their intelligence, their gifts, their mental abilities, their authority, their power, their wealth, their social position, etc. Yet, blessed and happy is the human soul that leans on her beloved, on the Lord and none but Him.

The three young men entered the burning fiery furnace, but they trusted and leaned on their beloved. They were accompanied by a fourth man whose form was *like the Son of God*, (Dan 3:25). They leaned on and trusted Him. That is why they did not perish.

David says, *Though I walk through the valley of the shadow of death, I will fear no evil*. This is not because of his bravery or strength but because, as he says, *You are with me. Your rod and Your staff, they comfort me,* (Ps 23:4). Leaning, as is seen here, is on the beloved, not on man's personality, intelligence or gifts.

Another example is offered in David's confrontation with Goliath, who trusted his own personal strength and leaned upon his strong physique and his armor. David, however, said to him, *You come to me with a sword, with a spear, and with javelin. But I come to you in the name of the Lord of hosts,* (1 Sam 17:45). Mine is a soul that leans on her beloved.

You also should ask yourself, Are you going through life leaning on Your beloved, our Lord? Or do you lean and depend on yourself?

Unfortunately, there are some who go through life leaning on the devil. Examples for this can be found with someone who lies to avoid a certain situation, someone who swears to avert certain consequences, or someone who accepts bribes to get by in life. There are those who go through life leaning on their spiritual infirmities and mistakes. There are many people who live in dishonesty and lean upon deception.

The soul referred to in *Song of Songs* is, however, one that is *coming out of the wilderness, leaning upon her beloved.*

Throughout its history, the Church has continued to lean on her beloved; *If it had not been the Lord who was on our side when men rose up against us, then they would have swallowed us alive,* (Ps 124:2-3), an indication that the Church has leaned on the Lord. The confidence permeating the following verse can also be traceable to that dependence on the beloved; *Though an army may encamp against me, my heart shall not fear; though war should rise against me, in this I will be confident, (Psa 27:3).*

Mine is a soul that leans on her beloved

Who is this coming up from the wilderness may also be used to refer to the Church in the Old Testament that came out of the wilderness of Sinai leaning on her beloved. They left without food, drink, clothes and other important provisions and necessities. However, they leaned on their beloved. The Lord explains this point to the people in the Book of Deuteronomy, Chapter eight:

> *And you shall remember that the Lord your God led you all the way these forty years in the wilderness.*
>
> *So He humbled you, allowed you to hunger, and fed you with manna which you did not know nor did your fathers know, that He might make you know*

that man shall not live by bread alone;

but man lives by every word that proceeds from the mouth of the Lord.

Your garments did not wear out on you, nor did your foot swell these forty years.

Deut 8:2-4

For forty years, this church walked in the wilderness leaning upon her beloved who divided the Red Sea for her and made its waters like walls on both sides so it could walk right through it. She also leaned upon her beloved in the wilderness: a cloud provided her with shade and a pillar of light led her at night. When hungry, her beloved sent her quails and manna from heaven. She lived in faith. The nations that rose up against her led by Og King of Bashan, and Sihon King of the Amorites (Numbers 21) were vanquished and defeated. Her beloved gave her victory over them and over all the other nations: *Stand still, and see the salvation of the Lord*, (Ex 14:13). What is the meaning of the salvation of the Lord? It indicates the leaning and the reliance of the soul upon the beloved.

The whole world is a wilderness

I would like to consider the words *leaning upon her beloved* from another perspective. There is no reference here to her leaning upon the almighty, omnipotent God who is strong and victorious at wars. While the Lord is truly almighty, strong and triumphant at wars, the human soul depends and leans upon Him as a *beloved*, a trait that inspires a sense of security and safety.

For what is the use of the Lord's power and might if you do not have a relationship with Him, and you do not feel that He is your *beloved* on whom you could lean? That church, however, spent forty years in the wilderness leaning upon her beloved. *Who is this coming up from the wilderness?*

Maybe the angels were looking at this people as the Red Sea was divided, as the rock brought forth fresh water, as the bitter water was transformed into fresh water, as bread was sent forth from heaven, and as the quails were provided to feed them. The angels approvingly and admiringly look at this church journeying in the wilderness and reverently praise it, saying, *Who is this coming up from the wilderness, leaning upon her beloved?*

It is also possible that the words *Who is this coming up from the wilderness* may be used to refer to the triumphant, ascending church, as it leaves the world and ascends to meet God on the clouds in glory and in splendor. The Lord and His angels praise it saying, *Who is this coming up from the wilderness, leaning upon her beloved?*

Why do we say *coming out of the wilderness?* This is because the world is considered a wilderness in comparison with Paradise and Heaven. The whole world is a wilderness. In Paradise, however, there is what *Eye has not seen, nor ear heard, nor have entered into the heart of man,* (1 Cor 2:9). Therefore, the whole world is but a wilderness. As the Church ascends to the heavens, the angels will praise her with this melodious song of praise: *Who is this coming up from the wilderness, leaning upon her beloved?*

It is also possible that the words *Who is this coming up from the wilderness* can be applied to the Church in its struggle and fight here on earth. The wilderness can be taken as a symbol of renunciation and denial. It can be a symbol of staying away from desires and lusts, averting pleasures, avoiding opulence and squandering, and turning away from extravagance, luxury, self-indulgence and sumptuousness. It is a wilderness, an arid and uninhabited place. It is *a dry and thirsty land, where there is no water*, (Psa 63:1), as David says.

The Lord favorably regards the soul of Lazarus the poor when it ascended unto heaven saying, *Who is this coming up from the wilderness?* Lazarus' was a life without any pleasure. It was more of an arid, barren land, a wilderness with neither pasture nor water.

Conversely, Solomon's life offers the opposite picture: he did not live in a wilderness. Where then did he live? I will tell you where Solomon lived. He says:

> *I made myself great, I built myself houses,*
>
> *and planted myself vineyards.*
>
> *I made myself gardens and orchards,*
>
> *and I planted all kinds of fruit trees in them. I made myself water pools from which to water the growing trees of the grove. I acquired male and female servants, and had servants born in my house.*
>
> *Yes, I had greater possessions of herds and flocks than all who were in Jerusalem before me.*
>
> *I also gathered for myself silver and gold and the special treasures of kings and of the provinces.*
>
> *I acquired male and female singers,*
>
> *the delight of the sons of men, and musical instruments of all kinds.*
>
> *So I became great and excellent more than all who were before me in Jerusalem.*
>
> *Whatever my eyes desired I did not keep from them. I did not withhold my heart from any pleasure.*
>
> *Eccl 2:4-10*

Is this the kind of life that one might lead in the wilderness? Absolutely not. What kind of wilderness is this? He is talking about *orchards* and *gardens* and not keeping from his eyes whatever he desired! Hence, the uncertainty of many concerning his salvation. Was he saved or not?

His father David, however, was not in the least interested in all these things. He renounced everything he had; he gave up his wealth, relinquished his riches, abandoned his authority, and turned away from all worldly desires. His one desire was the Lord; *One thing have I desired of the Lord, that I will seek: that I may dwell in the house of the Lord all the days of my life, to behold the beauty of the Lord, and to inquire in His temple,* (Ps 27:4). Aside from that, he had absolutely no other desire. It was the *one thing* that he desired. There were no other desires besides Him.

Lazarus' was a life without any pleasure

Such is an example of a soul that dwells in the wilderness: even if the whole world is in the grasp of such a soul, its attitude would be one such as that expounded by St. Paul in, *Those who use this world as not misusing it,* (1 Cor 7:31). He possesses money, but money does not possess him. There are no desires or lusts that control him. That is the soul that lives in the wilderness. That is why the wilderness may be taken to stand for renunciation, abandonment, and austerity.

It symbolizes the relinquishing of pleasures and the shunning of lusts and various forms of extravagance. It is the soul as it walks the dreary *narrow road*, enters through the *narrow gate*, and labors and toils for the sake of the Lord. Throughout its struggle and toil, the angels look at it and say approvingly, *Who is this coming up from the wilderness?*

How about you? Where will you be coming from when you go to meet the Lord? Will you be coming out of orchards and gardens? Or will you be coming out of the wilderness? You ought to ask yourself carefully. Will you come up from orchards and gardens after you have fulfilled everything that your eyes have desired, or will you come up from the wilderness?

Out of this internal peace and quiet, zealous, fiery and passionate prayers arise.

I am afraid that if your soul comes up from orchards, you would be met with that dreadful saying: *You have had your reward on earth.* Whereas if your soul comes up from the wilderness, as is the case with the rich young man to whom Jesus said, *Go, sell what you have and give to the poor,* (Mat 19:21), then the angels will receive you chanting and singing, *Who is this coming up from the wilderness, leaning upon her beloved?* That's it! That is the way it should be.

Yet, the words *Who is this coming up from the wilderness* may also be a reference to monasticism. The word *wilderness* does indeed describe the desert. I believe that when the angels look at the monks who live in the wilderness praying and worshipping, meditating and prostrating, reading the Bible, the Psalms and the life histories of the saints, practicing self discipline, selflessness and submission, and living entirely for the Lord, in prayers that ascend into the heavens as fragrant incense, they regard their prayers and chant *Who is this coming up from the wilderness?*

The wilderness, dear brethren, is a school that teaches serenity and tranquility, peace and quiet. In the serenity of its surroundings the soul, the senses, and the heart find their peace and tranquility. Out of this internal peace and quiet, zealous, fiery and passionate prayers arise.

There is a big difference between a prayer that arises from the midst of the hustle and bustle of city life, that all too familiar turmoil and commotion that you experience and see daily, and one that arises from out of the wilderness. The angels are pleased with those prayers that come out of the wilderness. In fact, there is something especially delightful and pleasing about everything that comes out of the wilderness.

Seeking the counsel of a person who lives surrounded by daily concerns is very different from seeking the counsel of one of the monks living away in the wilderness. While the former, like you, lives in the midst of the noise of this world, toils and labors, and is trapped and encircled by turbulence and problems, the latter lives in amazing peace, tranquility and serenity. He can impart a piece of advice that abounds with wisdom and permeates with love. When you meditate on this advice, you are bound to say *Who is this coming up from the wilderness!* Wow! That is amazing!

People were used to coming from the farthest corners of the land to visit our fathers in the wilderness to benefit from a useful word coming out of there. Such a word is said to be *leaning upon her beloved*; which is to say, leaning upon the guidance and support of the Holy Spirit who imparts His word to the teachers, and puts it in the mouths of some so they can deliver to others.

The wilderness has actually become a second heaven and the monks have become *earthly angels* or *heavenly people*. The heavens regards the wilderness and all the prayers and praises that come out of it and says, *Who is this coming up out of the wilderness?*

If we are to consider the significance of the wilderness in detail, time will not suffice. I will therefore try to be brief.

We read, *Who is this coming up out of the wilderness, leaning upon her beloved?* We also read: *Who is this coming out of the wilderness like pillars of smoke, perfumed with myrrh and frankincense, with all the merchant's fragrant powders?* This is an exceedingly beautiful verse! If one wanted to dwell on it for a year, time would not suffice.

Like pillars of smoke, perfumed with myrrh and frankincense, with all the merchant's fragrant powders? The first time I reflected on this verse, the censer, which we use in the church to raise incense, came to my mind. In the midst of the fiery coal, we place some beads of incense. These beads burn and go up like pillars of smoke *perfumed with myrrh and frankincense, with all the merchant's fragrant powders.* This is true with the soul as it rises up to God. It is also true with the Church itself. The Church rises up to God *like pillars of smoke perfumed with myrrh and frankincense, with all the merchant's fragrant powders.*

In the past, incense contained frankincense. Myrrh is a kind of liquid perfume. Aloes are semi liquid, and cassis was usually cut into pieces and strips. Incense in the past came in different types and various flavors. It contained cinnamon, carnation, aloes, cassia, and *all the merchant's fragrant powders.*

I used to imagine that in the midst of the censer of human life the Lord placed a number of beads. One of these beads was called Abba Anthony, another St. Philopater, a third Abba Bishoy, a fourth St. Athanasius the Apostolic, a fifth St. Cyril, a sixth St. Demiana, etc. All of these beads are burning and rising as a pure fragrant incense in the presence of the Lord *like pillars of smoke perfumed with myrrh and frankincense, with all the merchant's fragrant powders.*

The Lord and the angels regard this pleasing aroma coming up out of the wilderness and approvingly declare, *Who is this coming out of the wilderness like pillars of smoke, perfumed with myrrh and frankincense, with all the merchant's fragrant powders?* This is the meaning of pillars of smoke. That is the meaning of what we read in Psalms, *Let my prayers be set before You as incense, the lifting up of my hands as the evening sacrifice,* (Ps 141:2).

While it is true that incense rises up like pillars of smoke, how about the evening sacrifice? Does it also rise? Absolutely. Imagine the censer on the altar with the fire burning in it day and night. As this censer burns with the Holy fire, it is transformed into pillars of smoke *perfumed with myrrh and frankincense, with all the merchant's fragrant powders.*

The wilderness has actually become a second heaven

After the Ark landed on dry land and rescue was finally attained, Noah, the father of fathers, presented a burnt offering unto the Lord. In the Bible we read, *The Lord smelled a soothing aroma,* (Gen 8:21). This means that the Lord was pleased with the smell of the burnt offering, and He started to look favorably on humankind. In other words, while Noah was presenting a burnt offering here on earth, the Lord gladly received the sweet aroma that was rising up to Him as He says, *Who is this coming out of the wilderness like pillars of smoke, perfumed with myrrh and frankincense, with all the merchant's fragrant powders?*

St. Paul the Apostle also asks to *present your bodies a living sacrifice, holy, acceptable to God,* (Rom 12:1). You ought to present yourself as a sacrifice, a burnt offering, burning and ablaze with divine fire. Whether you are a bead of frankincense in the censer or a burnt, sanctified offering unto the Lord, you will be transformed through the fire into a pillar of smoke, *perfumed with myrrh and frankincense, with all the merchant's fragrant powders.*

What is the meaning of *all the merchant's fragrant powders?* The merchant's powders refer to myrrh, frankincense, cinnamon, carnation, aloes, cassia and many other things. You may examine all these elements related to incense in the Book of Exodus.

However, the implications of *the merchant's powders* in our spiritual life are varied and numerous. According to St. Paul, the fruit of the Spirit that is in you is *love, joy, peace, longsuffering, kindness, goodness, faithfulness, gentleness, (and) self-control,* (Gal 5:22). If we were to ask St. Paul what these are, he would respond saying that they are the merchant's powders.

Now, who is the merchant? It is written that the kingdom of heaven is like a merchant who likes to gather the best kinds of pearls. When he found the best pearl (the heavenly kingdom), he sold everything he has to purchase that particularly precious pearl.

There are extremely beautiful things in the Church

It is the merchant who traded with the five talents, he received and made profit. It is also the merchant who traded with the two talents and also made profit. He is well equipped with all the merchant's powders: he trades with the talent of love, and he wins people to Christ; he trades with his humility and meekness, joy and peace, kindness, goodness and longsuffering, and wins people over to Christ. Such a person is oftentimes surrounded by love from all directions.

He is always encircled by God, the angels and people. When you ask him for the secret for the success of his trade and profit, he will tell you that it lies in *all the merchant's fragrant powders*. These, as mentioned, are *love, joy, peace, longsuffering, kindness, goodness, faithfulness...* For this reason, when the spirit of such a person departs from his body and rises into the Lord, it is like a burnt offering *perfumed with myrrh and frankincense, and all the merchant's fragrant powders.*

And what of the church itself? There are extremely beautiful things in the church. In First Corinthians, Chapter 12, we also read about the merchant's fragrant powders:

> *And there are diversities of activities, but it is the same God who works all in all. But the manifestation of the Spirit is given to each one for the profit of all: for to one is given the word of wisdom through the Spirit, to another the word of knowledge through the same Spirit, to another faith by the same Spirit, to another gifts of healing by the same Spirit, to another the working of miracles, to another prophecy, to another discerning of spirits, to another different kinds of tongues.*
>
> *1Cor 12:6-10*

These are the merchant's fragrant powders. The Church, as seen here, abounds with all the imaginable talents and all the various works of the Holy Spirit. In it, there are all the works of Grace, all kinds of virtue, and all kinds of service. All these merchant's fragrant powders are placed like beads of incense in the crucible of life. They burn and rise before the Lord like pillars of smoke *perfumed with myrrh and frankincense, with all the merchant's fragrant powders.*

Which one of the merchant's fragrant powders do you have in your life? What do you have that burns in the censer and rises as fragrant incense and as pillars of smoke before the Lord? From amongst the merchant's fragrant powders, with which one are you equipped?

The merchant's fragrant powders is a reference to perfection. Everything is there; the Church lacks nothing. The human soul is not in need of anything, either. It is equipped with all the merchant's fragrant powders.

The Lord is pleased with and takes delight in the Church; He is proud of it. He talks about it in His Divine Book, *Who is this coming out of the wilderness like pillars of smoke, perfumed with myrrh and frankincense, with all the merchant's fragrant powders?* The Church is *prepared as a bride adorned for her husband,* (Rev 21:2). How so? It is perfumed with myrrh and frankincense and all the merchant's fragrant powders.

How about you, dear brethren? Is your soul likewise perfumed? Does it rise up as a fragrant aroma before the Lord? Do your works ascend to His presence as sweet smelling and acceptable? Are your prayers like the smell of incense in His Tabernacle?

If your prayers are like the smell of incense perfumed with myrrh and frankincense, the minute you pray, one of the twenty four priests standing in front of the throne of God would carry it and put it in his golden censer and ascend with this sweet aroma of incense, much like the prayers of the saints, and present it to the Lord. *Lord, I have brought You a worthy and acceptable prayer.* What kind of prayer could that be? It is one that is *perfumed with myrrh and frankincense and all the merchant's fragrant powders.* These are the perfumed prayers!

A weak, drifting and thoughtless prayer, one that

lacks in meditation and understanding cannot be described as one that is *perfumed with all the merchant's fragrant powders*. That is quite impossible! Such a prayer cannot ascend to the Lord as the smell of incense.

This is occasionally experienced at the death of some. When certain man's spirit departs from this world, one finds that the whole room is filled with the smell of incense. That is because his life itself was typically fragrant and aromatic like the smell of incense, rising upwards, *perfumed with myrrh and frankincense and all the merchant's fragrant powders*. Conversely, there are those on whose corpses bottles of perfume are hastily poured. People swiftly hurry to bury them to avoid the stench, that unpleasant smell that the body might emit. So, what will happen when the smell is emitted? It is not one that is *perfumed with myrrh and frankincense and all the merchant's fragrant powders*.

There are spirits that are perfumed with myrrh and frankincense when they ascend. I find the words *perfumed with myrrh and frankincense* fitting because when Jesus took human form to present Himself as an offering, the Wise Men came and offered Him myrrh and frankincense. As the spirit of Jesus arose, it was *perfumed with myrrh and frankincense and all the merchant's fragrant powders*. The gold, however, stands for the golden censer with which He ascended.

Which one of the merchant's fragrant powders do you have in your life?

As the Creator of every beautiful thing, and as a lover of beauty Himself, God wants our souls to be likewise beautiful and perfumed with myrrh and frankincense.

What else can we find in myrrh and frankincense? Myrrh is a symbol of the pain that man experiences and endures for the sake of the Lord. Frankincense symbolizes priesthood and the Sacraments that priests observe for your sake. In life, you need both. You need the sacraments that are symbolized by frankincense and the incense that priests raise, and you also need to toil, fight and struggle for the sake of the Lord. In other words, you ought to be perfumed with the Sacraments and works, myrrh and frankincense, and all the merchant's fragrant powders.

It would be worthwhile if you would examine and search yourself to see which of the merchant's fragrant powders are missing in your life. Which ones do you need? Which ones do you not have? Look for ways to have your soul perfumed when you go up to meet the Lord in the heavens.

Who is this coming out of the wilderness like pillars of smoke? The words *pillars of smoke* do not mean that your life was a sacrifice or an offering at a certain point in time. No! They mean that your life is an ongoing sacrifice, a continuous offering. The pillars of smoke are forever ascending, rising continuously and without intermission. Martyrs were just like that. Their lives were a sacrifice unto the Lord, an offering that went up as pillars of smoke *perfumed with myrrh and frankincense and all the merchant's fragrant powders.*

St. Demiana offers us a sticking example. She was exceedingly tortured, her flesh was cut, and she was put in boiling fat and oil. An angel must have looked at this saint as the smoke was coming out of her body and said, *Who is this coming out of the wilderness like pillars of smoke perfumed with myrrh and frankincense and all the merchant's fragrant powders.*

The Church is like that. It has all the merchant's fragrant powders. There are the prayers and the chants; there are the praises and the spiritual songs; there are the

Psalms, the thanksgivings, the prostrations and all the merchant's fragrant powders. It is a church that is complete; it is whole. The angels look at the holy Church and consider its beauty and beliefs, its rituals and history, and its worship and offerings. They chant saying, *Who is this coming out of the wilderness like pillars of smoke perfumed with myrrh and frankincense and all the merchant's fragrant powders.*

All I want to do is to give you an idea about the *Song of Songs* to help you when you read it. By so doing, I hope that we may avoid the excuses of some. The *Song of Songs* is a holy book that abounds with beautiful ideas. We ought to approach the book with godly love to benefit from its riches of myrrh and frankincense and all the merchant's fragrant powders. The book is, in fact, a treasure of spiritual concepts and ideas, thoughts that rise upwards like pillars of smoke perfumed with myrrh and frankincense and all the merchant's fragrant powders.

Let us pray.

May God have mercy upon us and bless us, and make His face shine with His Countenance upon us and have compassion upon us. With the prayers and intercessions that are raised on our behalf by the Mother of God, the Pure Saint Mary, and all the angels and apostles, and the prophets, and the martyrs, and the confessors, and the anchorites, and the saints who we ask to pray for us for peace at all times, and the blessings of the saint of this blessed day, and the blessing of Saint Mary first and last, may their holy blessings and the prayers and intercessions be with us all. Amen.

Peace be with you all.

May God make us worthy to say, Our Father…

Have You Seen the One I Love

I Have Compared You, My Love, To My Filly Among Pharaoh's Chariots

Song of Solomon 1:9

In the Name of the Father, the Son, and the Holy Spirit, One God. Amen.

Today I would like to talk about leading a strong and victorious life in Christianity. Let us start by reading this verse, *I have compared you, my love, To my filly among pharaoh's chariots*, (Song 1:9).

This kind of love is totally different from the love of a man to a woman

One can suggest with certainty that the kind of love depicted here can not be farther removed from the kind of love that exists between a man and a woman. No man in his right mind would liken his wife to a *filly among pharaoh's chariots*. If he did, she would kick him.

Let us also consider the following verses:
Behold, it is Solomon's couch,
With sixty valiant men around it,
Of the valiant of Israel.
They all hold swords,
Being expert in war.
Every man has his sword on his thigh
Because of fear in the night.
Song 3:7-8

Herein we see the picture of valiant, courageous men who are depicted as having expertise in the art of warfare.

We also read:
You are as beautiful as Tirzah, my love,
comely as Jerusalem,
terrible as an army with banners.
Turn away your eyes from me,
for they overwhelm me!
Song 6:4-5 (NRSV)

Again, these two verses depict the lover as *terrible as an army with banners*, another striking example that confirms that this kind of love is totally different from the love of a man to a woman. No man would compare his lover to a *terrible army with banners*.

And, finally, we continue contemplating the following verses:
Who is this that looks forth like the dawn,
fair as the moon, bright as the sun,
terrible as an army with banners?
Song 6:10 (NRSV)

Once more, it is inconceivable, even unthinkable, that a reference to physical love is made here. The image contains an oxymoron, a *terrible beloved*? How can the beloved be terrible? How can she be like an *army with banners?* Of course we can deduce that the beloved is not terrible in the eyes of the Lord. Rather, they are terrible and fearful in the eyes of anyone who dares attempt to snatch or grab them from the Lord.

Should such an attempt ever occur, the lover would instill fear and fright in the heart since they are like an *army with banners*. With one look the lover will inspire awe and trepidation. We should also notice that the word *banners* are used in the plural form. This indicates that a multitude of units, not just one battalion or detachment, are ready and alert. It is not even one brigade. Rather, there is a group of brigades forming an army, formidable and invincible.

Some people have an erroneous conception of meekness and humility

The image *terrible as an army with banners* is a reference to the human soul that has achieved harmony and unity with the Lord and has, in consequence, experienced vigor and strength drawn from Him. Some people have an erroneous conception of meekness and humility. They equate these concepts with the outward expression of various forms of weakness and helplessness. This is far from the truth. A man of God is, conversely, a strong, compelling person, *valiant* among those courageous experts at war, *terrible as an army with banners*, and a *filly among pharaoh's chariots*. Such strength and such vigor are drawn from the Lord.

For this reason, when Jesus sent forth His disciples, He did not send them unprepared, without the strength they needed. He did not want them to appear weak or irresolute. In fact, He wanted them to wait until He had provided them with strength which was granted them when the Holy Spirit descended upon them, *But when the Helper comes, whom I shall send to you from the Father, the Spirit of truth who proceeds from the Father, he will testify of Me. And you also will bear witness…*(John 15:26-27).

This is a clear example of what the Lord wanted for His disciples. He promised to provide them with strength from the Holy Spirit. Then they can *bear witness* of Him. Similarly, the Bible shows us that the Kingdom of Heaven was growing vigorously and rapidly. It was imbued with strength. Also, the children of God were strong and courageous. This strength and this courage were reflected and manifested in their service. An example of this is provided by St. Stephen the First Deacon who unwaveringly and courageously stood before synagogues and great multitudes of people who resisted the Spirit and the strength with which he was filled. The Kingdom of Heaven was growing with strength.

We are destined to wrestle and wage wars against Evil

Christianity as a religion has always reflected these aspects of strength and might. However, this strength is predominantly related to spiritual domains and realms; it has nothing to do with physical strength or tangible and worldly might. Moreover, it does not derive its strength from obstinacy or stubbornness. Rather, Christianity is about the strength of the Spirit as it works within the heart of man. Understanding this concept is of paramount importance if we are to come to grips with the seemingly conflicting images of the Church as *fair as the moon, clear as the sun.*

The children of God are those who are triumphant and victorious. During their life span in this world, they are the fighters and warriors. In the Book of Numbers, for example, when the Lord wanted to count His people, we read the following relevant verses in which the Lord asked Moses to, *take a census of all the generation of the children of Israel... from twenty years old and above, all who are able to go to war,* (Num 1:2-3). This is a clear reference to those who are of age, strong and valiant. Such men will be ready to fearlessly and valiantly take part in the Lord's army. It is this kind of people that the Lord uses to fight His wars to vanquish and conquer the world.

In Revelation, we encounter another striking example in which Jesus is seen as a leader leading us in a victorious, triumphant procession. Everyone of the angels of the seven churches heard the Lord's declaration that they would be rewarded for their victory. The angel of the Church of Smyrna heard the declaration, *Be faithful until death, and I will give you the crown of life*, (Rev 2:10). The angel of the Church in Philadelphia heard the proclamation, *He who overcomes, I will make him a pillar in the temple of My God*, (Rev 3:12). And the angel of the Church in Laodiceans heard the assertion, *To him who overcomes, I will grant to sit with Me on My throne*, (Rev 3:21). Many such assertions and pronouncements are promised those who live a victorious, triumphant life.

However, in this world we are bound to face the enemy. We are destined to wrestle and wage wars against Evil. We may be required to resist the desires of the flesh; we may have to stand firm against the lure of material possession and the enticement of material comfort. We may have to fight the power of the ego, to mention just a few of the various forms of clashes with the world. If we overcome, we will be granted a crown. But how can we overcome? How can we lead a victorious life?

God will lead us in His triumphant, victorious procession. Our Church is, incidentally, labeled and called the victorious, triumphant Church. When a member of the Church passes away in the faith, we say that they, *fought the good fight...finished the race... kept the faith*, (2 Tim 4:7), on this earth, and has finally moved to the triumphant Church in the heavens. *Finally, there is laid up for (them) the crown of righteousness, which the Lord, the righteous Judge, will give to (them) on that final day*, (2 Tim 4:8). This is a direct reference to the victorious Church that richly deserves the crowns of victory.

Christianity is, therefore, not an expression of weakness. On the contrary, it is a reflection of strength and victory. We have to achieve this victory. All manners of evil, sinful thoughts and images, lustful desires, evil doers,...etc, will face and confront us, but we have to remain steadfast, unwavering, resolute and victorious.

How can we stand firm and resolute? The answer to this question is provided by St. Paul the Apostle, *Finally, my brethren, be strong in the Lord and in the power of His might. Put on the whole armor of God, that you may be able to stand against the wiles of the devil. For we do not wrestle against flesh and blood, but against principalities, against powers, against the rulers of the darkness of this age, against spiritual hosts of wickedness in the heavenly places,* (Eph 6:10-12).

Essentially, we are in a state of war and we are advised to be strong in the Lord and in the *power of His might* because we are fighting against spiritual *hosts of wickedness*. Furthermore, we are urged to *put on the whole armor of God* in order to fight diligently and resist victoriously. St. Paul's advice on securing a successful fight continues, *Therefore take up the whole armor of God, that you may be able to withstand in the evil day, and having done all, to stand. Stand therefore, having girded your waist with truth, having put on the breastplate of righteousness,* (Eph 6:13-14). This is exceedingly essential in our fight against the devil.

St. Peter's words also resonate with a similar sentiment. He underlines the nature of the foe we are to confront, *Be sober, be vigilant; because your adversary, the devil, walks about like a roaring lion, seeking whom he may devour,* (1 Pet 5:8). He, therefore, urges us to, *resist him, steadfast in the faith,* (1 Pet 5:9). This is an invitation to resist the devil, not to retreat and appear feeble-hearted or fearful. In the Book of James, the words, *resist the devil and he will flee from you,* (James 4:7), reverberate the same theme. The picture emphatically depicted here is one of unwavering resistance in a ferocious war, a fierce fight conducted by the Lord's strong and valiant men *from twenty years old and above*, those who are ready to go to war and fight the Lord's battles.

> **The minute we have been baptized we are going to confront these spiritual wars**

The minute we have been baptized we are going to confront these spiritual wars. We will, however, be equipped with our breastplates and provided with the necessary armor. We are urged to *gird our waist* just as St. Paul had his waist girded. He was geared up, prepared and alert. *Girding the waist* is symbolic of fighting and wrestling against the enemy for the Lord's name. It is important to be prepared to *resist (the enemy) steadfast in the faith* because we will not be wrestling against *flesh and blood*.

Rather, we will be wrestling against the spiritual hosts of wickedness in high places. Fortunately, you do not have to be afraid. God has carefully and fully explained the nature of this spiritual warfare to Jeremiah, the prophet. He assured him not to be afraid of his enemies, *For behold, I have made you this day a fortified city, and an iron pillar, and bronze walls against the whole land...they will fight against you, but they shall not prevail against you. For I am with you, says the Lord, to deliver you,* (Jer 1:18-19). God wants us to lead a strong, triumphant life.

It is such a great joy for one to lead a victorious, triumphant life. Man will thereby feel that the strength he has drawn from the Lord has not gone to waste, but has rather been put to good use. He feels he possesses the armor of the Lord and that it has been usefully exploited to fight His wars. Everyday he moves from glory to glory for God's sake, and everyday he explores new territories and annexes new regions to His Kingdom; *the word of the Lord was growing and multiplying.* That can only be accomplished by the power and strength bestowed upon us by the Lord. With this power, God has granted us the authority over all the devils and the ability to *tread upon serpents and scorpions and every power of the enemy.*

The Lord has given us dominion over everything. Man was created strong and equipped with authority and dominion. In paradise, Adam was strong and he had authority. God gave him dominion over all the creatures in paradise. It is true that Adam was overcome in the war against the devil, but he was equipped with strength nonetheless.

The armor of the Lord has been distributed among the believers. It is, therefore, reasonable to suggest that the believers are equipped with the *whole armor of God.* This indicates that God has not given them only one weapon with which to fight, but that He has equipped them with His whole armor. The implication here is that believers are strong and well-equipped with a myriad of various weapons at their disposal in their arsenal. We have such weapons as faith, righteousness, patience…etc. Accordingly, we have the power and the ability to resist and to fight against all the various onslaughts of the enemy. This power and the confidence that it brings about are magnificently depicted in David's beautifully assuring song:

> **The armor of the Lord has been distributed among the believers**

Though an army may encamp against me,
My heart shall not fear;

> *Though war may rise against me,*
> *In this I will be confident*
>
> Ps 28:3

Indeed, David *prevailed over the Philistine with a sling and a stone,* (1Sam 17:50). Naturally, he extols the Lord's name, *I will sing a praise to the Lord.* There is no need to fret or worry if we are equipped with the armor of the Lord:

> *Some trust in chariots, and some in horses;*
> *but we will remember the name of the Lord, our*
> *God.*
> *They have bowed down and fallen;*
> *but we have risen and stand upright*
>
> Ps 20:7

What an exhilarating feeling of strength, power, and triumph when we have the *whole armor of the Lord!*

In fact, to compare my beloved to a *filly among pharaoh's chariots* is to show my beloved as being ready to fight, prepared to attack, and geared up for ferocious resistance. My beloved is like a *filly*, a warrior in chariots of war and fire, not in an excursion of sort of diversion. This is exactly what the Lord expects to see in the human soul. Do you consider yourself a *filly among pharaoh's chariots*? This is the human soul to which the Lord refers as *terrible as an army with banners.*

This *terrible* human soul is the Lord's pride and joy. He takes great delight in such strong, victorious people. He is confident that this kind of people are reliable, victorious, and triumphant at war. In Job, Satan pleaded, even bargained, with the Lord. The Lord said to Satan, *Have you considered My servant Job, that there is none like him on the earth, a blameless and upright man, one who fears God and shuns evil?* (Job 1:8).

God was seen as confidently using Job to challenge Satan. He was certain that Satan would not be able to conquer Job, not in a million years. The Lord saw Job as unparalleled and unmatched, *there is none like him*. Satan tried, but he could not conquer Job. He destroyed Job's home and deprived him of his possessions, but he could not change his mind. He killed his children, but he could not bend his will. He inflicted upon him vile sores and repulsive, abhorrent blisters, but he still could not conquer or beat him. In the sight of the Lord, Job was as *terrible as an army with banners*. What an amazing strength! What an incredible power! Satan tried in vain.

One should be like a *filly among pharaoh's chariots*, resolute, unyielding, and indomitable. There are some who, pathetically enough, cave in and yield, even collapse and fall apart, at the first encounter of some hardships or difficulties. They disintegrate and become dejected the minute they experience the slightest mishap in their lives. *I can't function ...I am overwhelmed... I feel lost... I can't go to church anymore... etc*. Such an attitude is, simply put, childish. It is immature, unbecoming and totally inappropriate.

It just does not fit the description of the man of God who is portrayed as, *valiant... of the valiant*, holding swords and as, *being expert in war. Every man has his sword on his thigh because of fear in the night*, (Song 3:7-8). Therefore, to grumble and complain that you cannot stand it anymore and that you are overwhelmed because of a certain situation is a course of impious judgment, one in which you portray negative feelings. It is an expression of depression, disillusionment and despair. It has nothing to do with the valiant, steadfast attitude of the men of the Lord. It is simply childish.

As long as one is well equipped with the *whole armor of God*, there is no place for fear or panic. On the contrary, it is Satan who will tremble in fear and shake in horror. This is natural since the word *terrible* means capable of inspiring awe and fear. It has always been the case that the righteous have instilled fear in the hearts of the devils. Here is an example; when St. Macarious went to the island of Fiala, the devils experienced great horror and panic. They cried in agony claiming that they had left the wilderness of Wadi-el-Natroon (Scete) only to be followed by the Saint. They screamed and complained in great agony at his presence.

This example shows how truly strong and valiant the righteous are. Another example that I mentioned a long time ago and which is recorded in *The Paradise of the Desert Fathers* tells of a certain Saint who was tempted by a devil. The saint tied the devil up outside his cell. Another devil tried to tempt the saint, and he met the same fate. A third devil tried to tempt the saint only to meet a similar fate. Before we proceed any further, we ought to ask ourselves what the meaning of *being tied up outside the cell* could be. One ought to sit and meditate on this phrase for some time. What could it mean and how could it be?

The devils having been tied up outside the saint's cell started to cry. The saint looked at them and reproachfully and admonishingly commanded them to, *go away and be humiliated and mortified.* Upon hearing these words coming out of the mouth of the saint, the devils departed howling and crying. How could they ever dream of conquering

This *terrible* human soul is the Lord's pride and joy

such a person? The Lord looks favorably at him and regards him as a *filly among pharaoh's chariots*. He looks at such a saint who had been able to vanquish these devils and likens him to a *filly*, ready and strong.

Spiritual life is one of strength and vigor. It is that Divine strength, that celestial, heavenly power that works within the human soul. These are exhibited in wrestling against sin, on the one hand, and in service, on the other. There are those people whose service is strong and effective. Every word that proceeds from their mouths is effective and powerful; it produces the results sought and achieves the goals set. The power of the Holy Spirit is felt in their every word.

Spiritual life is one of strength and vigor

Jesus manifested this power when He spoke. It was said that He spoke and taught the multitudes as *one having authority* and not as the scribes, (Matt 7:29). When people listened to Him, they proclaimed and confirmed that they had never heard anything like that before. Such a proclamation can only be attributable to the strength that permeated His words, the strength of a *filly among pharaoh's chariots,* one that is as *terrible as an army with banners*, and *valiant* among the valiant of the Lord. That also accounts for the fact that the word of God was *growing and multiplying*. This is only logical since the service rendered was one that was at once fervent and impassioned as well as imbued with the power of the Holy Spirit.

St. Paul provides us with another example. We know that he spoke with power even though he was a prisoner, a captive in chains and surrounded by guards. His words on righteousness, chastity and condemnation were awe inspiring to the extent that Agrippa, the governor, was afraid and felt uneasy. Never have we heard of a governor who shakes and trembles in the presence of his captives, nor have we witnessed a judge whose heart is filled with fright in the presence of a defendant. That, however, was exactly what had happened. The governor was awe-stricken because of St. Paul's effective and powerful words.

When Agrippa said to St. Paul, *You almost persuaded me to become a Christian*, St. Paul responded saying, *I would to God that not only you, but also all who hear me today, might become both almost and altogether such as I am, except for these chains*, (Acts 26:28-29). This response shows how fearless, dauntless and valiant St. Paul was. Even earlier in this encounter, St. Paul, a prisoner in chains asked Agrippa, the powerful king, *King Agrippa, do you believe in the prophets? I know that you do believe*, (Acts 26:27). The king, mighty and powerful as he was, was speechless and failed to respond.

It is, therefore, unsuitable to portray signs of embarrassment, hesitancy or awkwardness when we are serving the Lord or delivering His word. We cannot stammer or stutter; we cannot falter or fail. On the contrary, it is both natural and logical to exhibit clarity and strength of purpose and an unbendable and unswerving determination. David's words, *I will speak of Your testimonies also before kings, and will not be ashamed,* (Ps 119:46), provide a striking example of this power that fills the Godly and the righteous.

In this respect I would like to note what happened when St. Anthony went to visit St. Macarious. Having sat for a short time with St. Macarious, St. Anthony noted what great power emanated from this saint.

This also happens in our daily lives. Oftentimes, we meet people who are strong and uplifting. They are inspiring, enriching and inspirational. They can relieve you of the heavy burdens that you may be carrying; they may attenuate the terrible impact of sin on your conscience; they may lessen the weight of your problems and hardships; and they may even help you change your deeply-rooted harmful habits. They seem to be able to really carry others on their own shoulders.

Conversely, we sometimes encounter people who literally drag one down as we try to uplift them. They easily collapse and disintegrate and, no matter how hard one tries to assist and help them, such efforts are doomed to fail. This is sad and disappointing. The Children of God must be strong and valiant. They are equipped with the strength drawn from the Holy Spirit, from Divine Grace and from prayers. They have the *whole armor of God*.

In addition to this kind of strength that is manifested in service, God's children also reflect their valiance and strength in their conduct. Sometimes people resort to a lie in order to hide something. When this lie is revealed, they try to go around the issue by telling another lie and so on and so forth. What kind of strength of character is this? What kind of vigor could be implied in such a crooked, evasive behavior? Such people are destined to stumble and falter. They have become helpless. You feel pity for such pathetic individuals. When Satan approaches such people, he would say, *Woe unto you. What is it that you do and we do not? There is only one thing with which you could vanquish us and it is humility.*

Humility is a form of strength. Humbleness is a weapon that one can use to vanquish and conquer the devils. St. Anthony says, *I witnessed the snares of the devil spread on the ground and I inquired who could escape unharmed from them!* God assured him that the meek and the humble will not be touched. This is due to the fact that the meek and the humble have power that can obliterate and annihilate the devils. The strength drawn from humbleness is neither pretentious nor ostentatious. It has nothing to do with worldly power.

Goliath, the Philistine, was richly endowed with worldly might. He was physically strong; he was tall and well built. He had an army with weapons. Yet, David, who was ostensibly much smaller and appeared quite insignificant in comparison, was indeed much stronger. And why? His strength was drawn from the Holy Spirit, *I come to you in the name of the Lord of Hosts,* (1 Sam 17:45). The name of the Lord is filled with power; it is a strong tower. Do we have this kind of strength?

God's children also reflect their valiance and strength in their conduct

In the Bible, we read that, *God has chosen the foolish things of the world to put to shame the wise, and God has chosen the weak things of the world to put to shame the things which are mighty,* (1 Cor 1:27). Those who seem to everyone else as weak, humble and helpless are used by the Lord to put to shame the mighty and the strong. Has the Lord not used David to put Goliath to shame?

If we have a relationship with the Lord, we should draw strength from Him. We should not rely on our own human strength, nor should we put our confidence in man. We should, rather, trust the might and the strength of the Lord. Let us become soldiers and fight the Lord's wars and let us overcome. David expresses this sense of exultation and his jubilant feelings of triumph in his song:

> *They surrounded me like bees;*
> *They were quenched like a fire of thorns;*
> *For in the name of the Lord I will destroy them...*
> *The right hand of the Lord exalted;*
> *The right hand of the Lord does valiantly.*
> *I shall not die, but live,*
> *And declare the works of the Lord.*
> Ps.118:12-17

It is, as it were, a declaration of the victorious, triumphant life of those who have established a strong relationship with the Lord. However arduous or strenuous the difficulties or hardships they encounter, and no matter how strong and crafty the enemy they face may be, they will be victorious and they will overcome. *They surrounded me like bees; they were quenched like a fire of thorns; for in the name of the Lord I will destroy them...The right hand of the Lord exalted; the right hand of the Lord does valiantly. I shall not die, but live.* This is a song sung by a *filly* among pharaoh's chariots.

We should confess our limitations and acknowledge our weaknesses

One may sometimes sin and fail to seek the real power and the true strength that may uplift, *for (sin) has cast down many wounded, and all who were slain by her were strong men,* (Pro 7:26). This takes place when one depends on worldly power rather than trusting in the Lord. The strength of the Lord is like a *strong tower* for man. David acknowledges the strength of the Lord in his psalm, *The Lord is my strength* and in *The Lord is my salvation.*

Is the Lord our strength? Do we have the Lord in our lives? We cannot trust and put our confidence in worldly power. We see how David rejected the helmet and the breastplate. He insisted that he had no use for such symbols of worldly power. He sought a different kind of power, the name of the Lord of Hosts.

The martyrs also confronted judges and stood before governors and kings. They were in chains and they were subjected to various types of torture. They, however, remained steadfast, strong and they most boldly overcame their opponents. They were never frightened, troubled or apprehensive. They had amazing strength springing from within. No threats, no intimidation, no temptations would ever lure them into changing their position. They were in possession of great strength. They would rebuke Satan, *Flee away* and he would instantaneously flee.

Likewise, we need this kind of strength from the Lord, strength that is capable of performing wonders and miracles, one that *raises the poor out of the dust, and lifts the needy out of the ash heap, that He may seat him with princes, with the princes of His people,* (Ps 113:7-8). We should ask the Lord for this strength. We should confess our limitations and acknowledge our weaknesses. We should declare to Him that we are the *poor* that need to be plucked out of the dust, and the *needy* that need to be lifted from the ash heap. We should confess that we do not have strength on our own and that we need His strength to uplift us. We should confess that we do not have the means to fight and ask for His whole armor. We should come to the realization that we are nothing without Him, but with Him we can do everything. We have strength drawn from Him.

Not only do the children of God have power against Satan and sin, they also have strength in their relationship with the Lord Himself. We remember how Jacob struggled and prevailed. This is an example of the human soul to which the Lord says, *Turn your eyes away from me, for they have overcome me,* (Song 6:5). Also, Moses the prophet stood before the Lord pleadingly, and the Lord *relented from the harm which He said He would do to His people,* (Ex 32:14). It is almost inconceivable to suggest or hint that people have strength when they plead or wrestle with the Lord. However inconceivable it may be, there are people who do have power as they plead with the Lord.

This means that such people stand before the Lord, fighting, struggling and pleading with Him until they have been able to draw strength and power from Him, *I will not let you go unless You bless me,* (Gen 32:26). What is the meaning of not letting Him go? It is an admission of the human soul that even if the Lord regards it as a tiny insignificant insect, one will still persevere and cling to

Him until one has been able to draw strength from Him. This is an example of strength, one who is pleading with and beseeching the Lord.

There are those who exhibit strength in their prayers. They argue and talk with the Lord; they struggle and plead with Him. They have strength. This pleases God. The Lord said to Moses, *Now therefore, let Me alone, that My wrath may burn hot against them and I may consume them,* (Ex 23:10). Dwell upon this verse and meditate on it. The Lord Himself was seen as asking Moses to *let* Him destroy His people. Who on earth was Moses that the Lord was seeking his consent on what He wanted to do, *let Me alone.* We can only deduce that the Lord was *overcome* by Moses' clinging love and earnest, solemn appeal for forgiveness.

Such is the strength that people may manifest even in their relationship with God Himself. The Lord abides in the heart of such people, and He feels comfortable there, He is pleased with them. He looks at their hearts and longs to dwell there. They, in turn, draw strength from Him.

This is not surprising. Man draws strength when he is transformed into the image of the Lord and His likeness. Man also draws strength from the Lord when he becomes a true son to God. The son has a share and an inheritance and, therefore, strength.

We should lead a strong, victorious and triumphant life. We should not fail or falter, and we should not fear or cringe. We should not be apprehensive before the opponent. Only those who are proud and arrogant, vain and conceited would experience fear and trepidation. Putting one's confidence in one's own strength can be a source of misgivings and uneasiness. We should not attach importance to our own strength.

Rather, we should admit our weaknesses and be ready to receive the Lord's power. When this happens, we will be transformed to a *filly among pharaoh's chariots*. We should recognize that we do not have the means to fight, and that when the Lord provides us with His armor, we will be able to fight and overcome. It is God who grants us His strength and His power.

People have different manifestations of strength. Some are extremely intelligent, others exhibit strength in politics. Some are shrewd, astute and insightful and others are hard-working, thorough and conscientious. These are all realizations of worldly power. The Lord regards this kind of power as ephemeral and transitory. It is like counterfeit currency with which we cannot *buy gold refined by the fire,* (Rev 4:18). These various manifestations of worldly power are useless.

We should be equipped with the power of prayer and humility

We should be equipped with the power of prayer and humility. We should also have the power of humbleness and contrition before the Lord. We should manifest power and strength in our fights and wars against the devil. We should have the strength of purity and chastity so as not to succumb to or be defeated by the tricks of the opponent, nor fall in his snares and traps. A victorious life such as this one would sing new praises to the Lord and rejoice in Him with power and strength day by day.

This power and strength would be naturally reflected in one's life. Moreover, it would be reflected in the Church as a whole. This is power in the true sense of the term. Some people mistakenly believe that true power is the ability to overwhelm others in arguments and discourse. Wrong! Other people believe that exonerating and vindicating themselves in an attempt to be deferential and reverent is an expression of strength. On the contrary. Strong people are those who own and acknowledge their wrong doing and sin. Strong people are not those who claim that they are free from sin.

Rather, they are the ones who confess that they are wretched sinners and admit to the multitude of their sins. Strength does not mean overwhelming and defeating others. Rather, strength means winning others over. It also means being patient and long suffering towards others. Strength does not mean an eye for an eye. It is turning the other cheek; it is the ability to walk the second mile, and it is showing patience and tolerance, *We then who are strong ought to bear with the scruples of the weak...*, (Rom 15:1). We should be patient and long suffering towards those who are weak and helpless. It is such a wonderful thing to be strong; however, one ought to understand the true meaning of strength.

> **All those who have had a relationship with the Lord have been able to draw some strength from Him**

It is important for us to adopt the right attitude of strength and to understand the proper concept of power. We should shun and reject the worldly concept. We should have forbearance, leniency and patience. We should be able to stand everything and hope in everything. A person who is quick to anger is not strong. Neither is the person who clashes and collides with others. A boastful, immodest person also lacks strength. A strong person is one whose heart is pure and chaste and is, thereby, transformed into an amazing energy and an incredible power that is *fair as the moon, clear as the sun* and yet, *terrible as an army with banners.*

All those who have had a relationship with the Lord have been able to draw some strength from Him. They have come to understand the inadequacy of their human strength and have opted to place their trust and confidence in the Lord. Moses abandoned his former, human strength which he employed in knocking down the Egyptian. He headed to the wilderness where he forsook and deserted his physical strength. He only and truly experienced the true meaning of strength when he returned to God and confessed his limitations, *O my Lord, I am not eloquent, neither before nor since You have spoken to Your servant; but I am slow of speech and slow of tongue,* (Ex 4:10). He became equipped with humility and purity. He had been able to relinquish conceit and self importance. He stopped counting on his own strength.

We need strong people to fight in the army of the Lord. Their strength is drawn from the Holy Spirit, from righteousness and chastity, and from the work of the Lord within them. This strength will be embodied and exemplified in their service, in their prayers, and in their ability to lead a triumphant life. It will be exemplified in everything and everywhere. Let us pray.

May God have mercy upon us and bless us, and make His face shine with His Countenance upon us and have compassion upon us. With the prayers and intercessions that are raised on our behalf by the Mother of God, the Pure Saint Mary, and all the angels and apostles, and the prophets, and the martyrs, and the confessors, and the anchorites, and the saints who we ask to pray for us for peace at all times, and the blessings of the saint of this blessed day, and the blessing of Saint Mary first and last, may their holy blessings and the prayers and intercessions be with us all. Amen.

Peace be with you all.

May God make us worthy to say, Our Father...

Behold, You are Fair, My Love! Behold You are Fair! You Have Dove's Eyes

Song of Solomon 1:15

In the Name of the Father, the Son, and the Holy Spirit, One God. Amen.

The first thing that attracts our attention in this verse is that God bears witness and acknowledges that the human soul is a beautiful thing. Many people may talk about you, and sometimes their accounts and statements are not truthful. But the Lord's testimony is truthful and honest.

The Lord's testimony is truthful and honest

Many people may declare that you are fair and beautiful. Some may do so out of flattery, others out of a willingness to encourage others, especially the powerless and the helpless. Some may be motivated by attraction, while others may be motivated by love. Some may be motivated by deceit, some malicious desire, or the prospect of gain. However, the most important thing about this verse is that God Himself bears witness for you. Our Lord Jesus Christ says, *I do not receive honor from men*, (John 5:41), and, *There is another who bears witness of Me, and I know that the witness which He witnesses of Me is true*, (John5:32). He neither asked nor expected people to bear witness for Him.

The most important thing for the human soul is that God bears witness for it. One of the most beautiful verses that I have read about St. John the Baptist is that it was said about him, *he will be great in the sight of the Lord*, (Luke 1:15). He will not be great in the sight of people. Rather, he will be great in the sight of the Lord Himself. Who could that be who will be great in the sight of the Lord? The Lord's testimony can do that for you. All that we want in our lives, all that we need in our lives, is that the Lord look favorably upon our souls in the final day and declare, *Behold, you are fair my love! Behold, you are fair!* And, *Well done, good and faithful servant; you were faithful over a few things, I will make you ruler over many things* (Matthew 25:21).

A testimony from the Lord that you have been faithful and honest in your life resonates just like, *Behold, You are fair, my love*. It is the most beautiful word that the Lord may say to the human soul at the end of life's solitary journey on earth, when its holy wars and struggles have been completed and when it ascends to Him purified by His holy blood and sanctified with the tears of penitence. To such a human soul the Lord would say, *Behold, You are fair, my love*.

To have such a testimony in the final day is the important thing. There were people on earth who prophesied, cast demons out, and performed wonders and miracles. However, as the Lord says, *Many will say to Me in that day 'Lord, Lord, have we not prophesied in Your name, cast out demons in Your name, and done many wonders in Your name,'* and the Lord will respond saying, *I never knew you; depart from Me, you who practice lawlessness!* (Matthew 7:22-23). What a terrifying thought to hear a statement such as *I never knew you.*

The most important thing for the human soul is that God bears witness for it

Therefore, the Lord's testimony is the important thing. It is not important that you can cast demons out, or that you can perform miracles and wonders in the sight of people, or that you can do this and that. The important thing is that the Lord looks favorably at your soul on that final day and says, *Behold, you are fair, my love. Behold, you are fair!* and then invites you to, *Enter into the joy of your Lord.*

Let us consider a very important statement in God's testimony in *Revelation.* Jesus addresses every one of the angels of the seven churches saying, *I know your works.* This is a testimony. To the angel of the church of Ephesus He says, *I know your works, your labor, your patience.... And you have persevered and have patience, and have labored for my name's sake and have not become weary,* (Rev 2:2-3). *Behold, you are fair, my love*, for you have labored for Me and have not become weary.

Similarly, Jesus looks at the Canaanite woman and declares, *O woman, great is your faith!* (Matthew 15:28). *Behold, you are fair, my love.* You are fair when you say that, *Even the little dogs eat from the crumbs which fall from their master's table*, (Matthew 15:27). And the woman who in tears washes Jesus' feet in humiliation, her tears are mixed with the fragrant oil as she washes His feet and wipes them with the hair of her head. Jesus looks at her and says, *Behold, you are fair, my love. Behold, you are fair!*

Much has been forgiven her for, *she has loved much*. The Lord's testimony is the important thing. The Pharisee, a man of great knowledge of the Law, thinks to himself, *This man, if He were a prophet, would know who and what manner of woman this is who is touching Him, for she is a sinner,* (Luke 7:39). It is true that the woman is a sinner in the sight of people and according to their standards. However, the important thing is the Lord's view, His judgment. She has loved much and, consequently, much has been forgiven her. *Behold, you are fair, my love!*

It is this testimony that we should look for and seek. Many girls may long and yearn to hear a phrase such as *You are fair* from anyone's lips. They go to great lengths to hear a statement like this although such a declaration will get them nowhere. The important thing is to hear it from the Lord's mouth, *Behold, you are fair, my love. Behold, you are fair!*

Many girls may long and yearn to hear a phrase such as You are fair from anyone's lips.

God's assessment of beauty and fairness differs from that of man's. Therefore, the bride whom the Lord addresses saying, *Behold, you are fair, my love*, may regard herself differently as, *I am black and beautiful*, (Song 1:5). Despite her blackness the Lord sees her as fair and beautiful.

Similarly, a person who is leading a life of asceticism and austerity, worn out because of fasting, and frail because of frugality would raise a mother's concern and worry. What's the matter with you, my child? You do not look well! Are you feeling Okay? You look ghastly! You look pitiful as though you were dying! What is the matter? What is wrong? However, the Lord looks at the fading, diminishing strength and waning, deteriorating health of this person and addresses them saying, *Behold, you are fair my love.*

Abba Isaac, the mentor of St. Misael the Anchorite, was exceedingly distressed when he saw the Saint after many years had gone by. Although St. Misael was born into a wealthy family, he had become frail and exceedingly feeble due to his ascetic life. Abba Isaac wept when he saw him in such terrible health. He told him that he had had the appearance of loyalty, the strength and the vigor of youth. Now, all that had undergone a complete change. He appeared to be extremely weak, fragile and withered, *as a piece of firewood.* However, in spite of his shabby and ragged appearance, the Lord would look at him and declare, *Behold, you are fair, my love. Behold, you are fair.*

The saints who were maimed and disfigured during persecutions offer us another example. St. Samuel the Confessor lost one of his eyes when they pierced it. St. Jacob the Maimed had his limbs severed. All of those who were whipped until their bodies were mutilated, disfigured and appeared horrible to the eyes of the onlookers, the Lord looks upon all of those and declares, *Behold, you are fair, my love. Behold, you are fair.*

Anyone who labors and toils for the name of the Lord will be regarded as fair in His sight regardless of how people look at them. A woman who dresses conservatively and respectfully may be regarded as a "peasant" by other people. She does not use cosmetics extravagantly and unnecessarily, nor will she waste time fretting about her dress or observing the latest vogue. However, the Lord looks upon her and declares, *Behold, you are fair, my love.*

Behold, you are fair.

No matter how dark in sin she may be, the Lord's standards of fairness are different from man's. God even likens the beauty of this fair and beloved one to pillars of smoke. What is fair or beautiful about pillars of smoke? The Lord's values are truly different from those of man.

A person who confesses his sins and acknowledges his horrible deeds may offend others if they heard him mention what he had done. However, the Lord delights in this sinner who pours out his soul and empties his bosom in confession. He looks at the soul of this person, as he broken-heartedly and in contrition and humiliation confesses his sins, and declares, *Behold, you are fair, my love. Behold, you are fair.*

To God, fairness and beauty manifest themselves in many different means. It is easy to understand, *Like a lily among thorns, so is my love among the daughters,* (Song 2:2). However, *I have compared you, my love, to my filly among Pharaoh's chariots,* (Song 1:9), may not be readily understandable. No girl would probably appreciate being likened to a horse in the chariots of Pharaoh. Nonetheless, a steadfast, firm soul that triumphantly fights in the name of the Lord is as mighty as a horse among the chariots of pharaoh. It is such a triumphant, victorious soul that the Lord praises and beautifies its struggles, its labor, and its toil. It is to such a soul that the Lord declares, *Behold, you are fair, my love. Behold, you are fair.* You are like a horse in the chariots of Pharaoh. This is how God describes the soul that fights and toils for His sake.

The first thing we talked about is the testimony of the Lord; in other words, how God bears witness for the human soul. Then we talked about how the standards of fairness and beauty differ between God and man. For example, to some people, a person who turns the other cheek may be regarded as contemptible, despicable, and not worthy of respect. On the other hand, God favorably considers the patience, forbearance, forgiveness of this person, and delights in this ability to *bless those who curse (them)*, and declares, *Behold, you are fair, my love. Behold, you are fair.*

Also, people who become poor and without any material possessions for the sake of the Lord may be regarded as poor by some, miserable and helpless. The Lord looks at these people and testifies, *Behold, you are fair, my love. Behold, you are fair*. This fairness lies in the fact that they have given up the love of the world, its riches and material comfort, *As poor, yet making many rich; as having nothing and yet possessing all things*, (2Cor. 6:10).

It is noteworthy that the Lord reiterates this verse. He says, *Behold, you are fair, my love. Behold, you are fair*. It is amazing that the Lord testifies and repeats His testimony. It seems as though He is emphasizing, solidifying, and confirming it. The Lord's testimony is firm and unshakeable. Its repetition seems to infuse it with more depth and strength.

Our main concern should be how the Lord looks at and regards us, our moral fiber and inner life.

The body of Job the Righteous was infested with blisters from head to toe. His stench was such that everyone around him, even his nearest and dearest, shunned him. Everyone ran away from him because of his unpleasant, disgusting odor. It was unbearable even to his wife. Yet the Lord regards his patience and endurance declaring, *Behold, you are fair, my love. Behold, you are fair*.

We should not be concerned with the judgment of

people. Our main concern, rather, should be how the Lord looks at and regards us, our moral fiber and inner life. In the eyes of the world self-importance, pomp, and haughtiness are reflections of strength and power and manifestations of vanity and overconfidence. The Lord, however, looks at the meek and the humble, and those who are *poor in spirit*. He *regards the lowly state of His maidservant*. He exalts the lowly and the modest, and uplifts the trodden and the crushed to serve as ruler among kings. To this poor, miserable, and crushed spirit, the Lord declares, *Behold, you are fair, my love. Behold, you are fair.*

Seek the testimony of the Lord, His view and His judgment.

Standards differ. Standards vary. People seek praise and glory. They hunger for high status and ranks and long for dignity and self-respect. This, however, was not the case with one of the saintly nuns from the *Paradise of the Desert Fathers* who pretended to be a fool, faked weakness, indolence and idleness, pretended to be negligent of her spiritual duties and responsibilities. She made her virtues unknown and undisclosed to man, only to stand fully upright at night, while everyone else slept, before the Lord as a flame of fire and fervently prayed while being surrounded by angels. The Lord looks at this self-proclaimed fool and declares, *Behold, you are fair, my love. Behold, you are fair.*

St. Marina the Monk, who disguised herself as a man in order to join a monastery, patiently and silently endured scandal and disgrace when she was accused fathering a child. She did not defend herself and was thrown out of the monastery. Everyone looked at her as a fallen, adulterous monk, worthy of no respect. Nonetheless, the Lord looks down from the sky and declares, *Behold, you are fair, my love. Behold, you are fair.*

God's benevolent and favorable testimony for us is the important thing. Joseph the Righteous was wrongly accused of sinning against Potiphar. He was thrown into prison. The inmates regarded him as a sinner worthy of being locked up. Potiphar looked at him as a sinner sentenced to imprisonment. However, the Lord looks at Joseph in his predicament and declares, *Behold, you are fair, my love. Behold, you are fair.*

Therefore, seek the testimony of the Lord, His view and His judgment. I wish that everyone of us is ready and prepared before the Lord so as to be worthy of hearing, *Behold, you are fair, my love. Behold, you are fair.*

Let us now continue with the next verse. *Behold, you are fair, my love. Behold, you are fair. You have dove's eyes.* "Eyes" are meant to indicate vision. "A dove" symbolizes the Holy Spirit. This indicates that the Holy Spirit emanates from your eyes. In other words, you have a spiritual outlook, a saintly view. *You have dove's eyes.* A dove, in particular, has a unique and important significance in the Bible. I would like to contemplate on its status.

A dove has always had singular and unique characteristics throughout the ages. Saint Mary is likened to a dove. A priest censes to the north of the Sanctuary where the icon of the Virgin is located and says, *Hail to you, O Mary, the Beautiful Dove.* What is meant by a "Beautiful Dove"? The first beautiful and striking story about a dove occurs when it went into the ark of Noah the Righteous. It was a dove that was sent out by Noah to bring back tidings of peace. It was a dove that brought back a freshly plucked olive leaf, thereby symbolizing peace and indicating that the waters had receded from the earth.

These were good tidings. The Flood that had

prevailed upon the earth had ended. The plants started to blossom anew, and this beautiful dove had come back with that promise. That is why we consider Saint Mary the Virgin a "Beautiful Dove" foreshadowing, as She does, that the waters of the Flood no longer prevail upon the earth, that Salvation is at hand, and that the ark has almost come ashore. These are symbols of salvation, of peace, and of good tidings, *Behold, you are fair, my love. You have dove's eyes.* Every eye brings forth good tidings foretelling peace and salvation and carrying an olive branch to everyone.

A heavy-hearted sinner who is almost driven into despair would look into the eyes of a righteous, kind-hearted counselor, one who gives comfort, opens a window of hope, offers an opportunity for penitence and salvation, and explains God's boundless love, and this sinner would say, *You have dove's eyes.* This sinner's helplessness and despair have given way to hope and promise. It is as though those eyes are holding an olive branch thereby proclaiming to the ark that the waters has receded and that salvation has drawn near.

A dove is a symbol of simplicity. The Lord has said, *Be as...harmless as doves*, (Matt. 10:16). A simple eye is a token of simplicity in a human being. Jesus says, *If therefore your eye is good, your whole body will be full of light*, (Matt. 6:22). Eve lost this pure, simple vision when she looked at the fruit on the tree and desired it. Her eyes were no longer those of a dove's as they were made to be.

When the Lord created the human soul, He made it such that He chanted saying, *Behold, you are fair, my love. Behold, you are fair. You have dove's eyes.* God adorned this human soul with simplicity, chastity, and purity. It had no knowledge of good nor evil, and everything, to this human soul, was beautiful, chaste, and pure. It had known no evil whatsoever. Neither had it any evil desire. *Behold, you are fair, my love. You have dove's eyes.*

Then man lost this simplicity and purity. People's eyes have opened. They have started to look at things that were alien to them before, and they have become aware of things that were beyond their comprehension. In short, man lost the simplicity with which he was endowed. God can no longer say *You have dove's eyes,* because that purity, which is characteristic of doves, has vanished. Now, those eyes are filled with craftiness and slyness.

When you look at those eyes, you may find myriad, innumerable worlds at variance. You may find thousands upon thousands of thoughts, and thousands upon thousands of curses. You may even feel bewildered, puzzled, and even exposed as if they have been able to see right through you. Judgments are passed. You cannot say *You have dove's eyes.* This is quite inconceivable. There are those who have eyes like those of a vulture, frightening and fearsome. But you would look at a person who is simple, gentle, quiet, and kind, one whose outlook at everything is characterized by purity and say, *Behold! You are fair, my love. You have dove's eyes.*

> **God adorned this human soul with simplicity, chastity, and purity.**

A person who has dove's eyes is characterized by a spiritual and modest outlook, one that is filled with goodness and gentleness. Has anyone among you ever seen a sullen or grumpy dove, one that frowns and scowls? Never. A dove symbolizes gentleness, kindheartedness and meekness. By *You have dove's eyes,* we mean to say that you have a meek, gentle, and kind disposition.

Behold, you are fair, my love. You have dove's eyes. Doves always sing and chant. They have, therefore, become a symbol of chanting and praising. When we talk about the monasteries of the monks that chant and praise ceaselessly and without intermission, night and day, we refer to them as doves' towers. They sing and praise incessantly. This singing has become a symbol for endless praises and spiritual songs, a symbol of perpetual prayer. For this reason David was overjoyed and chanted for *the sparrow has found a home, and the swallow a nest for herself...Even Your altars, O Lord of hosts, my King and my God*, (Ps. 84:3). This beautiful dove has found herself a place.

Doves do not only dwell in towers, but they also live in the wilderness, in caves and caverns and in the cracks of the mountains. Therefore, doves do not only symbolize the spirit of praises and chanting, but they also embody solitude and seclusion as doves may live in solitude and in isolation in a cave. This is very similar to the monk who opts to dwell alone in a cave.

When God describes the beauty of the human soul, He turns to the dove to draw the similarities

David the Prophet chants about this saying, *Oh, that I had wings like a dove! I would fly away and be at rest. Indeed, I would wander far off, and remain in the wilderness*, (Ps. 55:6-7). David longs to have the wings of a dove that he may fly away, wander far off, and be at rest in the wilderness. Monks, like doves, dwell in the caves in the wilderness. The Lord favorably looks at every monk in his cave and says, *Behold, you are fair, my love*. They live to chant and give praises to the Lord.

It is amazing that we can observe that a dove has the ability to live with the crowd in harmony, love, loyalty, and peace, as well as the ability to live in solitude and seclusion in the wilderness. A dove has the unique ability to do both. Some may claim that when the Lord says, *Behold, you are fair, my love. You have dove's eyes*, He may only have those who live in solitariness or isolation in mind. However, we oftentimes hear about a flock of doves flying together in harmony and cohesion in the same direction. Flocks such as these represent the pure, undefiled life of an assembly.

The Lord regards the people of His Church as flocks of doves that gather together to fly in the wilderness of this world to chant and praise. He looks upon these flocks and says, *Behold, you are fair, my love. Behold, you are fair.* Furthermore, the Lord has most aptly described the Church in David's Psalms, *You will be like the wings of a dove covered with silver, And her feathers with yellow gold*, (Ps. 68:13). This picture of the beautiful church illustrates one consecrated to the Lord. At such a church, the Lord would look adoringly and say, *Behold, you are fair, my love. Behold, you are fair. You have dove's eyes*.

In addition to all of this, there is something uniquely singular about a dove. For the poor in the Old Testament, a dove was used to represent the burnt and sacrificial offerings. While a rich person would probably be able to offer cattle, sheep, or goat, a poor person, on the other hand, would only be able to offer a pair of doves: one as a burnt offering, the other atonement for sin. The Lord favorably regards these two sacrifices that are offered. He, likewise, looks at the Church that has this spiritual manner, one that presents such offerings and says, *You have dove's eyes*. One dove as a burnt offering, and the other a sacrificial one for the atonement of sin.

On the day of her purification which is the fortieth day after delivery, when a woman has given birth to a son, the woman would come to church and offer a pair of doves. This was the custom on the day of a woman's purification. The Lord would accept that benevolently and say, *Behold! You are fair, my love…You have dove's eyes.*

The dove did not only symbolize the Holy Spirit, peace, simplicity and praises in the Old Testament, but it also symbolized offerings and sacrifices. It was for this reason that the temple was always filled with caged doves. Our Lord Jesus Christ was not angry because there were doves in the temple. Rather, what angered Him was the selling and the buying that was taking place inside the temple. We read that, *Jesus went into the temple of God and drove out all those who bought and sold in the temple, and overturned the tables of the money changers, and the seats of those who sold doves*, (Matt. 21:12). However, He never overturned the doves' cages. He never even touched them. He requested the people to remove them.

Jesus loved doves. There are also those who do not eat doves at all because of all the beautiful symbols associated with them and which abound in the Bible. Suffice it to say that the Holy Spirit descended like a dove upon Jesus on the day of His baptism. Currently, people always think of doves when they talk about the Holy Spirit. It was no coincidence, therefore, that alongside the apparition of the Virgin Mary, white doves were always seen soaring over the domes of the Church in Zeitoun. And the Lord looks at the Church in Zeitoun and blesses it, *Behold, you are fair, my love. Behold, you are fair! You have dove's eyes.*

Thus, when God describes the beauty of the human soul, He turns to the dove to draw similarities. He considers the dove as an offering, a burnt one to please God on the one hand, and as a sacrificial offering for the atonement of sins, on the other. The human soul attains this sublime and lofty position when man offers penitence for his sins through the symbolic offering of the two doves, the burnt and the sacrificial, and thereby pleases the Lord.

Once atonement for sins has been granted through the offering of the doves, man starts to contemplate the dove that has brought the olive leaf promising peace and salvation, and assuring that the waters of the flood have receded and no longer prevail over or threaten the earth. And once man's ark safely reaches shore and man's redemption and salvation become certain and ensured, that old purity and simplicity, that have long been forgotten because of man's sins, return once again.

Doves represent forgiveness through the offerings, stand for the peace that the ark is finally ashore, and is a token of simplicity, purity, innocence and goodness. Doves give us an example of how the Holy Spirit works in man. It is impossible for man to live righteously unless there is union with the Holy Spirit. Once man lives righteously, man's life will abound with prayers and praises like the everlasting songs of the doves, their towers that resonate with their chanting night and day, and the doves that fly into the wilderness to live in unity and oneness with the Lord. Once there is this curious integration of all of these blessed qualities, the Lord will declare, *Behold, you are fair, my love. You have dove's eyes.*

Doves give us an example of how the Holy Spirit works in man

Let us pray.

May God have mercy upon us and bless us, and make His face shine with His Countenance upon us and have compassion upon us. With the prayers and intercessions that are raised on our behalf by the Mother of God, the Pure Saint Mary, and all the angels and apostles, and the prophets, and the martyrs, and the confessors, and the anchorites, and the saints who we ask to pray for us for peace at all times, and the blessings of the saint of this blessed day, and the blessing of Saint Mary first and last, may their holy blessings and the prayers and intercessions be with us all. Amen.

Peace be with you all.

May God make us worthy to say, Our Father…

The Voice of My Beloved!
Behold, He Comes

Song of Solomon 2:8

In the Name of the Father, the Son, and the Holy Spirit, One God. Amen.

The voice of my beloved!
Behold, he comes
Leaping upon the mountains,
Skipping upon the hills.

Song 2:8

A person who loves the Lord can discern, be moved and affected by His voice. As soon as the voice of the beloved sounds in one's ears, it penetrates and reaches deep into the inner recesses of the heart. The minute St. Elizabeth heard the voice of St. Virgin Mary, she said to her, *For indeed, as soon as the voice of your greeting sounded in my ears, the babe leaped in my womb for joy,* (Luke1:44). St. Elizabeth was filled with the Holy Spirit. Perhaps we may be able to visualize St. John the Baptist still an embryo, leaping and proclaiming, *the voice of my beloved.*

When Jesus was in the flesh, He had a peculiarly profound and particularly effective voice that influenced and affected people. He talked to the multitudes as *one having authority,* (Matt 7:29). He captivated their hearts, dominated their feelings, swayed their thoughts and mesmerized their will. A great number of people proclaimed that they had *never heard anything like that before.* The voice of Jesus has always been a distinct voice because, *His mouth is most sweet, Yes, he is altogether lovely,* (Song 5:16).

Jesus' voice is fascinating in a uniquely peculiar way. We feel awe-stricken when we consider the story of St. Matthew the tax collector. St. Matthew had a job, a responsibility to collect the taxes. As soon as he heard the words *follow Me,* he abandoned everything. He gave up his job, his responsibilities, his source of income and material comfort, and his future. He even started a journey into the unknown. Why? It is because of *the voice of my beloved.* It is a voice that moves and influences. It is unfortunate, however, that we did not have the chance to live at the time when Jesus was in the world in the flesh. It is sad we did not have the chance to enjoy His unique, profound, and effective voice.

Let us also consider the story of Zacchaeus. Even though Zacchaeus was a chief tax collector, his heart was thoroughly transformed the minute he heard Jesus' words, *Zacchaeus, make haste and come down, for today I must stay at your place,* (Luke 19:5). The words of Jesus drastically changed Zacchaeus' heart. He repented and said, *Look, Lord, I give half of my goods to the poor, and if I have taken anything from anyone by false accusation, I restore fourfold,* (Luke 19:8). The mere utterance of the words *make haste* and *come down* had changed him altogether. It is *the voice of my beloved.* Jesus' voice does have an incredibly amazing effect.

Some of the people who were contemporary of Jesus have recorded some of His intriguing characteristics in the available literature that have come down to us. They described his eyes as penetrating and piercing. No one could look steadily in His eyes. They also described His voice as particularly unique and profound and astoundingly effective and moving.

A great number of people followed Jesus because of His voice. As a shepherd, Jesus knows the effect of His voice, *My sheep hear My voice, and I know them, and they follow Me,* (John 10:27). They do not hear the voice of strangers. They can differentiate between His voice and the voice of strangers. It is very unfortunate that in the days of Jesus they did not have such things as tape recorders to record His voice. If we had had such technology then, we would have been spellbound and captivated by listening to but one sermon.

Even though man ought to distinguish the Lord's voice from other voices, not every man is capable of doing so

The Lord's mere utterance of words such as *follow Me* would render people helpless and powerless. People would instantaneously feel enthralled and enchanted. *Follow Me, and I will make you fishers of men,* (Matt 4:19), said Jesus to Simon and Andrew. They immediately abandoned their ship and the nets and left family and relatives. St. Peter even left his wife to follow Jesus. They all were mesmerized by that sweet, beautiful voice, *the voice of my beloved.*

Even though man ought to distinguish the Lord's voice from other voices, not every man is capable of doing so. Some are not even worthy of hearing His voice. Saul of Tarsus was able to hear the Lord's voice while the others around him were not able to. They saw the light but did not hear Jesus who was talking to Saul. They were unworthy to hear His voice. Not everyone is worthy. It is for this reason that in the prayer preceding the reading of the Holy Bible we say, *we beseech our Lord and God that we may be worthy to hear the Holy and Divine Gospel.* Therefore, in order to hear the Lord's voice, one ought to be prepared and worthy.

God has always made His voice clear and accessible to people

God had spoken to the prophets and the fathers in many different ways. The Lord's voice has been hovering over the many generations since the dawn of creation. The first manifestation of the voice of my beloved is that as a Creator, *'Let there be light;' and there was light,* (Gen 1:3). *Let there be life, and there was life. Let Us create man, and man was created.* That was the first voice of the Lord as was recorded in the Scriptures. Then the voice of my beloved was manifested in the Lord's bestowal of blessings, *Be fruitful and multiply; fill the earth and subdue it,* (Gen 1:28).

Thus the voice of the Lord was manifested first as a Creator and then as a giver of blessings. Then we hear the Lord's voice as an instructor, *Of every tree of the garden you may freely eat; but of the tree of the knowledge of good and evil you shall not eat.* God instructed man to be careful and not to eat from that particular tree or they *shall surely die,* (Gen 2:16-17). God has always made His voice clear and accessible to people.

Yet, even though the voice of the Lord is made accessible to everyone, not everyone can readily discern His voice. We therefore pray to have those well trained and capable ears that can hear and discern. When Samuel the prophet was still a child, he heard the Lord's voice. However, he was unable to distinguish His voice and mistakenly thought it was the voice of Eli, the priest. Only after the third time was Samuel able to discern the Lord's voice, *Speak, (Lord,) for Your servant hears*, (1 Sam 3:10).

The Lord also spoke to St. Mary Magdalene, but she was unable to recognize it as the Lord's and she incorrectly thought it was the gardener's. The Lord had chosen to hide His identity from her. However, when He wanted her to be able to discern His voice, He called her in His all too familiar voice, *Mary*, a voice she had always loved to hear. Upon hearing His familiar, beloved voice, Mary melted and instantly responded, *Rabboni! (which is to say, Teacher)*, (John 20:16). The Lord's voice also reached Balaam, but Balaam failed to recognize it and he sinned. The Lord's voice has reached a great number of people that have failed to recognize it. The Bible likens this to, *people...who have ears and hear not,* (Jer 5:21). People have on numerous occasions failed to understand and discern the Lord's voice.

It is such a blessing if we are able to hear and discern the Lord's voice. The first thing is to discern the Lord's voice and come to the realization that it is the voice of the Lord reaching and seeking us. St. Anthony heard a verse in church, a verse that everyone else in the congregation must have heard. What distinguished him from the others in the church is that St. Anthony knew and realized that God was directly speaking to him, *Go your way, sell whatever you have and give to the poor...*, (Mark 10:21). He knew that that verse was directed at him. It was *The voice of my beloved*. The Lord was coming, *leaping upon the mountains*, and *skipping upon the hills*. It was as if the Lord was sending him a special message. Also, at the beginning of his life as a monk, a woman came to him and told him that if he were a monk, he should have taken abode in the mountain since the place in which he dwelled then was, according to her, not fit for a monk. He recognized in her God's voice and realized His will.

The Lord may speak to us in various ways, and it is our responsibility to recognize His voice. The Lord may speak through a word in some book. He may use someone in the street to impart His message. We may hear the Lord's voice in the Church. He may use a friend or even a foe to deliver His message and make known His voice to us. The Lord may use many different ways. The important thing is to discern His voice as the *voice of my beloved*. It is important to recognize that it is the Lord's voice to us.

One may become seriously ill only to discover that the Lord's voice is seeking them out through sickness. We may experience some difficulties, problems and harsh conditions. Or, we may even go through adversity, hard times or hardships. Yet, in the midst of all these difficulties and hardships, we may be able to recognize the Lord's voice to us. Upon such a recognition, we come to the realization that it is the *voice of my beloved*. The Lord is imparting a specific message. The Lord is talking to, and seeking us.

An example for this is when Joseph's brothers found themselves in trouble after the governor's cup was found in one of their sacks. They realized that they were facing a great ordeal. In their distress they heard the voice of the Lord pointing out their guilt for turning a deaf ear on their brother's entreaties and ignoring his supplications: *God has found out the inequity of your servants,* (Gen 44:16).

We may be able to hear the voice of the Lord speaking directly to us in a clear voice, or we may feel His voice in our inward parts, in our hearts or in our consciences. His voice may direct us to do this or not to do that. He may instruct us to stay away from this place or to change that thing and so on and so forth. This is the voice of God penetrating to our inner recesses and calling us.

No man on earth has ever been bereft of the chance to hear God's voice. Even criminals and murderers have been visited by His voice. God spoke to Cain, *Where is Abel your brother?* (Gen 4:9). Judas, the traitor, also heard the voice of the Lord, *Judas, are you betraying the Son of Man with a kiss?* (Luke 22:48). The voice of the Lord chases us at all times. Sometimes even murderers who perpetrate such heinous atrocities are chased and even haunted by the Lord's voice. It oftentimes urges and induces wrong-doers to confess. The Lord's voice reaches everyone in a variety of ways.

The Lord may speak to us in various ways, and it is our responsibility to recognize His voice.

Sometimes, the voice of the Lord reaches us in a soft, mild, pleasant and serene way. We may hear His voice in a word of consolation or encouragement. Jacob, the father of fathers, fled from his brother Esau and traveled a long distance until he became weary and fell asleep. In a dream, he saw a ladder set up on the earth, and its top reached to heaven. He heard the voice of his beloved, *Behold, I am with you and will keep you wherever you go, and will bring you back to this land,* (Gen 28:25).

Such a voice imbues the soul with solace and instills encouragement and comfort. It is a voice that reaches man at a time of difficulty or distress. The Lord's voice also came to Joshua in his distress after the death of Moses, *as I was with Moses, so I will be with you. I will not leave you nor forsake you,* (Josh 1:5). It is the voice of consolation and encouragement. The disciples, awe-stricken, troubled and afraid in the midst of the tumultuous waves of an angry sea, also heard the voice of Jesus, *Be of good cheer! It is I; do not be afraid,* (Matt 14:27).

We often hear the voice of the Lord in the middle of trouble or distress and when we are overwhelmed and weighed down, *Fear not, for I am with you,* (Is 41:10). *The Lord is your keeper; the Lord is your shade at your right hand. The sun shall not strike you by day, nor the moon by night,* (Ps 121:5-6). One cannot but acknowledge that this is, *The voice of my beloved! Behold, he comes leaping upon the mountains, skipping upon the hills.*

We should note that the bride heard the voice of the beloved from a distance while he was *leaping upon the mountains* and *skipping upon the hills.* He has not arrived yet. However, she was able to feel his most welcome and much anticipated arrival. He is approaching and she can hear his voice coming from afar upon the mountains and the hills. He will surely come. This gives us hope. When we are weary and overwhelmed, we may mistakenly feel that we are abandoned and that God is not coming to our deliverance.

A man who is equipped with faith and hope would be able to hear the voice of the Lord even from afar

Yet, faith will help us overcome this unfounded feeling of abandonment. With faith we can still cling to the unshakable conviction that *the voice of my beloved* is coming, and that he is coming *leaping upon the mountains* and *skipping upon the hills.* He will certainly come. He will come even in the last hours of the night. Indeed he may be late, but he will definitely come.

A man who is equipped with faith and hope would be able to hear the voice of the Lord even from afar. There is a distinction that one ought to consider in this respect. Hearing the Lord's voice from a close distance may entail witnessing the Lord. Hearing His voice from a far distance, on the other hand, implies faith. The Lord is definitely coming. Even though He is late, one feels that He is making haste to arrive speedily, He is *leaping upon the mountains* and *skipping upon the hills*. In spite of the fact that He has not arrived yet and we have not seen Him with our eyes, we know that He is on His way and that He will be here speedily. It is true that we do not see Him with the naked eye, but we are filled with the conviction and the assurance of His certain, unquestionable coming. Faith endows man with many such comforting feelings.

People may, on occasion, reproachfully criticize our faith in God. They may sarcastically enquire about our God, Where is your God whom you worship? Where? Why has he not hastened to your help? Why has he forsaken you? Such a sentiment is reminiscent of what has transpired between the angel and Gideon. When the angel said to him, *The Lord is with you, you mighty man of valor*, Gideon responded saying, *O my Lord, if the Lord is with us, why then has all this happened to us?* (Judg 6:12-13).

We should not feel this way. Even if the Lord seems to be far from us, we should have the conviction that He is coming, *leaping upon the mountains* and *skipping upon the hills*. He is hastening to our rescue and deliverance. He will arrive. However, this arrival will only take place in due time. It is a conditional arrival based as it is upon the Lord's own timing.

What are these mountains and hills that the Lord is jumping and skipping upon? The Bible instructs us that *His foundation is in the holy mountain*, (Ps 87:1). The Lord is coming *leaping upon the mountains* and *skipping upon the hills*. The verse *Behold, He comes* fills the heart with solace, hope and assurance. For this reason they used to say that the Lord is coming, *Maranatha,* in the first generation. He is coming. Do not lose heart. Do not despair.

The voice of my beloved. The Lord's voice provides us with solace and consolations and with help and encouragement. In addition, it also provides us with blessings and rewards. It is such a thrilling feeling to hear the beloved's voice saying, *well done, good and faithful servant; you were faithful over a few things, I will make you ruler over many things. Enter into the joy of your Lord,* (Matt 25:21). This is truly the voice of the beloved: that joy-inspiring, blessing-filled voice; the *voice of my beloved.*

Dear sisters and brothers, you will experience joy and gladness in the voice of the Lord only if He is your beloved. Let me explain. You will feel happy and joyful with God's voice if He is precious and dear to you. Then you will proclaim that it is the voice of my beloved. If, however, the Lord is not your beloved, His voice to you would be terrifying and scary, *It is a fearful thing to fall into the hands of the living God,* (Heb 10:31). It is terrifying indeed.

We all know the parable of the foolish rich man who heard the voice of the Lord saying, *Fool, this night your soul will be required of you; then whose will those things be which you have provided?* (Luke 12:20). The rich man has heard the voice of the fair Judge, not the voice of a beloved. *It is a fearful thing to fall into the hands of the living God.* The voice of the Lord reached other people declaring, *Verily I say unto you, I do not know you.* The Lord is thereby rejecting and denouncing them. It is frightening to have the Lord wash His hands of, or turn His back to, someone.

The voice of the Lord also came to Cain asking him about his brother Abel, *Where is Abel your brother?... So now you are cursed from the earth, which had opened its mouth to receive your brother's blood from your hand,* (Gen 4: 9-11). This, too, was the voice of the Lord. Therefore, it is important to maintain a good relationship with the Lord if you want to hear the Lord's gentle, kind and pleasant voice. Only then will you be able to declare that this is *the voice of my beloved*.

The voice of the Lord was also heard gently reproaching, *Saul, Saul, why are you persecuting Me?* (Acts 9:4). What does the voice of the Lord mean to you? Is it a voice of blessing? Of reproach? Of condemnation? Or is it help and encouragement? Which one is it for you? Those who have a good relationship with the Lord pronounce that they hear the *voice of the beloved* when the Lord speaks to them. They feel overjoyed. This is typical for those who experience pleasure in meeting the Lord and hearing His voice.

> **You will feel happy and joyful with God's voice if He is precious and dear to you**

The voice of the Lord reached Adam. However, Adam was deprived of this happiness and joy after his fall. When he heard the voice of the Lord, he hid himself from Him. He was afraid. How could that be? Was that not the voice of his beloved? Indeed it was before he sinned. At that time, he used to feel joyful and happy when the Lord would come to the garden to sit with him. Now a barrier had been placed between Adam and the Lord. Sin had created a great barrier between Adam and God.

In this respect, Adam's words were striking and remarkably alarming, *I heard Your voice in the garden, and I was afraid because I was naked, so I hid myself,* (Gen 3:10). There was no way that Adam regarded the Lord's voice at that particular juncture as that of the *voice of the beloved*. It would be a disgrace, a shame, if the Lord's voice reaches us when we are naked and unprepared, not wearing the garments of righteousness or clothed in our heavenly attire.

The voice of the Lord reached Ahab, the King, through Elijah the Tishbite. It is amazing how Ahab regarded the voice of the prophet of the Lord. He said to Elijah, Have *you found me, O my enemy?* (1King 21: 20). People would normally be overjoyed at seeing a prophet coming from the Lord. However, rather than feeling joyful and peaceful at seeing the Lord's messenger, Ahab experienced fear and anxiety. He was not happy to hear the prophet's fear, inspiring voice saying, *In the place where dogs licked the blood of Naboth (the Jezreelite), the dogs shall lick your blood, even yours*, (1 King 21:19). Of course, this was not the voice of the beloved; rather, it was a prophecy for discipline, a decree of judgment and a verdict of condemnation.

No one knows when or how the Lord will talk to them.

Therefore, we should make a distinction between the voice of the Lord in general and His voice as my beloved. It is His voice as the beloved that we should strenuously and diligently seek. It is the *voice of my beloved! Behold, he comes, leaping upon the mountains, skipping upon the hills*. It is this voice that brings about happiness and joy to the human soul.

Those who love the Lord find His voice pleasing and delightful, *I rejoice at Your word as one who finds great treasure,* (Ps 119:162). It is, therefore, important to have a loving relation with the Lord in order to be able to say *the voice of my beloved*.

The Lord's loving voice had sought people out. Moses the prophet was tending the flock in the desert when the Lord unexpectedly spoke to him from the midst of a burning bush. He took his sandals off his feet for the place where he stood was holy ground, (Ex 3: 5). No one knows when or how the Lord will speak to them. The Lord's voice comes without any previous warnings. His voice is not subject to our mental speculations or calculations, but His voice will come to us, nonetheless. The important thing is to be prepared, at all times, to hear the voice of the Lord as our *beloved*.

When we read the Scriptures, we should meditate, contemplate, even *devour* every word in it, because it is the voice of the beloved. The voice of the Lord will not necessarily be audibly heard. *I have found your words like honeycomb, so I ate it*, because it is the voice of my beloved.

The *Song of Songs* abounds with examples of the loving voice of God, a voice that is filled with praise, emotion, veneration and eulogy. It is a testimony on the Lord's part to the human soul. The Lord describes that human soul in His, *Behold, you are fair, my love, Behold you are fair, You have dove's eyes,* (Song 1:15). How sweet such a testimony is when it proceeds from the mouth of the Lord! This is truly the voice of the beloved. Will we hear such a testimony in the Final Day? I wonder.

It is a well known fact that the world bears witness for many people who are trained to be experts in various fields. People are acknowledged as professionals in Medicine, Engineering, Accounting, and many other areas of expertise. However, the important question that we need to ask ourselves is, Will our beloved bear witness for us in Judgment day? Will the Lord acknowledge or bear witness for us as those saved by His blood? Will He acknowledge that *salvation has come to this house?* (Luke 19:9). Will we hear His voice saying, *well done, good and faithful servant; you were faithful over a few things, I will make you ruler over many things. Enter into the joy of your*

Lord, (Matt 25:21). Such is the testimony, the acknowledgement, that we should long for and seek.

What kind of testimony does the Lord have for us? What will be the nature of His voice? We may hear the voice of the Lord tonight asking us to repent, change our ways and turn over a new leaf. He may direct our attention to a sin and ask us to be vigilant and cautious, *Sin lies at the door. And its desire is for you, but you should rule over it,* (Gen 4:7). Or we may hear the voice of the Lord inviting us to spend the night in His presence, *Lift up your hands in the sanctuary, and bless the Lord*, (Ps 134:2).

Whatever the nature of the Lord's voice may be, we should be prepared to discern and distinguish it. We ought to obediently follow and seek whatever He is asking us to do. We should always be ready to ask Him to, *show me Your ways, O Lord; Teach me Your paths*, (Ps 25:4). We earnestly want to hear Your voice. It is in our ears like honeycomb in our mouths.

The Lord's voice is multifaceted; it performs many things. Consider what David the prophet said, *The voice of the Lord divides the flames of fire. The voice of the Lord shakes the wilderness,* (Ps 29:7-8). We long to hear the voice of the Lord and we ought to seek it even if it were meant to admonish, scold or discipline us. We ought to seek His voice even if He is holding a whip in His hand and reproachfully saying, *My house shall be called the house of prayer, but you have made it a den of thieves,* (Matt 21:13).

We long to hear Your voice. We seek Your voice in the midst of current events. We seek it in the middle of difficulties and tribulations. We yearn to hear Your voice lavishly bestowing love, encouragement, solace and comfort.

Before the birth of Christ, the Lord's voice had

been seldom heard for a long period of time. There were no prophesies or visions in dreams. The Lord had not visited people with His Angels as He used to before. The voice of the Lord was direly needed since He had not spoken to them for a long time. Consequently, people longed to hear but one word from the Lord. Now, however, the voice of the Lord is ever present. It is daily seeking and chasing you. Will you heed His voice? Will you listen to Him? If you truly seek the voice of the Lord, pray and say *Speak, Lord, for Your servant hears*, (1 Sam 3:10).

Let us pray.

May God have mercy upon us and bless us, and make His face shine with His Countenance upon us and have compassion upon us. With the prayers and intercessions that are raised on our behalf by the Mother of God, the Pure Saint Mary, and all the angels and apostles, and the prophets, and the martyrs, and the confessors, and the anchorites, and the saints who we ask to pray for us for peace at all times, and the blessings of the saint of this blessed day, and the blessing of Saint Mary first and last, may their holy blessings and the prayers and intercessions be with us all. Amen.

Peace be with you all.

May God make us worthy to say, Our Father...

Have You Seen the One I Love

Behold, He Comes

Song of Solomon 3:6

In the Name of the Father, the Son, and the Holy Spirit, One God. Amen.

We continue our contemplations on the *Song of Songs*. We read:

> *The voice of my beloved!*
> *Behold, he comes*
> *Leaping upon the mountains,*
> *Skipping upon the hills.*
>
> *Song 2:8*

I have previously given a lecture on *the voice of my beloved*. Tonight we will consider *Behold, he comes leaping upon the mountains*. The words *Behold, he comes* are reassuring and consoling. You do not feel lonely. Rather, you feel that your beloved, the Lord, is coming; *He comes*.

Regardless of the difficulties, tribulations, troubles and problems that you face; no matter how depressing, overwhelming and disheartening the world becomes, you can still hold unto the words, *the voice of my beloved! Behold, he comes*. The Lord will definitely come sometime, someday. Even if He seems to be late, He will come, if even during the late hours of the night.

These words are often mentioned in tribulations and difficulties. For example, I can imagine one of the disciples saying, *Behold, He comes* as they were wrestling with the tumultuous waves and turbulent sea, in a boat about to capsize and sink. As the disciple see Christ coming from afar, he won't feel forsaken or lonely in his predicament.

I also recall the people grunting under the heavy yoke of servitude and the humiliation of slavery at the hands of pharaoh. The words *He comes* must have been consoling and comforting. The Lord will hearken to the cries of the people and will come, even after a short while.

These comforting words are readily available to individuals, and also to the Church, as they encounter difficulties and hardships and face problems and tribulations. They can also prove uplifting and helpful for a person who has had a difficult time trying to rid himself of a certain sin. For example, someone may be torn apart by a particular sin that he cannot shun or avoid. No matter how often he confesses his sin, he goes back to it. He calls upon the name of the Lord, *Save me, O Lord, from this sin*. The Lord's deliverance is at hand, and will soon hear an inward voice supporting and encouraging, *He comes leaping upon the mountains, skipping upon the hills*. He will never leave nor forsake you. He will come to rescue and save you from this sin.

I can also imagine these same words said by the lost sheep as he had gone astray. Journeying away from the fold and becoming lost and bewildered amongst the thorns, he reconsiders and deliberates, *He comes*. The

Shepherd is coming. He definitely will. If He does not come today, He will come tomorrow. At a certain point and in a particular minute, I will find an uplifting hand pulling me up from amongst the thorns, and the lost sheep will chant, *He comes leaping upon the mountains*.

These words do not only lend themselves merely to situations where rescue and salvation are needed. They are symbolic and representative of visitations of love, as well. I can, for example, envisage Mary and Martha hearing the gentle hand of the Lord knocking at their door as He has come to spend some time and to speak and converse with them tenderly and encouragingly, *Behold, he comes*.

> **The words *He comes* are loaded with hope and promise**

The words *He comes* are particularly relevant to the whole of humanity as it awaits salvation. They are pertinent to those who have already fallen asleep in hope of resurrection. Every soul beseeches and implores, *For You will not leave my soul in Sheol, nor will You allow Your Holy One to see corruption,* (Ps 16:10). As these souls were waiting in Sheol, they witnessed the angel announcing the birth of Christ to St. Mary and they proclaim, *Behold, He comes*. The Lord is coming!

These were the same words that were in Simeon's mind and which found their way to his lips when he carried Christ, *Lord, now You are letting Your servant depart in peace, according to Your word; for my eyes have seen Your salvation*, (Luke 2:29-30).

The words *He comes* are loaded with hope and promise. A person who does not become overwhelmed with hardships and tribulations and does not fall a victim to despair and depression is one who is fortified and equipped with hope. He believes in *He comes*. The Lord will surely come at a particular moment. He will come to solve problems and work miracles. He will even make the impossible possible: *He comes*.

Nor should one think that the Lord will come when it is too late. No! *He comes leaping upon the mountains, skipping upon the hills*, indicates that He is coming swiftly. He is running. That is why we read these fitting, uplifting words in the Book of Isaiah, the prophet:

> *But those who wait on the Lord*
> *Shall renew their strength;*
> *They shall mount up with wings like eagles,*
> *They shall run and not be weary,*
> *They shall walk and not faint*
>
> Is 40:31

Those who wait on the Lord renew their strength. When you feel that the Lord is definitely coming, you feel this certain internal strength empowering you. Your morale becomes high; you feel elated and jubilant and you experience joy and exuberance. *You mount up with wings like eagles*. God is coming. Do not lose heart or despair. The Lord will surely come.

He has come to transform weakness into strength and despair into hope

Those who feel the Lord will never come are, unfortunately, victims of despair, dejection and a prey to weakness and gloom. They may seem alive, yet they are dead indeed.

The words *He comes* imbues power, instills courage and inspires hope. Think about the condition of the disciples as they witnessed the crucifixion and burial of Christ. Imagine their feelings as rumors started to spread around them, and as the Jews proudly and gloatingly mocked them. Consider their state as they were facing this predicament and difficult time. Yet, in the midst of all of these difficulties, they regard the Lord coming to them through closed doors. At a moment like this, they would say, *He comes*. The Lord has come. He has come to change everything; He has come to transform weakness into strength and despair into hope.

I wish that everyone of you would always keep this verse in their hearts. Always ponder on *He comes*. The Lord will definitely come; He will come at a particular time to accomplish great deeds, *Now I will arise, says the Lord; I will set him in the safety for which he yearns*, (Ps 12:5). Arise, O Lord God!

The verse *He comes, Maranatha*, was the form of greeting among Christians during the apostolic era. It was also used as when bidding farewell. *Mar* or *mari* means *Master* or *Lord*, *Atha* means *come*, and *maran* means *our Lord*. So, together *maran atha* means *The Lord or our Master Jesus Christ is coming*. They used to comfort and solace each other by acknowledging at the end of their messages or speeches that, *The Lord is coming! Maranatha*.

The promise entailed in *He comes* is both consoling and uplifting. It was used for the first time at the birth of Jesus *Maranatha, He comes*. He is coming to publicly accomplish salvation and to seek and redeem the souls of those who have perished. He is coming to restore the divine, godly image to man. *Behold! He comes*. To do what? He is coming to change this image that we currently have and transform it to a godly image. He is coming to restore unto man his first state and the dignity which he has lost. He is coming to bring salvation and redemption.

It was also said in His Resurrection. He came to overcome death and destroy it. He came to eradicate and eliminate Thomas's doubt and suspicion. He came to wipe out Peter's sadness and lighten his burdens. He came to put a stop to Satan's tricks, deception and treachery. I recall some of the verses that I wrote in the 1940s about Christ's Resurrection:

Arise and Satan destroy and obliterate,
his kingdom demolish and annihilate;
Arise! Your shepherds' faith fortify and make strong;
Gather Your scattered flock unto a mighty throng.
Peter's infirmities and weakness forgive and forget,
Wipe out Magdalene's tears, take away her fret.

Arise! It is a message that inspires hope. The Lord is coming. He is coming to perform great deeds and carry out wondrous accomplishments. He is coming to strengthen and fortify the faith of the shepherds. He is coming to gather unto His tender bosom His scattered, wretched flock. He is coming to forgive Peter's weaknesses and wipe out Mary Magdalene's tears.

He comes is a message that imbues power and strength. One feels that something great and magnanimous is about to take place; some miracle or wondrous deed is about to happen; something supernatural and incomprehensible is about to occur: Divine Providence and intervention is at hand, *Maranatha!*

The words *He comes* may also be a reference to the Second Coming of our Lord. *Behold! He comes!* He is coming with ten thousand upon ten thousand of His saints. He is coming on the clouds with the angels. He is coming to judge the living and the dead. He is coming to sit on the throne of His glory. *All the nations will be gathered before Him,* (Mat 25:32).

Behold, he comes are words that please the saints and instill fear in the hearts of the ungodly, the unprepared. The saints will gladden and become joyful, *I will see you again and your heart will rejoice,* (John 16:22). So, the words *Behold, He comes* are a reference to the

Lord's Resurrection and can also be used for His Second Coming.

Jesus said, *I go to prepare a place for you. And if I go and prepare a place for you, I will come again and receive you to Myself; that where I am, there you may be also,* (John 14: 3-4). These words should cause joy and happiness to those who are ready. The righteous become joyful and shout *Amen. Come O Lord Jesus.* We need You, Lord.

However, the ungodly will not experience this joy at hearing *Behold, He comes.* All the tribes of the earth will mourn and moan for their sake; they will bewail them. With the advent of Jesus, *they shall say to the mountains, 'Cover us!' and to the hills, 'Fall on us,* (Hosea 10:8). They will be utterly ashamed and exceedingly mortified. Where will they hide? The words *Behold, He comes* will be the cause of joy to some and sorrow to others.

The Lord is coming. He is coming to perform great deeds and carry out wondrous accomplishments

This is reminiscent of the Resurrection of Jesus, an event that caused the disciples to become exceedingly joyful while at the same time alarmed and distressed the chief priests of the Jews. They became anxious and fearful; in fact, they were exceedingly frightened and terrified.

The words *Behold, He comes* can also be a reference to the life of every human being. There is a time when every one of us will pass away. We must remain spiritually alert. *Blessed is that servant whom his master, when he comes, will find so doing,* (Mat 24:46). Hence, the coming of Jesus was a cause of joy for the wise virgins on the one hand, and a source of anxiety and trepidation for the foolish virgins. *Lord, Lord, open to us,* (Mat 25:11).

Assuredly, I say to you, I do not know you, (Mat 25:12). How incredibly difficult to hear the Lord saying this? How harsh to hear the Lord saying, *I do not know you* upon His arrival?

As I mentioned earlier, *Behold, He comes* are words that can be regarded as a reference to Christ's birth and resurrection, the passing away of any human being, the general resurrection of the human race, or the Second Coming of our Lord. Yet, we cannot fail to realize that the words permeate with love. The words *The voice of my beloved! Behold, He comes leaping upon the mountains, skipping upon the hills* express a visitation of love.

When Jesus came to the world, He did indeed come leaping upon the mountains and skipping upon the hills. We can trace this right from the beginning.

The first mountain was the mountain of Judea in which the Virgin carries Christ in her womb and heads to Elizabeth leaping upon the mountains and skipping upon the hills.

When Jesus came to the world, He did indeed come leaping upon the mountains and skipping upon the hills.

Likewise, throughout His life on earth, Jesus kept moving from one mountain to the other. We first see Him on the Mount of Temptation where He spent time in prayer, worship, and fasting. There, having been tempted by the devil, we see Him coming out victorious and triumphant. The victorious Church in the heavens, likewise, beholds Christ and hails Him as He comes *leaping upon the mountains, skipping upon the hills.* This is the first mountain that Jesus came to after the mount of Judea. He came out victorious.

After, we see Jesus on another mountain. It was the

Mount of Preaching where Jesus went up a mountain to speak, preach and teach the thousands that had gathered to hear Him. People were greatly astonished at His teaching for He had taught them as one *having authority,* (Mat 7:29). The multitude marveled at His sayings, those awe-inspiring, sublime spiritual principles that humanity has ever come to know. Once again, we see the Lord leaping upon the mountains. Angels hail Him saying, *The voice of my beloved! Behold, He comes leaping upon the mountains.*

From the Mount of Preaching, the Lord went to the Mount of Olive. Having ended His teaching of the multitude, everyone went his way. However, Jesus went to the Mount Olive where He sought serenity and tranquility and where He spent the whole night in solitude contemplating and praying to God the Father.

From there Jesus is seen on the Mount of Transfiguration, the Mount of Tabor, where humanity was mesmerized and awestruck. There His *face shone like the sun.* Even His clothes became *as white as light,* (Mat 17:2). His amazingly incredible appearance was like a token of our existence after our own resurrection for we will become like Him. On the Mount of Transfiguration, Jesus gathered representatives of the whole of humanity around Him. There He united Moses the prophet, who represents family life, and Elijah the prophet, who represents celibacy. He gathered the two around Him at the same time.

Around Jesus on that mountain were the Law, as represented by Moses, and the Prophets, as represented by Elijah. On that mountain emblems of manhood and virility as well as symbols of senility and old age surrounded Jesus. While Moses lived for one hundred twenty years and represents senility and old age. Elijah symbolized vigor and masculinity. As Jesus stood on the Mount of Transfiguration, Elijah who represented the life of solitude, seclusion and contemplation on the Carmel Mount stood on one side. Moses represented the life of service as he ministered for hundreds of thousands of people, leading them for decades surrounded the Lord. Once again, we witness the Lord leaping upon the mountains there.

On the mountains, those like Moses who passed away as well as those who ascended to the heavens and remain alive as Elijah surrounded the Lord.

The Lord jumped from the Mount of Temptation to the Mount of Preaching and then to that of Olive. From there He moved to the Mount of Transfiguration and finally to the Mount of Golgotha. The Mount of Golgotha represents the life of sacrifice and pain, as the Lord gave Himself up as a sacrifice unto mankind. The picture that the Mount of Transfiguration offers us is utterly different from the one that is represented by the Mount of Golgotha. While the former shows the Lord in all His Glory and depicts Him in His brilliance and splendor, the latter portrays Him in His suffering, His pain and His passion on the Mount of Golgotha. Yet, the two pictures ought to be witnessed and taken together.

Leaping upon the mountains indicates that you will by no means be confined to one mountain only. Rather, you will have a taste of every one of them.

When the Lord left the Mount of Golgotha, He went to the Mount of Ascension where He ascended to the heavens in great glory; from one mountain unto another. In the meantime, the whole of humanity looks at the Lord in awe and proclaims *my beloved! Behold, He comes leaping upon the mountains, skipping upon the hills.*

Yet there are other mountains in the history of mankind that the Lord has allowed us to witness and experience and which had also been a source of unexpected beauty. Perhaps the oldest and the most important among these mountains in the Mount of Ararat where the Lord provided humanity with an ark to grant us a new life after the death and destruction caused by the Flood. *The voice of my beloved! Behold, He comes leaping upon the mountains.*

Such are the sweet memoirs that the virgin in the *Song of Songs* recollects. She seems to mull over them one at a time. Having remembered the mount of Ararat, she reconsiders the Mount of Sinai where the Lord had provided the Law and instilled awe and fear. On that Mount the people pleaded with Moses to speak to them because they could not speak directly with the Lord. I wish they had maintained this spirit of awe and reverence. In that moment, the people experienced fear and were awe stricken. They were physically consecrated and sanctified. Yet, they could not directly speak with the Lord. They would rather have Moses talk to Him on their behalf. Sadly, however, after the awe and fear that engulfed them on Mount Sinai had worn away, every one of them went their way and did as they pleased.

What is important, my dearly beloved, is to realize that we have been experiencing all of these mountains in our lives.

Then humanity experienced another mountain, the Mount of Gerizim where blessings were continuously granted: *Blessed shall you be when you come in, and blessed shall you be when you go out…Blessed shall be the fruit of your body, the produce of your ground and the increase of your herd, the increase of your cattle and the offspring of your flocks,* (Deut 28: 4-6). *The voice of my beloved! Behold, he comes leaping upon the mountains.*

There is another mountain that we encounter in *Song of Songs,* Chapter four. It is mountain of myrrh and frankincense. The bitterness of myrrh is not necessarily what is emphasized here. Even though myrrh is bitter, it is a sort of fragrance. *All Your garments are scented with myrrh, aloes and cassia,* (Ps 45:8). It is true that myrrh is sour, yet it is sweet smelling and fragrant. This is similar to spiritual life that may taste bitter as myrrh, yet is sweet in its incense and fragrance.

On the holy mountain, one is away from the world, its clamor and uproar, its hustle and bustle and its chaos and confusion.

Let us consider myrrh and frankincense. Does frankincense not emit sweet smelling incense as it burns? The two processes take place simultaneously. The Lord has experienced the mount of myrrh and frankincense, and the Book of Songs abounds with instances of myrrh and frankincense. We will consider this in more detail later.

What is important, my dearly beloved, is to realize that we have been experiencing all of these mountains in our lives. For just as we behold our Lord and proclaim, *The voice of my beloved! Behold, He comes leaping upon the mountains,* Jesus Himself also wants to look at us and proclaim, *The voice of my beloved… He comes leaping upon the mountains.* Which of these mountains have you ʾerienced?

The Bible likens the Apostles to high mountains. symbolic of ascension, the act of climbing and ʾhe Lord. High mountains represent the peaks and those spiritual pinnacles that humanity has witnessed along the ages. They also symbolize the renunciation of the earth with all its hustle and bustle, problems and concerns. It is a journey upwards towards heaven and God.

When people found themselves incapable of reaching the tops of the mountains, they decided to build high minarets on top of each church to symbolize their desire to seek the Lord. Such minarets represent the desire to soar upwards, seek the heavenly and reach the Lord. The church with its symbolic minaret is but a representation in miniature of those high mountains pointing towards heaven.

The voice of my beloved! *Behold, he comes leaping upon the mountains, skipping upon the hills.* What should you do if you want to hear His voice well? You should ascend with Him that holy mountain. Otherwise, if Jesus is on the mountain's top and you are at its bottom, or in the valley or the plains, you will hardly be able to reach Him. You have to ascend the mountains with Him.

While I cannot tell how you perceive the mountains from practical or symbolic perspectives, I would like to mention these two dimensions. From a practical perspective, one may want to consider how people regard the holy wilderness and those who dwell in them in the faith of God, and how the mountains effect their spirituality. Saint Isaac poignantly mentions that *the mere contemplation of the wilderness dissipates even annihilates the heart's lusts for worldly desires.* On the holy mountain, one is away from the world, its clamor and uproar, its hustle and bustle and its chaos and confusion.

Even though the notion and symbolism of the mountain is not readily accessible to everyone, I thought I might mention it to you. The seed may come to fruition in due time. When some decide to go to the mountains, hills and holy places, they board a bus with forty or fifty others. In so doing, they transplant the uproar of the world to the peace and quietude of the mountain. Rather than benefiting from and experiencing the serenity and peace of the mountain, they unwittingly cause commotion and uproar and disturb its peace and tranquility.

Yet, this is not the point I would like to stress here. What I want to emphasize here is this situation in which one goes to the mountain to seek the Lord in privacy. One wants to be with God alone, *Lord, I have come to sit with you alone. Let us sit together, just the two of us on the mountaintop. Alone on the holy mountain.* The Bible therefore declares, *His foundation is in the holy mountains,* (Ps 87:1).

These mountains are symbolic of the Apostles. They also stand for moving upwards, elevating and uplifting the self in an attempt to reach for and seek the Lord, *I will lift up my eyes to the hills from whence comes my help,* (Ps 121:1). I will lift my up eyes towards those saints who resemble these high mountains in their grandeur and magnificence. I lift up my eyes to them asking for their intercession and help from *whence comes my help,* for my help is with the Lord. These saints have come to know and experience the love of the Lord and they are, therefore, in a position to take from Him and enrich us with these blessings.

One is tempted to talk about the mountain of Scete, the mountains overlooking the Red Sea, and the many other mountains that abound with holy monasteries. ⸱. I will not talk about them now.

The important thing here is to decide which of ꞌntains have you come to know and experience ꞁ life? Have you been to the Mount of

Temptation? You may say, I have always been on that mountain. I have not seen the mount of the Transfiguration, or the Mount of Gethsemane. The only Mount that I have thus far experienced is that of Temptation.

Well! It would indeed be magnificent if you were on the Mount of Temptation provided that you are leading a victorious life there. There is nothing wrong in the Mount of Temptation per say. Jesus Himself was on that mountain. He faced one temptation after another, but through them all He had come out victorious and triumphant. On the Mount of Temptation, Jesus said, *It is written, 'Man shall not live by bread alone, but by every word that proceeds from the mouth of God,* (Matt 4:4). On the Mount of Temptation, He said *Away with you, Satan,* (Matt 4:10). There were temptations, but He was victorious.

> **For us, the Mount of Temptation is the Mount of Victory and Triumph over all manners of temptation.**

There are people who feel burdened when they experience temptations. They regard temptations as tribulations. That should not be the case. For us, the Mount of Temptation is the Mount of Victory and Triumph over all manners of temptations.

Have you been to the Mount of preaching, the sermon on the mount? Do you always keep the Lord's words in your heart? Do the beatitudes of Jesus resonate ceaselessly in your ears? Have you kept the Lord's words well hidden in your heart? Or are you far away from that Mountain, from His teachings and commandments, His hidden manna? Does the Lord beckon to you and whisper in your ears every now and then as if He were on the

Mountain of preaching? Have you reaped the benefits and blessings of the sermon on the mount from certain books or certain spiritual mentors or counselors? Or are you incapable of chanting, *The voice of my beloved! Behold, He comes leaping* upon the Mountain of Preaching? Ask yourself!

Have you experienced the Mount of Olives in its serenity and tranquility? Have you enjoyed peaceful times of meditation there? And have you experienced the Mount of Golgotha in all its tribulations and suffering, and have you carried your cross in silence and patience everyday? If you can patiently wait, God will grant you the blessing of the Mountain of Transfiguration in the life to come. To us, this Mountain is to be experienced in the life to come, *It is sown in dishonor, it is raised in glory... It is sown in a natural body, it is raised a spiritual body,* (1 Cor 15:43-44). This is the Mount of Transfiguration in the life to come.

However, this transfiguration may oftentimes materialize on this earth as well. Examples of this can be found in the revelation of some saints in the form of luminous and resplendent events that would oftentimes bring happiness and joy to many people. These revelations are indicated by light, shimmering and brilliant. These saints can now reveal themselves. We have all seen and witnessed the Virgin Saint Mary when she appeared in the form of radiant, glowing light on the Church of Zeitoun. These are examples of human nature as it transcends its humanity and attains glory and splendor.

Every human being can likewise attain such glory. This can only happen, however, if such a person walks in the same way and declares, *The voice of my beloved! Behold, He comes leaping upon the mountains*. The Lord is ready to reveal Himself as He did on the Mount of Transfiguration even before ascension. The only condition is that you should prove victorious on the Mount of Temptation, carry your cross on the Mount of Golgotha, lead a life of meditation on the Mount of Olives, and keep the teachings of the Lord on the Mount of Preaching in your heart.

The voice of my beloved. Behold, he comes leaping upon the mountains. If the mountains are too difficult for you, you may at least try to jump over the hills in accordance with your ability. Or you may try to go upwards gradually, one step at a time as befits the spiritual growth that man should experience.

He comes. You may tell the Lord, *You are coming. Your Grace is coming to strengthen and support me. It will provide me with the power that I need to climb up Your Holy Mountain.* But to lead a life characterized by casualness and indifference will avail you nothing. Nothing good will come out of this attitude.

When Jerusalem was built a long time ago, it was built on the mountains. Mountains surrounded it. People used to climb up the mountain to get there. Hence, there are praises and spiritual songs that are called the songs of ascension. Some of these songs are mentioned in the evening vespers. They were used in chanting these praises as they were ascending the Holy Mountain.

I cannot forget that time when I was five or six years old when we attended the feast of Saint Mary at the mount of Drunca near Assyuit. We would climb up the mountains, on and on and on. We would leave in the middle of the night or at the crack of dawn. We would keep on walking and climbing up until we got there. Sometimes we would get there before the sun was up. This is my recollection of the image of going up the mountain to get to that church at the mountaintop at that young age. What an image! It is simply unforgettable. The image of climbing up that holy mountain has persisted throughout the years.

It so happens that the Lord may oftentimes allow concrete images to cast spiritual projections and inclinations. For example, He allows the mountain with its height, its altitude, its prominence, its pointing forth towards God and heaven in order to meditate on how we can likewise attempt to go upwards, ascend and get to the high peaks and elevated pinnacles that the Lord desires us to reach. If you can climb up the mountains, you may be able to reach the mountaintop of the mount of Gerizim. There you will find someone announcing and declaring: *Blessed shall you be when you come in, and blessed shall you be when you go out,* (Deut 28:7). He will also bestow upon you all the various blessings that are mentioned on the Mount of Blessing in Deuteronomy 28.

The voice of my beloved! Behold, He comes leaping upon the mountains, skipping upon the hills. These verses also give us an idea about spiritual growth; one ought not to stop at a certain stage. Rather, one ought to keep on ascending and reaching to the highest peaks. There are people who become satisfied and content, even complacent, at reaching a certain spiritual position. This is not suitable. The Lord is *leaping upon the mountains and skipping upon the hills.*

Go! Climb up the mountain with Jesus.

If we are to meet the Lord, we must try to reach Him over there on the Holy Mountain. This is what our Lord and Master Himself used to do. He would take His disciples and climb up the mountain with them. There He would spend time with them. *And seeing the multitudes, He went up on a mountain, and when He was seated His disciples came to Him. Then He opened His mouth and taught them,* (Matt 5:1-2).

Go! Climb up the mountain with Jesus.

May God have mercy upon us and bless us, and make His face shine with His Countenance upon us and have compassion upon us. With the prayers and intercessions that are raised on our behalf by the Mother of God, the Pure Saint Mary, and all the angels and apostles, and the prophets, and the martyrs, and the confessors, and the anchorites, and the saints who we ask to pray for us for peace at all times, and the blessings of the saint of this blessed day, and the blessing of Saint Mary first and last, may their holy blessings and the prayers and intercessions be with us all. Amen.

Peace be with you all.

May God make us worthy to say, Our Father...

Made in the USA
Lexington, KY
02 June 2017